MW00632806

THE ANATOMY OF A RECORD COMPANY

HOW TO SURVIVE THE RECORD BUSINESS

Dr. Logan H. Westbrooks
and
Dr. Lance A. Williams

Ascent Publishing
Los Angeles, CA

Ascent Book Publishing
1902 5th Avenue
Los Angeles, CA 90018
LoganWestbrooks.com

Edited by Dee Robinson the RightWriter
Cover Design by Jessica Godbee

Printed in the United States of America

ISBN: 978-0-692-85152-4

SAN: 990-0306

Library of Congress
Control Number: 2017936121

On his decision to delve into Black music marketing in the early 1970s…

"I noticed the Black motion pictures were coming out such as "Shaft" and one or two others that were getting a large audience. It appeared to me that the time was ripe to sign artists with potential who could develop into album sellers, as well as singles sellers."

CLIVE DAVIS
Former President of Columbia Records Group
(CBS/Sony Records)

On imagining the future of music innovation…

"When I came up with the term Jazz Fusion, I didn't want the music to be defined in commercial terms. I also wanted to define it in a way where it would embrace the future because Jazz is an adventurous art form and had been open ended in its past innovations, but it had stopped doing that. It had become ossified with certain conventions."

DR. DON MIZELL
Attorney, Grammy Award-winning producer

Reflections on the Harvard Report 45 years later...

"Bottom line is that our thesis project "A Study of the Soul Music Environment Prepared for Columbia Records Group" was simply a feasibility study and suggested marketing strategy for success."

MARNIE TATTERSALL
Formerly with
ABC Radio, MCA New Ventures,
Source Records, CBS Records

IMPORTANT MESSAGE

Material in this book is presented from an historical standpoint only and represents the opinions of the author and contributors. Readers should use caution in applying material contained in this book to his/her specific circumstances. There are constant changes in the music industry and some information may be out of date between the time of writing and the time of publication. Accordingly, the author and publisher assume no responsibility for liabilities based upon the advice contained herein. Product or corporate names that are trademarks are used only for explanation or identification with no intent to infringe.

To my wife Geri…

TABLE OF CONTENTS

FOREWORD
1981

Unfortunately, there are not enough active executives in the recording industry writing books about their activities and observations while they are on the firing line. Logan Westbrooks bridges that gap with this volume. I personally met Westbrooks when we both were working for Mercury Records in Chicago in the mid '60s. I was immediately captivated by his ability to self-start an assignment.

I was, at the time, the Publicity Director for a group of labels operated under the Mercury Records umbrella. As a part of creative services, I had to deal with so many different executives, each of whom were part of a different label structure. Westbrooks came to me only on occasion. He had his own well-rounded ideas about publicity. I was struck by this young man's initiative and some 15 years later, I still am.

Westbrooks's complete honesty has always amazed me. It still does. It is manifested in every page of this book, and most importantly, it's documented with his varied experience in an industry where he has shown that personal initiative can pay off.

In the mid-60s, Westbrooks was essentially an R&B National Promotion Director; however, today he is the basic record label president, well-versed in each and every function, with a record of corporate success to prove it.

John Sippel
Marketing Editor
Billboard
1981

PREFACE
2017

It's been 35 years since this book was first published, and I have witnessed a transformation of the music industry that is comparable in scope to the Industrial Revolution when there was widespread replacement of manual labor by machinery. Some of the driving forces at that time were the steam engine, steel, electricity, and the automobile.

The major driving forces today are the Internet, digitized music, and the mobilization of music. The major labels no longer hold autonomy as to who enters the 'gates'. Though this influence is still powerful, it is no longer seen as the only avenue for artists to break into the music industry.

Political, sociological, and psychological factors have also contributed to a major shift in the paradigm of the entire notion of music—how it is delivered and how it is received by today's music consumers. The late '90s development of peer-to-peer file sharing, where you could get the music free if you chose to, presented a huge dilemma as well as a loss of revenue for the major labels.

Radio has been consolidated by corporations, which are virtually monopolies such as Clear Channel Media and Entertainment. So now, corporate entities rather than program directors decide what music does and does not get played. This shift has diluted the sense of familiarity and the 'flavor' radio's appeal has on local communities.

The major labels have gobbled each other up and now there are only three remaining: Universal Music Group, Sony Music Entertainment, and Warner Music Group. Nowadays, many artists prefer independence and choose Indie labels. They opt for freedom of creativity rather than the conformity of commercialized music.

Also, there are now independent acts that have become major acts on their own. They have turned down contracts from major labels, yet, they can fill stadiums with their adoring fans. Ten years ago, this would have been impossible.

The question I have is how did the major labels allow themselves to be pushed aside by technology that was as available to them as it was to the independent artists and consumers that have embraced it and utilized it to their advantage? The fact is that the tables have turned and the business of music is wide open because the gates have come crashing down.

Dr. Logan H. Westbrooks

ACKNOWLEDGEMENTS
1981

The idea for this book was first suggested to me by my students at California State University, Los Angeles. Through the persistence of Althea and William Davis, I started creating notes on the work that I was doing in the music business. To Beverly, who taped all my lectures for transcribing, and Sheli, Marcelene, Jaunese, Pat, and Holly, the typists who worked so diligently, thank you.

To George Gerkin and Ronnie Mosley, who introduced me to the record business; Irwin Steinberg, Lou Simon, who taught me record marketing. Special thanks to Bruce Lundvall, and Walter Yetnikoff, who provided me the opportunity to enter the realm of International Music. To Carol Carper, thank you for all your creative inspiration throughout the idea development and writing process. Special thanks to Greg Franks for his canny insight, which aided in the completion of the manuscript.

To Dr. Van Christopher and Dr. Aida O'Reilly, who provided me the opportunity to teach at California State University, Los Angeles. Thanks to Tommie Smith of Jackson State University for all your hard work. Finally, I'd like to thank Wendel Bates, who gives his all to college students through sharing his experiences.

ACKNOWLEDGMENTS
2017

A big thank you to LaRita "Jazzy Rita" Shelby for contributing her excellent interviewing skills.

INTRODUCTION
2017

This book was first published in 1981. It was a limited edition, since it was primarily a text book for The Anatomy of a Record Company class that I taught at Cal State in Los Angeles.

Since that time, I have had many inquiries and requests for a copy of this book. It has also become a collector's item, selling for as much as $50 a copy. I have also been requested to update and release it, and have elected to do so.

In analyzing the music scene today, I have noted many changes, especially in Rap, Hip Hop and Gospel. However, the basic business principles of the music business are the same; it is a business.

The original idea and concept of this book was to deal with the business aspects of the music industry, and that concept remains the same. I've added several new chapters dealing with Rap/Hip Hop, Gospel, Chuck Brown, Source Records, updates from Dr. Don Mizell and Marnie Tattersall, and the Harvard Report.

It is still my intention for the layman to read this book and upon completion, have a basic understanding of the music business. One must understand that this book is an account of the music scene in the 60s, 70s and 80s, and should only be looked at from a historical standpoint. At the time of its publication in 1981, many colleges and universities decided to use it as a reference guide.

The participants in this book were the movers and shakers in the record business at that time and were the gate keepers in deciding who came in and how they would be exposed and exploited. They were all known names in the business and controlled it all. It can be said that they were the ones responsible for setting the stage and creating the climate that forced the unknown and creative individuals to create the music scene as we know it today.

INTRODUCTION
1981

This trade-text offers a generic description of the inner structure of record companies. Our intention is to effectively communicate with students, professionals and interested lay people as to the interaction of various segments of the music and record industry.

The record business is a very exciting commodity worldwide, a "glamour stock" if you will, yet little information as to its formal structure and the interrelated functioning of industry segments has been developed in textbook form. "The Anatomy of a Record Company" is a first step in filling that information gap.

The approach we have taken is *inductive*, setting forth a series of basic facts in the narrative commentary, then allowing for additional viewpoints to be expressed by "Informed Sources" —the multitude of experts who graciously consented to be interviewed for these purposes. Their commentary at the end of each chapter and section is offered to further clarify issues discussed in a narrative context.

The fact that they are full-time participants in the varied segments is of key value because of the first-hand knowledge thereby imparted. And, in situations where they contradict one another—or the narrative—the diversity of opinions and approaches underscores the *old saw* that it takes all kinds to make a successful world.

Section II provides more specific insight, a practical application of Section I's information, via analyzing the activities of one specific company, the Columbia Records Group (CRG).

Conceptually, the book flows from a simple delineation of the inner functioning of a record company's structure in Chapter I, replete with departments and chairs of command to the analysis in Section II of the CBS Harvard Business School Study that launched the entry of major companies into marketing Black music on a major scale. I, Logan H. Westbrooks, was a participant in that process as an executive of CBS during that time.

Dr. Williams and I have reconstructed the development of the Black Music Marketing (BMM) effort as a business and cultural phenomenon of America in the seventies, BMM is disbanded now, but its spirit will remain alive, as Afro-American Music continues to be recognized within the industry as a most viable and desirable commodity.

As a final concern, we offer this text as a *humanitarian gesture*. Nowhere is there a concise work that serves as a transition mechanism for persons interested in entering the music business.

Those of you already familiar with the structure and functions of companies, the relationship of marketing and promotion, the role of producers and so forth, may find those discussions pretty basic. Yet, there are a wide range of areas covered in here that *will* strike your fancy if music, records, radio, and trade publications interest you at all.

The Anatomy of a Record Company will serve many purposes—a ray of hope, food for thought, or directions out of the wilderness for your developing career. We sincerely hope so…

Dr. Logan H. Westbrooks
Dr. Lance A. Williams

SECTION I:

IT'S A BUSINESS

CHAPTER 1

STRUCTURE AND FUNCTIONS OF A RECORD COMPANY

The question posed is, what does this business of music entail? Beneath all of the glitz and glamour lies the obvious—making money. Much like most domestic and international businesses, the music industry is structured on a *for* profit basis. Those of you who are absorbing the information in this text have an important role in the process, as *consumers*.

Time and time again you may indeed find yourselves rushing out on impulse to buy the hottest CD, take it home and groove to the music. Unfortunately, many of you have never stopped to ask yourself, *"What goes on within the hierarchical structure of the music industry?"*

When the legendary soul groover Teddy Pendergrass released his first solo album, it quickly took off. More recently, when the R&B phenom Alicia Keys released her debut album, it also quickly took off. Needless to say, both albums were major sellers.

As a result of the album sales, advertisements—on the radio and on display in stores—revered Pendergrass as "the world's greatest singer" and Keys as a major contender within music. One has to wonder why the name of the individual who made such proclamations was never released. Perhaps it's because an ad said it.

The issue of promotional journalism, better known as *hype*, is discussed in later chapters. But briefly, a label has the opportunity to make large sums of money from an artist if they can sell the public on his or her talents.

Marketing campaigns often use such tactics as the one mentioned above. Although, in the late 70s and 80s, Columbia Records had an estimated 40 plus additional candidates for such distinctions, it was Teddy Pendergrass who won the brass ring regarding album sales because "crowning" him stimulated a media blitz, which sold a platinum-quantity volume.

Placing Teddy Pendergrass on the hearts and minds of eager fans, translated into dollars and cents for Columbia Records regarding the total number of units sold and the frequency of standing-room only concerts. At the end of the day, it can be said that "it's just business."

Record Company Organizational Chart

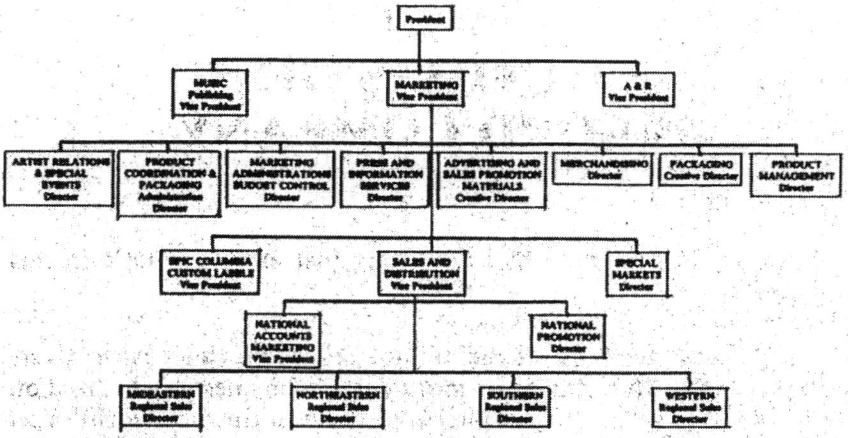

The figure depicted above is a generic organizational structure of the typical record company. The above-mentioned positions are the basic functional lines of power of a *formal system*. The roles of sector within the formal system are quite explainable.

The *President* of a record company is usually the titular head of the company. This individual functions in the same way as in other businesses, and takes on the role as the decision-making leader. He or she most likely works on contract, and reports directly to a *Board of Directors*.

Next in succession are the *Vice Presidents*. More often than not, it is the trend to have a Vice President for everything from Community Relations to Sales and Promotion. This, in turn, effectively diffuses the power instilled in the title role.

As a department head or controller, the Vice President(s) often have more effective, functional power than many company presidents. The following are a few categorical examples:

1. Vice President of Marketing: This is the single most important position in a record company other than the President. Individuals holding this position report directly to the President of the company, and eventually become the President of the company. Additionally, this position requires the individual who holds it to plan, develop, and administer all marketing operations of the company in order to achieve the fundamental company objectives.

2. Vice President of Sales: Individuals holding this position report to the Vice President of Marketing, and are responsible for setting up and delegating selling assignments. Additional duties include directing a field staff for the implementation and execution of selling assignments. In short, this person meets the demands for the product that has been created in the marketplace.

3. Vice President of A&R (Artist and Repertoire): The Vice President of A&R has the key responsibility of shaping the music that the company sells. This individual signs acts, and oversees both talent scouting and music production. Consequently, *A&R* is a very important element of a record company, moreover any mistake made within this department is crucial and may cost the record company thousands of dollars to rectify. *A&R* people are on the move observing talent and making evaluations both in and out of clubs. Most often, such individuals will agree to see an act based on the recommendation of an opinion from someone they respect.

4. Vice President of Music Publishing: *Music publishing* is a major profit-making area for a record company. A hit tune, or a collection of hits by a superstar artist may be re-recorded indefinitely. Each rendition represents money to a publisher. The publishing arm solicits business with Agents and Managers, hoping to place songs with an artist that is currently in the studio, but lacking a full complement of hit material. Most companies have their own publishing arm, as do many artists. Printed sheet music is another source of publishing revenue.

5. Vice President of Business Affairs: The *Business Affairs* division coordinates with both the *Administration* and *Budget* divisions to provide a stable business foundation for working with acts. The Vice President of Business Affairs is usually a lawyer who reports directly to the President. This department interfaces with every other department in a company about fiscal matters, and also conducts the majority of negotiations with outsiders.

6. Vice President of Promotion: The *Promotion* department has the core responsibility of making everyone in the product chain, including consumers, fully aware of the availability of a company's product. The simplest way to accomplish this is to secure airplay on radio stations by supplying program directors and air personalities with demonstration copies of a record. Also, buying advertising time as additional support aides in paying a station's operating expenses, and is therefore, a most beneficial form of reciprocity.

CHATTING WITH THE VICE PRESIDENT OF MARKETING AT ELEKTRA/ASYLUM

Commentary by Oscar Fields

1981

Perhaps, the single most important person within a record company is the Vice President of Marketing, while the most important division of the company is A&R. The Artist and Repertoire department is made up of the people who get the product recorded and assemble the raw materials. Then they come to the other divisions within the record company and say, "This is a record that we want to put out."

The second most important division within the record company is the Promotion Department. In my estimation, 75-80 percent of the business is promotion. People don't buy anything unless they hear it over the air, which obviously entails getting the record promoted.

Next is the Sales and Marketing department, headed by the Vice President of Marketing. Though each record company had a different physical makeup with different departments and so forth, the common link of most importance is the Vice President of Marketing.

It is the duty of this individual to ensure that the promotion, sales, and marketing teams are working together, while also ensuring that the product's visibility in street sales and radio airplay fall at the same time. In short, the Vice President of Marketing handles the interfacing and communications of all the departments within the record company.

Regarding the anatomy of a record company, it's important to note that while there are consistent similarities between all record labels (major or independent), it's also important to distinguish that each company may indeed function differently.

In all record companies, there are Vice Presidents of Sales, Marketing and Promotion. These three individuals, in turn (and along with the President), work closer than any other three people at a company. It is their cohesive relationship with each other that will make a company successful, other than having hit records.

DEPARTMENTAL FUNCTIONS

The **Promotion Department** usually has the most personnel in a company, because getting airplay on a record is a much harder process than simply requesting and having it happen. Both personal relationships and rapport established between record companies and radio stations are very important.

Failure here spells failure in the overall marketing plan. It's simple: the hits that are played over and over on the air are the biggest sellers for companies. With the high turnover rate, promotion is a good entry-level position to gain experience and understand the realities of the music business.

The functions of the **Press and Public Relations** (or *Publicity*) department coordinates with the *Promotion* department in order to seek out as much visibility as possible. Publicity executives place artists on radio stations for on-air interviews, contact magazines and newspapers for feature stories, blurbs, record reviews and choice gossip that is "leaked" for a buzz effect. Additionally, publicity executives perform many functions characteristic of their counterparts in other industries.

The **Artist and Repertoire** department exists for the purpose of maintaining a stable environment for artists. The executives within this department regularly "stroke" the egos of signed acts by providing special gratuities and favors.

Having a position within this department is one of the best jobs to have in the company, but also one of the hardest to keep. For instance, when a company faces financial cutbacks, Artist and Repertoire personnel are among the first to be laid off.

Executives within the **Advertising and Sales Promotion** department are primarily concerned with the nature of display advertising generated by a comprehensive marketing campaign. This department requisitions ad copy, graphic art and other elements necessary to sell music in mass media and newspapers, as well as on displays in music stores.

Relative to this department is the little acknowledged nerve center of activity within a record company, or the *Art* department. All graphic requests of a creative or promotional nature are routed through this department. In most cases, all the artwork is done in-house.

However, if the artist is a platinum seller, and demands that **Francesco Scaullo** photograph his or her next cover, the *Art* department will still plan the overall art layout of the promotional package on an artist or group.

Within the general area of marketing is *Merchandising*, which much like the *Promotion* department, is yet another entry level position that provides a panorama on one's abilities to move up the company ladder.

Merchandisers assist with the implementation of the marketing plan, or overall sales promotion approach for a given album. Innovative managers of merchandising eventually become Vice Presidents of Marketing.

The term *Special Markets* is most often used when referring to music aimed at a target segment of a particular market. Latin, Jazz or Gospel are all examples of special market genres of music.

The purpose of this department is to identify geographic regions where interest is high within these genres, and to structure a tailor-made campaign to exploit the value of products. For instance, a campaign promoting Salsa music might utilize Spanish language promotions extensively, while ads aimed at a Gospel-appreciative audience might play on a Sunday morning.

Custom Labels are production-oriented, smaller entities that are tied to a larger corporate distribution outlet. A *Custom Label* generally has an artist under contract and secures a larger label to manufacture and distribute the artist's music for a pre-established fee. Each *Custom Label* has the responsibility of promoting the music, even if only to protect its initial investment. After all, "It's a Business."

AN EVENING SESSION AT THE QUINCY JONES PRODUCTION WORKSHOP

Commentary by Ewart Abner

1981

First and foremost, a record company exists to make a profit for its owner and is not in the business of philanthropy, but functions like any other business in a capitalistic society. As with most businesses, the record company can take on several legal forms such as: proprietorship, sole ownership, a family-run operation, a partnership, or a corporation. Whatever form it takes on, it is always a *manufacturer*, securing profit from manufacturing a product and selling it for more than it initially cost to make.

So, you ask, what is the product of a record company? The product is a record, and a record is a recorded performance from an artist, either singing, speaking, or playing an instrument. Therefore, the product is the performance of an artist, and an artist is, of course, a person. The product, or record, is really a derivative of an individual's efforts.

This differs from selling the inanimate product of *Campbell's Soup*, because *Campbell's Soup* is something that once created, has both intrinsic and continuing value when it is shelved. A record, however, has no intrinsic value when it is released. It is not even worth the vinyl that it costs to make it, and only achieves value if the public accepts it.

What do I mean by that? In itself, a record is valuable. A record, however, has no intrinsic value when it starts out. It is worth nothing. Now we're getting the elements together.

We have a company that makes a product, the product is a record, the record is the pre-recorded performance of a human being, and the performance itself has no value until accepted by the public.

What the product has is its brand of uniqueness. It is one of a kind. That would be its innate product value. Additionally, the uniqueness is also the value assigned to the artist as well.

It is important to remember that, because unlike most industries, the record industry can only thrive on new creations. Such creations are made by people; therefore, the life and vitality of the creation is the artist. He or she is, in effect, the product.

Let us discuss the shape and form of a record company. Who or what is it? Is it big or little and how many people does it take to make one? As our economy has grown and the level of sophistication and technology increased, *size* has made it almost impossible for a new record company to be formed.

There is no mystery shrouding a record company because they all started out small or on the micro level. We have not gotten to the stage within the music industry—as within the auto industry—of having only three majors. Therefore, it is still possible today to be the artist, the writer, the producer, as well as the record company.

Indeed, it's possible to be all of those things. There is no mystique behind the average record company because its basic needs are simple. It needs an artist. So, if you are the artist and you sign yourself, you become a record company with an artist.

In this situation, I hope that you have some money, because as a record company you'll need to be able to record yourself (the artist). However, if you cannot record your artist, then you will not have a record, which is the product to be bought and sold.

Now, let's say that you are a talented artist—and you must believe that you are—you could then go to someone within the music industry available to show you how to start or become a record company.

If you excel in singing or playing an instrument, first and foremost, polish up your talents. The next step is to find friends and/or relatives who believe in you enough to give you money in order for you to schedule a studio session and record your performance.

To record an album today can cost anywhere from $100,000 and up, not including recording costs, studio time, musicians, digital or analog accessories, artwork (photos), etc. A single can cost roughly $6,000 and up, which may be enough to interest someone into making an additional investment in you as an artist.

The issue that ties the record company and the artist together is a contract. The recording contract marks the beginning of your relationship with the record company. There was a time in the old days, when a company simply paid someone "X" amount of dollars, and they went into the studio and sang.

It was the company's album, and the artist never got anything more. A one-time payment is all the artist ever received, and because of the contract, the company made all the money.

Today, there is legislation that has been enacted to protect artists from the above-mentioned scenario. Unfortunately, issues relative to artist-label relations become a double-edged sword when an artist is protected, because they are not getting an opportunity, which they may normally get, to do something else.

Now, let us say that having a contract with a record company protects you and governs what you will get from, and what you must do for, a record company. The record company has the responsibility of placing its resources at the disposal of the artist, which includes its money, personnel, ability to get records pressed, advertising skills and any other management skills that it has to take what the artist gives it.

Furthermore, a record company is supposed to do the following for you: take your recorded product and expose it in discotheques, provide in-store airplay, give it to radio stations, and place you on television shows.

What is your responsibility to the contract? Normally, it is the responsibility of the artist to be exclusive to the record company. When you sign a recording contract, typically it is not an employee-employer relationship.

In this instance, you are an artist *by contract*. It specifically states in the contract that you are not an employee, and the record company is not your employer. You enter into an arrangement whereby you agree that your talents are unique, special and extraordinary. The company agrees or it would not invest the $50,000 in you. So, both you and the company agree that you are unique.

For a certain period of time—from the company's point of view—it wants you for as long as you are attached to the label, for as little an investment as possible. You, in turn, want as high a royalty rate from the company as possible for an artist to receive.

At the same time, you only want to be with the company for as short a period as necessary, in case you get *hot*. At that point, you will probably want another company to offer an even bigger contract or offer you a royalty at a higher rate.

The basic relationship of the artist to the record company is as follows: XYZ Record Company has the resources and the artist has the talent. The merging of the two takes quite an effort, not merely as partners or as in an employer-employee relationship, but simply to make a profit. So, basically, when you go in to make a deal, the record company is going to make a profit off of you.

If they don't make any money, then you are of no value to them, and vice versa. That's why when you go in and get your deal, get it for a short period of time, or try to get an escalating deal. Remember, "It's your contract and your future, so never let anyone talk you out of it by being greedy."

QUESTIONS FOR REFLECTION

Answer each numbered question with a brief essay.

1. Is the structure of a record company complex? Why is there a need for diversity of departments within a single company?

2. Discuss the formal structure described in the narrative. In what ways do various departments and department heads interact? What is the purpose of each department? Who controls communications and budget allocations?

3. Why is Marketing such an important department within a record company?

4. Analyze the differences between Sales, Promotion and Marketing functions.

5. Why does A&R enjoy such favored status within a company?

CHAPTER 2

IMPORTANCE OF THE MANAGER, ACCOUNTANT & ATTORNEY:

Relationships with Record Companies, Other People's Money, and the Basics of Music Publishing

The business representatives working with an artist perform clearly defined tasks, including but not limited to: personal management, money handling and overseeing legal matters.

Seemingly, all the above-mentioned responsibilities are succinctly self-descriptive activities. These functions are so indispensable to a successful career within music that a very harmonious rapport must be well-established if the serious business of making hits is to begin.

The Personal Manager is one of the most important people regarding the relationship between an artist and the record company. For a nominal fee of nearly 15-20 percent of gross earnings, a personal manager buffers his/her clients from the outrageousness of the industry.

The Personal Manager commiserates with the artist, telling him/her that in the long run, the long, lengthy hours in the studio will one day pay off handsomely. The manager also interfaces with the company, taking the welfare of the artist into their own hands. This individual gets the client booked for performances and image-building personal appearances. When necessary, managers will often scream, rant and rave in order to get their way.

A good manager-artist relationship is best described as a *partnership*. Shrewd managers totally free their acts of non-creative responsibilities, which allows all their energies to flow into the marketable package of an album or stage show.

Meanwhile, the manager wheels and deals through the industry network to position his artist well within the promotion/publicity hierarchy. They dream up marketing strategies, headline-grabbing promotional campaigns, and otherwise coordinates the non-creative functions of the artist's life.

To paraphrase Attorney Lloyd Zane Remick's comments in an issue of *Inner Visions*, published by the Black Music Association (BMA), "a manager is similar to a coach with an all-star quarterback. Not only does he groom the player and call the plays, he sees that they are executed as well."

Personal rapport is crucial to such a close relationship. Emotional compatibility and trust are key ingredients, since managers invariably have their hands in so many areas of an artist's life.

The professional arts are one of the prime occupations in which personal concerns between artist and manager continuously overlap with business affairs. Therefore, the developing artist must be open to suggestions from their manager, including the selection of clothing and places to socialize.

As time and experience mellow the successful relationship, more equality and personal autonomy by the artist will be appropriate. At that point, the successful manager is capable of maintaining his or her star client while developing others who are up and coming.

The manager-artist relationship is central to the operation of the record business. Successful managers are those who position themselves into a power conduit from which they exert all sorts of leverage. In the past, successful managers evolved to positions of label control, à la David Geffen, who founded Asylum Records.

Many managers tend to utilize the visibility of their star acts as a foundation, as with the *Eagles'* Irving Azoff and Front Line Management, or Cavallo-Ruffalo with *Earth, Wind and Fire*. In those cases, the success of the act was thoroughly correlated to the manager's ability to leverage them once a wedge in the door was established.

As an effective check and balance, most successful artists have a separate accountant. Ideally, the accountant isn't the manager's brother-in-law, unless one's trust is *that* overwhelming. But remember, *'It's a business.'*

Accounting separated from management simply tends to keep important matters free from second-guessing. For example, when the stakes in an artist's career get bigger and bigger. Customarily, accountants receive 1-2 percent of the artist's gross earnings.

Yet another individual who is of great importance is the attorney. Attorneys are hired to check the merits of all contracts offered to an artist. They work for a preset fee, on an as-needed basis. Many attorneys have the ability to perform managerial functions, and many evolve to that status once they learn the ropes of the music business.

A brief overview reveals that record companies prefer to deal with the above-mentioned formal business representatives, because they are both knowledgeable about dealings within the industry, and provide a direct, accountable link to the artist under contract.

The Value of *Other People's Money* or OPM

In their fascinating book *Your Introduction to Music-Record Copyright*, which dissects the basics of music business contracts and law, authors Walter E. Hurst and William Storm Hale, assess the value of *Other People's Money* or **OPM** for short.

Hurst and Hale heartily suggest, "Other people's money is the best thing available to an up and coming act." Furthermore, the authors concluded that most often artists work on **OPM** furnished by their parents. Other sources of **OPM** include banks, moneylenders, stores that sell on credit, friends and family members, or a personal manager.

We definitively concur with that notion. To the fledgling record company entrepreneur, **OPM** can be a godsend, better yet, a cool honeydew melon on a hot day. Since this *is* a book about record companies, we offer the following song lyrics to go along here:

The OPM Blues

Other People's Money, sugar-sweet, ah honey
Makes your life real sunny
Evathang be funny!
No better cure for the chills
--Brought on by empty pockets, foreclosed mortgage,
And overdue bills...

In all seriousness, the ability to attract the kind of investment capital necessary to run a small business offers tremendous value to a project. There is potential to reach high levels of motivation and enthusiasm when a bank, Small Business Association (SBA), or private lender kicks in venture capital bucks the size of a small fortune.

Remember, we're talking about six and seven figure sums of money necessary to run a company. That is, to say the least, a formidable vote of confidence for your ideas as an artist, wouldn't you agree?

ON BEING AN ENTERTAINMENT MANAGER

Commentary by John Levy

1981

John Levy was an entertainment manager years before many of today's stars were born.

Complete confidence and trust in each other is the best working relationship between an artist and manager. It is very personal, and, to me, it can be the closest social relationship that is publicly recognized other than marriage.

As a former musician, I had a natural feeling for the field of management. Everything just sort of fell into place once I slipped into the role of the manager. I felt that I'd gone as far as I could as an artist and needed a change.

Despite the fact that I was a competent musician and could have made a solid living off of making my music for the rest of my life, I just felt there was something more to it than that.

I had a knack for business and liked working with people. The balance came through the artistic part of the business, also known as the developmental stages of the artist, which is what I enjoy most.

BEFORE CHOOSING A MANAGER CONSIDER THIS

Commentary by David Banks

1981

In the instance of dealing with a record company that may have 75-80 artists signed to the label, the function of the manager is to see that certain things are done promotion-wise for the artist. If I go into a meeting concerning my artist, and the company tells me how well it's doing with another act, that's of no interest to me.

What's being done for my act is *my* primary concern, and, if you (the artist) do not have a person representing you like that, then your situation is indeed *weak*. As a manager, your primary responsibility is your artist, from promotions to artist development and everything else in between. You are the liaison connecting your artist to the record company.

Now I'd like to review how a manager functions on behalf of an artist. For example, you (the artist) have decided to record an album, but before you do so, you want a certain person to manage you.

Why would you want this individual over any of your other possible choices? The first thing you would probably be interested in is getting a solid education about what kind of clout a potential manager has, and what this person can do for you as opposed to someone else.

Many major Black artists today feel that they may not get ample management service through working with a *brother*, because they feel that he does not have the clout, economic resources or anything else that can help them. Unfortunately, there is a lot of truth in the prior statement, but things are slowly getting better.

The manager, per se, would be the person who represents you in all forms, from securing your deal and ensuring that you get the best exposure, to making sure that your records are being promoted properly. If the record is not selling, he must be knowledgeable enough to ask why that is. If the record is not good, there are certain reasons why it couldn't sell.

If you just released a record, and it's being played, but there are no sales for it, then automatically it should hit you that it is a *stiff.* So, when the situation is dissected, and you discover that it was actually played in Los Angeles, but there was no stock available, you should be able to understand why people cannot buy something that is not available for sale.

Record companies have too many artists to be concerned about any one in particular. The bigger the conglomerate, the more chances of the artist getting lost in the shuffle, therefore, the greater the need for a manager.

The first responsibility of a manager is to secure a contract with the best terms possible for the artist. In dealing with the contract, the manager is not so much concerned with the dollar value, as with the effort behind it, which eventually will wind up being a dollar amount.

One of the most misleading things occurs when you read that an artist signed a contract for Two Million Dollars. Most people actually think that the artist received that exact amount upon signing the contract.

What it really means is that the life of the contract would be worth Two Million over a five-year period, so that when the first album is delivered, he or she will get $300,000 that is recoverable against album sales. The next albums, it escalates—$350,000, $400,000, and so forth.

There are two ways to go about choosing a manager:

(A) You can go to a firm that has established a number of acts; most likely their successful track record will lure you to work with them.

(B) You can go for another manager whose track record may not be as successful as that of the firm, but it is understood that in order for this manager to make money, he or she will have to keep you working.

Manager B's value is dependent upon the ability to get you jobs, and you may become very dependent on his efforts. This is the advantage of having a Black manager who is usually hungrier, and will work harder for you (the artist).

The Black manager might crash down doors and represent you just as well, if not 100 percent better than the well-established manager. The last thing that an artist wants is a manager that is too content, and, therefore, thrives off your total dependency on them, as opposed to the manager being totally dependent on you.

TYPES OF LEGAL RESPONSIBILITIES

Commentary by Larry Stephens

1981

Within the industry, attorneys can function in a number of ways. They can be an Attorney/Manager, which really brings him/her into the day-to-day aspects of the artist's career. Contrast that with an attorney who functions just as an attorney with the major focus of their time being spent on contract negotiations with the record company.

If there are certain built-in follow-up procedures within the contract, the company will have to be monitored to make sure that all provisions are met. When the attorney functions in that capacity, he or she will not be involved in the career of the artist on a day-to-day basis.

His or her role will be more of an as-needed consultant, when matters arise. Despite, this, more attorneys are moving into the role of a manager.

As an attorney for a record company, I am required to be involved in negotiating contracts, signing artists, and amending agreements for artists. In short, I draft, negotiate, and follow up on deals with artists, lawyers, and their managers. I also get into administering contracts.

For example, a normal agreement is for one year plus successive options. If we do not want to elect to obtain the services of an artist for another year, we have to give the artist 30 days' notice prior to execution according to the contact.

If, indeed, we decide to pick up the services of an artist, we don't have to say anything. We just renew the contract for a new year. But someone has to watch that, just to be aware of when the 30-day limit approaches.

For example, if a company does not want to renew a contract for a particular artist and forgets to send in the notice, then by default, it is stuck with them for another year, which you can imagine costs a lot of money. In a sense, being an attorney who works with a record company is almost like being a corporate lawyer in any other situation.

Whatever the outcome, someone will always feel like they have been given less than their fair share of justice. We generally do not handle litigation, which is why we have outside counsel who may be geared up to go to court every day to handle that.

Other very active areas of legal concern include uses of music on soundtracks for films and on television, which involves licensing agreements. Producers also have to be cognizant of their agreements with record companies. For example, one album may have as many as three producers and everyone needs a contract, which is how one gets involved in Producer's Agreements.

Publishing Agreements are also of interest and sometimes entail single song contracts. So, when someone wants to use a published tune in a movie, they will need to have a Sync License for that song.

Piracy or record bootlegging are issues which continuously occupy much of a corporate attorney's time. In such cases, there is a composer who has been denied his or her share of the Mechanical Royalties.

A certain portion of sales from each record will go into the American Federation of Musicians (AF of M) Health & Welfare Fund. In this situation, the record company and the performers do not realize their just due because the bootlegger does not pay the artist his/her royalties, or for the right to use the composition.

The bootlegger gets a free ride all the way around, riding on all the promotional dollars and publicity. Additionally, the bootlegger unknowingly affects the employment picture within the music industry. Occasionally, when record companies have had to let people go, it is quite possible that it was a result of the loss in receipts due to the activities of pirates.

A typical instance that I have dealt with regarding record piracy revolved around an incident in Greenville, South Carolina. A printer had been making up labels for a year without really knowing what the labels were for.

He had done at least $70,000 worth of business with an alleged pirate. He cited one order in which he had made six cases which contained 25,000 labels. That represents 150,000 tapes in one batch—no artist royalties and no mechanicals—and that was just one guy operating in Greenville, South Carolina.

Imagine how many millions of dollars' worth of tapes were being sold without a single dime paid to companies. Seemingly companies are not selling as many records as they could because people are buying them from bootleggers.

PIRACY AND ATTORNEYS REPRESENTING MAJOR ARTISTS

Commentary by John Mason

1981

John Mason has represented major artists such as Quincy Jones, Kenny Rogers and Donna Summers. Below is his viewpoint on the effects of piracy and how attorneys represent artists signed to major labels.

From the viewpoint of many artists, a longer record contract period provides security for the future, whereas a shorter contract provides an adequate leeway for negotiation. As attorneys, we do not get into the career planning aspect of an artist's life nor do we decide where, what, or whom they play or record for. Those decisions are best left to the managers who represent them.

Our interest is solely on behalf of the artists that we represent, and is further related to their overall non-creative business within the record company. It is our goal to make sure that they are protected to the maximum extent possible, vis-á-vis the terms of their record deal, financial planning, tax planning, business planning, investments and every other aspect of an artist's business life.

We want to make sure that every benefit available from a record company is obtained for our client. That's probably different, I suppose, than a record company whose true interest is in setting records and maximizing their profitability from record sales.

I think company attorneys should be concerned about the long-range financial picture for the record company, as well as any one particular deal. Our concern is for the one client, for their long-range planning. I advise artists to check out a firm's reputation very closely before making a decision. Talk to a number of artists and people in the business. Get some references and check them out. Meet with several people, then make a choice about who will represent you.

NEGOTIATING RECORD CONTRACTS

Commentary by Marc T. Little

© Law Offices of Marc T. Little

2003

Marc T. Little is an entertainment attorney whose work acumen has given him the opportunity to work with many of music's greatest contemporary artists. Following are a few pointers he gives to anyone who is negotiating a record deal.

The ten most important points in the negotiation of a record deal are crucial, and I have listed them below. Artists, regardless of genre, should always keep these questions in mind before signing off on anything.

(1) How long will the contract last and what are the terms of renewal?

(2) How many sides will a performer record, and is the label required to release finished recordings commercially?

(3) How much money will you receive from the sale of original singles, albums, cassettes, CDs and videos?

(4) What are the reduced royalty clauses? (This establishes what you will receive for sales in foreign countries, record club or TV album collections and low-priced budget albums.)

(5) What expenses will the label deduct from your earnings —from the cost of album covers and special inserts to limousines and travel expenses? (You need to have this spelled out.)

(6) As your sales rise, will royalties automatically increase?

(7) How many copies of product can a company give away for free or at a discount without paying royalties to you?

(8) How much money can be withheld from your royalties in anticipation of product returned by the stores for credit?

(9) What criteria is used in establishing cash advances?

(10) Will you be paid lower songwriter royalties when you perform your own songs? (Keep in mind that a successful best hits collection could mean financial fiascos to a writer/artist if other songwriters on the album won't reduce their royalties.)

THE SERVICES OF A BOOKING AGENT

Commentary by Don Fischel

1981

Basically, we find employment for the artists. In effect, we are an employment agency, and in the State of California we are licensed similarly. More than that, a good booking agent is not simply going to seek out any sort of work for the artist—he or she is, however, going to seek out the right work for the artist.

A manager guides the career of an artist and has to wear many hats. Being an expert on everything is increasingly hard for a manager to handle. If a manager has a qualified agent, he's got to rely very heavily on that agent.

I'm in the personal appearance marketplace daily. Not only do I seek out the employment, but I realize that the manager has to rely heavily on me or any other booking agent to come in with recommendations:

- *Do we play at the Santa Monica Civic Center now?*
- *Do we play at the Forum now?*
- *Do we play in a large building?*
- *Do we play in a small building?*
- *Do we accept a specific offer to play on a particular night?*
- *Are we better off accepting an offer for a show a month later?*
- *Is it time for an artist to play at a certain venue?*
- *Is it time for an artist to perform in Las Vegas or New York?*

These are all questions that are asked daily by managers. It's not just booking the acts and taking a commission that I'm concerned with; it is, however, booking the acts into the right venue, at the right time of year, with the right promoter. As you can see, I work very closely with managers.

This is a very exciting and stimulating business; financially it can be extremely rewarding. People get into the agency in various ways. Most people stumble or fall into this line of work, but I started out in a training program. A guy that I worked with at Regency Artists started out as a former promoter and entertainment chairman.

Booking can be accomplished in several ways. If there was a concern, or a one-nighter, the booking agency would route out the tour, reserve the buildings, and assign promoters. Another instance may be that promoters in various markets have buildings available and as the booking agent, I would negotiate with them depending upon the stature of the act.

With very large acts I would go and route my own tours, as well as decide who the promoters should be in the various markets. In the case of the smaller acts and the acts coming up, the promoter will have gotten his headliner one way or another and he makes you an offer for your support talent.

There are a lot of meetings that take place between agent and manager, sometimes including the artist. We all learn from each other. At the end of it all, my job is much deeper than just booking a date.

BASICS OF MUSIC PUBLISHING

A publisher is the legal intermediary between writers and record companies. They screen music and lyrics for commercial content, and secure protection for proper writer credits. Publishers provide lead sheets, copyrights, demo tapes, and otherwise promote artists to all potential buyers of songs. They also grant the rights to record companies for commercial uses, to television producers and to foreign publishers.

There are three performing rights societies in the United States: the American Society of Composers, Authors & Publishers (ASCAP), Broadcast Music, Inc. (BMI), and the Society of European Stage Authors and Composers (SESAC). These societies acquire the rights to license usage from members, and thus serve as clearinghouses for non-dramatic public performance. Terms of membership vary for each organization.

There is no initiation fee to join ASCAP, but annual dues of $10 for writers and $50 for publishers is charged. To become eligible, you simply need either a commercially recorded composition or a musical composition that has been regularly published, or a composition performed by an ASCAP licensed user. The duration of ASCAP agreements is usually ten years.

BMI charges publishers an initial fee of $25, with no initial fees or annual dues for writers. A writer may join BMI if that person has written a musical composition which is either commercially published or recorded, or otherwise likely to be performed.

Publisher members must demonstrate that they have the necessary finances to capitalize on musical compositions, and should have some songs already circulated.

To join BMI, it is necessary to file an application and sign a contract. The usual duration of a BMI writer's contract is two years. The usual duration of a publisher's contract is five years.

SESAC is similar in representation as the other two societies, covering mechanical, synchronization and performance licensing. Agreements with writers generally have a three-year duration, while publishing agreements last five years.

Three additional agencies that serve publishers include, The Harry Fox Agency, the Copyright Service Bureau, and the American Guild of Authors and Composers. The Harry Fox Agency provides a clearinghouse for licensing rights, other than for performance.

Fox is a publishers' organization that was established by and for them to license mechanical and synchronization rights, as well as rights of use in commercials. For a 3.5 percent fee, the agency issues licenses, collects royalties and distributes them to publishers.

The Copyright Service Bureau (CSB) services writers and publishers by filing copyrights—preparing basic publishing agreements, licensing copyrights, auditing and maintaining various clients' books and records. The American Guild of Authors and Composers (AGAC) is primarily a songwriters' organization. AGAC collects royalties and administers both copyright renewals, and a writer-publisher catalog. The basic AGAC licensing agreement is recognized throughout the industry for its thoroughness.

PUBLISHING CRITERIA

What is a publisher?
A publisher is a legal go-between for a writer and a record company.

What does a publisher do?
The publisher screens your work, music and lyrics for its commercial content, and secures the proper protection for you to receive proper writer credits. Publishers can provide lead sheets, copyrights and even demo tapes.

Publishers are the songwriter's promoter to the record company, production company, artist, and the A&R directors. Publishers are responsible for issuing a license to the record company for commercial release when a song has been recorded.

If I wanted to start my own publishing company, what tools will I need?

Songs, songwriters, a computer, stationery, publisher office manual, turntable, tape recorder, and if you are going to do your own lead sheets, you will need music manuscript paper, onionskins, etc.

Additionally, you will need ordinary things such as file cabinets, file folders and a closet for your dubs and tapes. You will also need some forms such as copyright forms and BMI songwriter forms.

For ASCAP, you will need index cards, publisher clearance forms, publisher songwriter-to-publisher forms, publisher/co-publisher forms, publisher-to-record company forms, mechanical license and letters of transmittal.

Remember: "YOUR SONGS ARE YOUR STOCK IN TRADE." PROTECT THEM! There are certain grants we must deal with, such as songwriter grants in the song to the publisher. A publisher grants the right to the record company to use the song for commercial use, rights to use TV producers and other uses. Publishers grant the rights in ownership to foreign publishers.

Is there a difference between BMI and ASCAP?

No. BMI is Broadcast Music, Inc, and ASCAP is American Society of Composers, Authors and Publishers. Both are performing rights organizations.

What are performing rights?

They are the rights granted under the U.S. Copyright Act, given to owners of musical works to license the work. Some examples include songs to be publicly performed on radio, television, or at nightclubs, hotels and concerts.

What are some of the things that BMI and ASCAP do for artists?

Since it is impossible for any one person to license all of these works to each music user, BMI or ASCAP acquires the rights from songwriters and publishers, and, in turn, licenses the music. BMI and ASCAP also collect fees from each user of music it licenses.

BMI and ASCAP pay all monies collected to its writers and publishers as a performance royalty, except what is needed as operating expenses and licenses for phonograph records. They do not license any other rights, such as stage plays or the legitimate theater or stage. Dramatic stage plays must be obtained directly from the creators of the show.

LAW OF COPYRIGHTS

Congress has the sole and exclusive power to regulate copyrights. *Where does Congress obtain the power?* Under *Article I, Section 8, Clause 8* in the Constitution, power is granted and maintained by Congress regarding *patents and copyrights.*

> "To promote the progress of Science and Useful Arts, by securing for *limited* times to Authors and Inventors the exclusive right to their respective writings and discoveries."

Note: *No copyright lasts forever.*

> "Generally, a copyright on a work created on or after January 1, 1978, endures for a term of 50 years from its creation and 50 years after the death."

NOTE: (Copyright Law as of 2016)
The term of copyright for a particular work depends on several factors, including whether it has been published, and, if so, the date of first publication. As a general rule, for works created after January 1, 1978, copyright protection lasts for the life of the author plus an additional 70 years. For an anonymous work, a pseudonymous work, or a work made for hire, the copyright endures for a term of 95 years from the year of its first publication or a term of 120 years from the year of its creation, whichever expires first. For works first published prior to 1978, the term will vary depending on several factors. To determine the length of copyright protection for a particular work, consult Chapter 3 of the Copyright Act (title 17 of the *United States Code).* More information on the term of copyright can be found in Circular 5a, *Duration of Copyright*, and Circular 1.

Suppose you cannot prove that the person is dead, would it be possible for you to use his/her work without facing a lawsuit for copyright infringement?
The answer is YES. After a period of 75 years from the initial publication of the work, or a period of one hundred years from the year of its creation, (whichever expires first), any person who obtains a certified (or sealed) report from the copyright office assumes that the records within the copyright office disclose nothing.

Further, any person indicating that the author of the work is living or has died less than 50 years after the inception of the work is entitled to the benefit of the presumption that the author has been dead for at least 50 years. Reliance in good faith upon this presumption is a complete defense to copyright infringement.

COPYRIGHT VIOLATION
Anyone who violates any of the exclusive rights of the copyright owner or who imports copies of either records or compact discs into the United States without the authority of the owner, is deemed an infringer of copyrights.

What happens if you are sued for copyright infringement?
Should this occur, the judge would issue an injunction court order to make the individual stop violating your copyright.
(1) Money, or the actual damages
(2) Profits made by the infringer or
(3) Statutory damages as follows: Not less than $250 or greater $10,000, but if you prove that the violation is willful, you can recover up to $50,000.

NOTE: You must elect before judgment to have statutory or actual and loss profits.

(4) Attorney's fees (Don't forget your honest workers)

What rights do a copyright disclose for a recording?
(1) Reproduction
(2) Distribution
(3) To perform the copyright work publicly

(4) To display the work publicly
(5) To prepare de-route works

Must you give notice on the musical product of the copyright to be protected?
Yes. It is necessary to site 17 U.S.C. Section 402.

What form should the notice be in?
The notice appearing on the compact disc or phonorecord shall consist of the following three elements:
(1) The symbol ® (the letter R put in a circle)
(2) The year of the first publication
(3) The name of the owner of the copyright

Where should the copyright notice be placed?
The notice should be placed on the surface of the compact disc, phonorecord, or on the record label or contained in such manner and location as to give reasonable notice of the claim of copyright.

Can you transfer or will (bequeath) copyright?
Yes. It is personal property.

THE LIFE OF A SONG
Commentary by Mabel John
1981

Music publisher, singer and songwriter Mabel John compares the life of a song to the birth cycle of a baby.

A publisher will screen a song for commercial value while also promoting the song. My theory is that we would do a song like you would handle a baby's birth record. When a baby is conceived, not born, the mother goes to the doctor. She seeks care to nourish the baby so it'll be healthy and strong.

Your publisher handles your creation in the same way so that the song is nourished as a good commercial piece of material. If the lead sheet is done when you take it to the publisher, they won't reject it because it does not look like 'homemade' material.

It appears professional, meaning that a copyright has been secured so there is no doubt as to who authored and composed the tune. This is all included in the process of making a song. If the publisher has done these things correctly, they will then showcase your song to producers, to the recording artist who is looking for material, and to A&R directors who screen material.

The above-mentioned people will listen to the songs and find an artist within their company structure who the tune is best suited for. As a publisher, I may know that you are looking for a particular type of tune, and knowing that there are good tunes in the catalog, I can say to the record company or the artist that I have a good tune best suited for a particular artist. This is where the publisher becomes a liaison between the writer and the record company.

One of the major jobs of the publisher is to secure a U.S. Copyright from the Library of Congress, to be sure that your tunes have been copyrighted in your name, then you own the copyright. So, you find a publisher, take your lead sheet and copyright to him or her, and you let them handle it. Then, it's up to the publisher.

Ask them certain questions such as the following: M*ay I have a copy of the copyright? Will you sign it over to the publishing company?* This gives the publisher the legal right to negotiate your song and copyright your work on your behalf. The publisher is also a responsible party to the record company to issue a license when a song has been recorded.

The writer cannot issue a license, only a publisher has the authority to issue a recording license. Once a writer gives a song to the publisher, he or she sees to it that the lead sheet is done, the copyright is done, and a good demo is made. Then, if the record company decides to use the writer's song, the publisher grants them the right to put this song on the market for commercial sale.

At some point, you may want to have your own publishing company. In order to do so, you need the following: songs, song-writers, stationery, and a publisher office manual. Every publishing company should have that manual in the office. It is your reference. There are dummy copies of contracts so that you can always have a guideline, because every situation in any contract deal is always negotiable.

You should never be in such a big hurry to get your song recorded that you just dump it anywhere. You should take time to analyze the situation. If you took pride in putting the material together, then you should choose a publisher who feels the same way about you and your song.

We categorize music so that it all falls prospectively into place. Whether *Country, Pop, Rock, Jazz* or *Blues,* it takes a certain kind of person to know the true potential of a song.

Other needs in starting a publishing company include a good CD player to hear the product, and a good tape recorder to duplicate from the CD. Those are just some of the basics, but most importantly, a publishing company is a very important aspect of the record industry.

No two artists will sell a song the same way. Every artist will be original in his or her concept, and will never change the words to a song, unless they are going to do an ad lib. An artist might add some words, but will never take the writer's words out.

You cannot take the exact same melody from a song and put it with another song and call it original—that would be sampling. If I come up with an idea, and another person might come up with something similar, that is a bit different.

Sometimes certain writers and certain publishing companies will not even allow you to even mention the title of the song you are singing. In every case, you have to ask permission, and permission always comes from the writer and the record producer.

A TYPICAL WORK DAY
Commentary by Brenda Andrews
1981

Former publishing executive Brenda Andrews *provides an overview of a typical work day for her.*

My daily routine consists of listening to songs that are given to me by songwriters, and making contacts with producers and artists to see who is currently recording. I want to know when a group is going into the studio, and what type of material they are looking for.

You are the creator of your whole day. No one is giving you anything, nor are they putting any paper in front of you. It's up to you to keep things going every day, which is a 24-hour job. We get the songs recorded, make new deals with writers, and listen to new music all the time because it's constantly changing and getting into the streets where things are happening.

The revenue comes in the form of royalties from tunes, not only recorded but on television, motion pictures and commercials. Publishing is an investment, like money in the bank. It just keeps generating money from performances to radio airplay, and every time it's played in doctors' offices.

After the artist is deceased, the money flows to their children. Many songs generate hundreds of thousands, even millions of dollars consistently.

ADVICE FOR PROSPECTIVE SONGWRITERS

Commentary by Janie Bradford

1981

Janie Bradford offers advice to prospective songwriters.

I started with Motown during its inception. I was still in my teens and was fortunate enough to co-write one of the company's earliest releases titled "Money" with Berry Gordy. I was a lyricist, which was how I grew as a writer. But I was still working every day at a regular job.

I was never the kind of writer who lived off of royalties. I always worked, even when I picked up my biggest royalty checks. I began as a receptionist, but it wasn't like it is today. I took care of artists' contracts, publishing, copyrights, and everything else. I even ordered records.

As the company grew and formed separate departments, I moved into publishing exclusively. For twenty years, I've been working in publishing, and it's a very lucrative end.

The publisher copyrights the song and knows the length of the copyright's life. He or she licenses the music to other record companies and actually works a song.

If, for instance, I was a writer who went to Motown's Jobete Publishing with a song that may not be right for a Motown act, they may take it to an outsider.

Publishing companies are separate entities from record companies, though the same person may own both. It is a publisher's job to offer songs to anybody, their associated company or anyone else they can get it to.

When I talk to many young writers as they're coming up, the first thing they want is a part of their royalties. I ask them if they know anybody in the business to get the song to, or whether they know about licensing, collection, or making a foreign deal.

Writers should go to a company first as a writer. Then, as you grow as a writer, learn these things and get your name out there where somebody's requesting a Holland-Dozier-Holland or Stevie Wonder tune, then you can talk publishing.

You're in demand and these things will be automatically done. You will get a call from a foreign territory where your song is wanted. In the beginning, I think all writers should deal with a reputable publisher that actively works the songs and knows the best form of protection for the writer.

QUESTIONS FOR REFLECTION

Answer each numbered question with a brief essay.

1. Discuss the relationship between a manager and an artist. What are the objectives of the partnership? What role does each play?

2. What are a few of the qualifications of a manager? Who is best qualified to manage? How is success in this field evaluated?

3. Describe the roles and functions of attorneys, booking agents and accountants in the music industry.

4. How important are songwriting/publishing holdings to a company?

5. Who is Marc T. Little? Why are protective laws important in specific situations?

CHAPTER 3

CREATING A HIT ACT

Now that the company has a definite structure with roles and functions defined, and the business of managing the artist has been described, likewise, what is next? It is time to develop a hit act.

First, a clear distinction must be established. There is a striking difference between a hit act and an act capable of hits. Though many contemporary artists fall into both categories, few remain a hit act very long.

Hit acts are artists that are capable of selling out concerts and events to generate massive fan appeal with personal charisma and otherwise sustain themselves at a high level for a long time. *Billy Eckstine, Lou Rawls, and Frank Sinatra*, and more recently *Nelly, Janet Jackson, and Michael Jackson,* are all prototypes of hit acts, for all the years and moments they've given the world.

Eckstine has thrived nearly half a century, establishing his career during the first twenty years and benefiting from a prudent image self-development campaign ever since. Ever debonair in his senior years, *"Mr. B"* draws on a repertoire of elegant standards to maintain a worldwide following. But he hasn't had a gigantic hit record since Truman was President.

Sinatra was not always a hit act. In his earliest days, he was a teenage idol dependent on the fluky whims of fans tied superficially to his charisma. He grew to *hit act* status only after the personal misfortune over a shattered career convinced him to diversify his appeal. His moves became *image-related,* and he got very serious about his acting, as the tour de force showcase in the movie *From Here to Eternity* demonstrated.

From the early '50s onward, Sinatra successfully cultivated the identity of a figure of modern American legendry, a personification of the successful artist-businessman. He periodically cut records and made films, which kept him in high visibility. Sinatra's talents were showcased and publicized through all available media channels. Even as his initial claim to fame—his vocal talents—were on the wane, his image accelerated.

Reviewers today soft-pedal criticism of his periodic concert performances, emphasizing in larger-than-life overtones the momentous significance of such appearances. Sinatra's hit act carries the connotation of being an American institution, though he has long since stopped being in the forefront of artistic innovation.

Acts that are capable of hits are a different story. The recent portrait reveals numerous *one hit wonders* who had an ear for a currently-appreciated style, and the ability to put a hit together in the studio. But such raw talent is only one element in the making of a hit act. With the issue of longevity in mind, artists should undergo the necessary training and preparation for a diversified career.

The intelligent record company, then, has the responsibility to develop the artist, create an image which reaches out to the public's demand, and to test the waters through showcasing and profuse airplay.

Indeed, image development and airplay are a necessary triad to create a hit act today. Tour business has slumped tremendously since its peak in the early 70s. Placement of an artist is, therefore, all important in diversified markets for maximum publicity, exposure and seasoning.

An artist's image must carry maximum impact to transcend run-of-the-mill candidates for public adulation and support. Radio airplay is the best means of communicating with the public, and an integral part of the sales strategy.

A well-known truism in this business maintains that groups move in cycles. They are here today, and gone tomorrow. Consequently, the prudent record entrepreneur looks to create a hit act that will make money over a long period of time. Once the first stages of signing and seasoning have taken place, the artist should be exposed through a good public relations campaign.

Good public relations is essential to anyone's image, and in the record business it translates directly into dollars and cents. The public buys records, for the most part, based on awareness of the artist's music correlated with familiarity to his identity.

The ideal mix is an artist with high visibility potential through good looks, personal charisma and wide public identification, also able to perform well and to project an articulate pose. Are the Bee Gees a simple enough example to provide a context?

A good public relations firm projects the artist from an angle, which builds interest beyond immediate perception of a record or a film. So it was that John Travolta's canonization as a media idol was fabricated in the public relations heat accompanying the movie *Saturday Night Fever*.

The hype became so intense that the star's story superseded the film; personal experiences took on epic trappings in the hands of the copywriters, who played on the immediacy of the public's need for an identifiable symbolic role model.

His attraction was based on his own raw talent—his youth fed into the gristmill, which creates commercial American idols. The image was built for him; a necessary function of the selling process connected with a major movie. Travolta has since spring boarded into a full-fledged personality.

Elvis Presley may have been the single most successful beneficiary of an image campaign in the history of the music business. His manager Tom Parker built his star's following to fever pitch early.

He exploited classic promotion devices such as a sense of the absurd in relation with the press, making the angle of Elvis' sex appeal, and institutionalizing him in celluloid via a film or two per year. The result? Elvis was elevated to near-royalty status, grossing as much as six million dollars a year during his prime.

The image contrasts which accompanied the Beatles' and Rolling Stones' rise to superstardom deserves commentary as well. Early on, the Beatles hit American soil with lightning speed and hurricane force.

Their strange new music was accessible enough in the beginning, but certainly not light years ahead of the pack, as sales figures from the period have indicated to be the case. The extra ingredient was the element of personal identification of fans, which suddenly realized via public relations hype that this particular group of musicians was worthy of undying love and admiration.

The 'Mop-Top Fab-Four' conveyed an undercurrent of winsome wholesomeness. Paul McCartney looked squeaky clean, which pleased teenage girls to no end. They screamed their lungs out from the initial Ed Sullivan Show appearance to the final Shea Stadium concert.

Ultimately, when parents started humming their sweet tunes like "Michelle" and "Yesterday," the image of the Beatles became thoroughly accessible to a cross section of people.

The Rolling Stones, however, never aimed their appeal at suburban mothers. Their public relations in the early years was a studied contrast to the Beatles. They conveyed a rebellious, aberrant image.

Whereas the Beatles dignifiedly acknowledged the influence of Blues and R&B in their sound, the Stones tried to live out a fantasy act as a group of space-age 'New Negroes.' Mick Jagger's voice approximated bluesman Jimmy Reed, which was certainly a hard sound for a square family living in the English midlands to readily digest.

But 'city-fied' teenagers appreciated the Stones for the alternative they represented. Their image as satanic-majesties and street-fighting men was well drawn for the culture of youth so defined in the late 60s. But, significantly, there was room for only one kingpin in this rivalry. The Stone's greatest image and commercial success happened after the Beatles breakup.

There are many sidelights and dimensions to this process. Obviously, it is easier to generate and publicize one hit than it is to develop a series of ongoing successes that will secure a career indefinitely. In each case cited above—including Travolta's—timing, persistence and longevity have played a huge role in image building.

One's creative abilities are not necessarily the key element. Another truism worth voicing is the reality that the best talent is not always hooked up with the best outlet/exposure network. A lousy public relations campaign can spell the death of a budding career more quickly than anything else. To an unproven act with lots of potential, public image is the only thing that matters.

In the one shot suicidal world of records, it's okay for Rick James to get up and curse at his audience because he's milking a clientele. They expect their favorites to project a defiant pose. But such behavior might spell death to a sophisticated balladeer's career. To be most successful, the balladeer needs an image of loving warmth and joy. As support, feature articles and press releases must have similar overtones.

In a successful image marketing campaign, great pains must be taken to correlate the artist's product with the market his image best plays to. Once again, each artist described above fits into a given category of public appeal—Travolta and Elvis, the matinee idols; the Beatles, helping bring off an important musical revolution; Sinatra, Rawls and Eckstine, "long-distance runners" with plenty of stamina.

Each fulfilled an identifiable public need, or a need was artificially manufactured, helped along via public relations writing, public showcasing and word of mouth. To that end, a company with a keen sense of PR can have a flashy impact. That's the nature of the business. It is image oriented with success calibrated by tangible manifestations of largess...big cars, glittery jewelry, and so forth.

The classic PR portrait of successful artists paints them as champions, à la the Beatles. Biographies and film treatments convey a strong feeling of inevitability about their destiny. Even bumbling Ringo is seen as a beautiful loser. His goofiness a fun counterpoint to the others' antics.

A good copywriter/public relations campaigner can make a difference in a group's repertoire of tools. Think of a few outstanding advertising and public relations-oriented articles that you've read over the years. Much of it has been stunningly hypnotic, no doubt, buttressing your own particular prejudices about a specific act.

At other times, you may have been motivated to run out and buy some delectable looking album package on the strength of the *image*: for example, a strikingly beautiful woman on the cover or an inventive article which touts a given group as the greatest thing to hit planet earth ever. Surely, you've read one of those stories.

Such items of hype run a dangerous risk. In a free market, as the saying goes, "fair exchange is no robbery." However, if you are shoving a dog meat piece of product down the public's throat in a $250,000 PR marketing campaign, your ethics are reproachable.
If you compare a new artist to Chopin on the premise that they both played piano, then you're a fool. Inevitably, you might draw a crowd of classical lovers to a punk rock concert.

Hit acts differ further from the others in various regards. "Manufactured" groups like Humble Pie and Blind Faith, popular during the acid Rock era, typified the reflexive relationship between high fan interest and record companies exploiting a trend. Both were "super groups" (note the PR hype) formed to capitalize on the moment.

Stevie Winwood, Ginger Baker, and the others became instant geniuses by all the press puffery aimed at them. But the recorded output in each case was far inferior to the cult of personality mystique developed around the principles; Blind Faith's record was no better than an extended jam, despite Eric Clapton's occasionally great licks.

As for Humble Pie, its major claim to fame was signing an advance contract for a healthy $900,000 on the strength of the players' overblown reputations. Surely, Peter Frampton and Steve Marriott were recognizable names, but subsequent recordings put a lie to the belief that this group was all-star or immortal. Again, that's the value of a successful PR machine in an image-conscious medium.

We cannot overstress this reality: The most successful contemporary acts have longevity attached to the public relations efforts. When groups like Ted Nugent, Foghat, and Bob Seger finally broke big, the seemingly endless days of entertaining on the road finally paid off.

'Paying dues' is nowhere captioned better than in songs about the record business. Blacks have the legacy of the 'Chitlin' Circuit' to fall back on in such matters. The Chitlin' Circuit, as it is routinely called, is the unofficial successor to the TOBA circuit. Blacks as diverse as Bessie Smith and the classic Blues singers, Duke Ellington and Louis Armstrong, Black minstrels and operatic virtuosos, cut their teeth in these all-Black settings.

Nowadays, the popularity of Black music demands classy showcasing on Sunset Boulevard, rather than across the tracks. But years of struggling on the Chitlin' Circuit has helped thoroughly prepare many acts—especially in the matter of inner poise, persistence and development of a hit formula.

Two types of settings are most appropriate for showcasing today's hippest talent. There are 'Tastemaker Clubs' located throughout the country where the local music scene makers congregate. If the club is in the Exit/Inn in Nashville, the Bottom Line in New York, or L.A.'s Roxy, most sets will be viewed by observers able to help your act along.

Writers, A&R, and promotion executives love to catch sets in these places—both to see and be seen. They pass the word along through the industry grapevine regarding an act's relative merits, and promotional efforts are often geared up accordingly. The other setting appropriate is to appear as an opening act for a major headliner. The aim in such an instance is to secure some of the headliner's fans, to continue developing as a performer, and build a base of support.

Pitfalls of appearing as an opening act are legendary, quietly spoken by artists who've crossed over to star billing. Politically, an opening act should be aware of the repercussions of upstaging a top-lining band.

Also, groups who require a lot of equipment on stage shows are needlessly limiting themselves. Travel costs are high as it is, and a cumbersome band creates extra logistic problems…but only briefly. The minimum wage salary a new group earns will not keep them on the road too long if they cannot meet expenses.

THE ROLE OF FORMULA IN DEVELOPING AN ACT'S IMAGE
Commentary by Ed Wright
1981

Black Music Association (BMA) co-founder Ed Wright, discusses the role of formula in developing an act's image.

I think each situation is a case by itself, and everybody has their own way of doing things. The way I try to deal is to first find out what that artist wants to be. All the public relations, publicity, and hype in the world will not get it, if it's not honest.

The key thing is to try and create an honest image, and develop it through the various areas of media that you bring in to play on the direction of the campaign. You try to devise a campaign that touches the artist's areas of strength. If an artist has a Black base, you want to touch it through the various publications, radio, and television shows that can help encourage that image.

If they have a strong base of development, you'll be able to expand their market into other areas. Television exposure and reviews in the daily newspaper are very helpful. But, I wouldn't want Leonard Feather to review Donald Byrd, now that he has turned to electric music. The only thing Leonard's going to talk about is the purity.

However, I'd want Leonard to do a Pharaoh Sanders. You have to know what the tastes are of critics and reviewers. Then again, you don't promise an act a *People* magazine cover when you know that only two or three Blacks are going to be on the cover of *People* in a given year. A lot of acts want covers all the time, without acknowledging that a piece in a magazine is still reaching a large consumer market that they might not have had access to.

There are certain discussion-type shows that are significant. But a spot on the Tonight Show that's not under the right premise may be the wrong type of promotion. Doing a song, without being talked to, isn't all that valuable as exposure. It's similar in a politician's case when he decides to run and takes a sophisticated poll, finds out the voter concerns and tries to address them with statements made through the media to the constituency they're trying to reach.

THE ROLE OF ANGLES IN PROJECTING AN ACT
Commentary by Bernice Sanders
circa 1981

Publicist Bernice Sanders comments on the role of angles in projecting an act.

I don't think there's a consistent formula for establishing an artist's image. You have to deal with each artist individually, look at their potential, and gear the particular campaign to the artist. It has to be something the artist can sustain. If you use a formula—let's say—to make a quiet homebody-type into a wild man, after a while they can't sustain it.

There is, however, a formula for approaching magazines for placement of stories about an act. There are smaller, weekly newspapers that you can go to when an act is smaller. There are ethnic newspapers that you place stories in to secure interest there.

During a nationwide Bob Marley tour in 1979, I wanted to expose him to as wide an audience as possible. We started with all the cult papers—the Reggae papers that naturally would want Marley on the cover. Those are the people who supported him from the word 'go.'

You build from there, and get further and further away from his base. Ultimately, you build Marley an image suitable for consumer publications. As you get further away from the base, you have to cover up with more creative angles.

I think we were very successful in exposing him this way. I have a whole box of clippings from all over that attest to that fact. Results are measured in the amount of placement beyond the base of Reggae magazines into CBS news.

In looking for angles, I personally spend a lot of time with the artist. Most people are pretty well rounded, and you can come up with things that are applicable to a lot of publications by just talking with them.

You might talk with the members of the group and find out that someone is a racing car enthusiast. So then, you call the racing car magazines if his enthusiasm is to the point where he has invested in a formula car. But you can only find these things out when you spend time with the artist. It's a very personalized process.

THE PERILS OF PUBLICIZING JAZZ ARTISTS
Commentary by Terri Hinte
1981

Terri Hinte critiques the perils of publicizing Jazz artists.

In doing publicity for Jazz artists, there's a lot of elitism involved. You'll get more Rock & Roll people interested in an act than the Black press. The amount of press that a Jazz artist gets has nothing to do with record sales.

Art Pepper, for instance, has gotten a bonanza of press coverage, but still sells extremely modestly. That situation is unlikely to change. I think there is very little correlation between Jazz publicity and record sales. The elitism is a big part of it. A lot of these Rock writers like the idea of writing about Jazz because it makes them hipper than thou.

In fact, you can't deny the Jazz artists' musical credentials and interesting facets of his or her life. I think that more credibility is afforded to Jazz musicians than any other musicians in the business.

The people who made Rock & Roll, and Rhythm & Blues records may be just as accomplished, but they are not going to achieve as much acclaim for their musical skills as a Jazz artist will. It doesn't mean that people are going out to buy a Jazz record. Critics will just talk about how wonderfully someone plays the piano.

How is a Jazz artist's image developed? Well, take a Sonny Rollins. For a long time, it was an 'in' thing to write about how horrible his records sounded, and how wonderful he played live. "Isn't it too bad he doesn't make a live album?" is a typical response.

Then, when we made a live album, we encountered the same thing. Sonny just doesn't like to record, but he's still aware that the tape machines are rolling.

Even though a few critics that maintain their anti-Rollins bias, Sonny is now a critic's darling. You can milk that for all it's worth, with stories in the *Village Voice*, cover stories in this magazine and that magazine, and features in *Rolling Stone*. People are willing to go out on a limb because he's the 'new' thing. You milk that as long as you can because the critics may be bored with him next year. You try to capitalize on the critic's opinion of the moment. It goes in cycles.

THE NUTS AND BOLTS OF A PUBLIC RELATIONS CAMPAIGN

Commentary by Sandy Wardlow

1981

Sandy Wardlow disclosed the nuts-and-bolts of a nationwide PR campaign. Wardlow was a former publicist with Norman Winter & Associates.

Our office handled—in conjunction with Solar Records and its manufacturer, RCA Records—the total support for the "Solar Galaxy of Stars 1980" tour, which encompassed some 80 cities nationwide. Acts involved were the Whispers, Shalamar, Lakeside, and Dynasty.

To support such an in-depth and widespread personal appearance tour, the following duties were performed. There was total coordination with the record label, the manufacturer and our PR firm.

We tied in the promotional personnel in each city where they had representatives. We contacted the individual promoter for each city's concert. We also made sure that individual biographies of each of the groups on tour were developed. We had an abundance of publicity materials and photography available in each city.

Press kits were serviced to record company PR departments, to the actual facility where the concert was taking place, to all of the local newspapers and magazines in each of the 80 markets.

In addition, we re-contacted newspapers after the initial mailing, to make them aware of the dates in their city, and to provide any further information about the acts on tour.

This particular tour was unique in that all four acts recorded for the same record label. We had more of a family atmosphere versus a tour with different acts and labels, when each group does their thing and gets off. In this instance, the acts performed together, in addition to their particular segments of the new show.

We contacted key consumer press, columnists and reporters in each market. We then set up personal interviews with our acts. Some interviews were set up once they reached the locale. If it behooves us to get features placed before the date, we set up phone interviews. We had a press person who actually traveled with the groups on tour.

Additionally, we contacted local television and radio station personnel for interviews and, wherever possible, we also did live news pickups of the show itself. In key markets, we had the press out, covering the various promotional parties. We also did a lot of phoners for radio spots, to make the general public aware of the dates.

In certain key markets, we organized press parties to follow the concerts—which entailed development of a complete guest list and invitations to people who appeared on that list. We selected locations for the parties, and worked on details regarding what food was to be served, refreshments, hiring photographers and limousines to get the acts to and from the parties.

While the acts were in particular towns, we set up autograph signing appearances at the various record stores nationally. We checked in advance to make sure the store had enough stock of product, that they had enough promotional-type gimmicks, in-store and window displays.

We did a lot of guest appearances on talk shows. In many cities, there were other major events that were happening simultaneously with our particular tour. Our office coordinated it so that Solar acts made guest appearances and gained extra visibility in a market by securing invitations to various parties in the city.

Additionally, we arranged with our label, manufacturer, and distributors to have product of all our acts stocked and displayed—to take advantage of the public appearances, interviews, and concert reviews. Part of a tour to any market—in addition to bringing the public what is heard on the road—is to garner additional record sales.

QUESTIONS FOR REFLECTION

Answer each question with a brief essay.

1. How would you define the distinction between a hit act and an act capable of making hits? Name other performers who fall into each category, and discuss why you have placed them there.

2. In your judgment, was Elvis Presley a legitimate American culture hero? What were his contribution, his legacy? In what ways did he influence a segment of American life? What role did image development play in this process?

3. Choose a hypothetical act and structure a publicity campaign for them. What is the group's image? How will you utilize angles to your advantage? What are your strategies for seeking national press coverage?

4. Is there truth to the statement "Good PR has monetary value."? Discuss the importance of successful image development to an overall marketing plan.

5. Describe the logistics of press coverage for a touring band.

CHAPTER 4

TIP SHEETS, CHARTS & TRADE PUBLICATIONS

Many of you regularly read magazines like *Rolling Stone*, *Maxim, Blender*, or *Right On*, and probably think those consumer-oriented publications are the definitive word as to happenings in the music business. Contrary to popular belief, these magazines are not the industry bible.

Actually, such media often receive information about breaking acts and star-studded attractions months after the tastemakers—who run the in-house industry publications—and decide which acts merit attention.

These tastemakers own or control the various tip sheets and trade magazines. Their names are frequently as colorful as the special information they print. *Mickey Turntable, Jack the Rapper, Kal Rudman's Friday Morning Quarterback, Impact*, and *Bill Gavin* are but a few.

They function as gatekeepers of information between the various industry segments of radio, retailers and record companies. Trade publications such as *Billboard, Record World, Cashbox, Black Radio Exclusive,* and *Radio & Records* are usually more detailed in content than tip sheets, which sometimes are one page in length.

A wide-ranging variety of subjects vital to the daily operation of the music business are reported in these magazines and newsletters. The most significant of these publications are printed weekly.

With so many on the market, there is bound to be a tremendous overlap of featured news items and ads, which run in four different publications simultaneously. And, compared to the millions who read *Time* and *Newsweek, Billboard* has a mere fraction of that total subscribing.

Because of stiff competition for advertising dollars, these publications utilize a wide diversity of means to stay afloat. This is no easy task. Many smaller publications are forced to justify their very existence every week to indifferent record companies, who have committed large sums in advertising campaigns to the major trades but omitted them from the largesse.

Some stage regularly scheduled conventions which showcase acts and pay tribute to deserving professionals within the business. Others project and enlist state-of-the-art snobbishness regarding music styles, garnering a "king-making" reputation in the process. All thrive on hype to promote records like a sweat hog thrives on you-know-what.

Some publications appeal to a specific industry segment, while others are of wide general interest. The *Goodphone* and *Fred* are examples of two distinctly radio-oriented publications. True to its name, *Radio & Records* straddles the fence between coverage of radio and other key areas, while *Black Radio Exclusive (BRE)* is a specialty magazine basing its appeal on the need for broad-based coverage of Black-oriented music by a major trade.

The collective importance of such publications may be summed up in a nutshell: They offer an opportunity to 'program the programmers.' Though some of the publications are circulated to as few as 500 people, each subscriber might be a key program director or major retailer hungry for a tip about a new record.

Of utmost concern is the element of timing: product is reviewed and projected as hit material in trades and in tip sheets as a preliminary, promotion-oriented device at the time of release. Consumer publications help the process along with stories and such, but it is the early reporting trades and tip sheets who get the ball rolling initially.

Press relations, promotion and advertising are departments within a record company that interface most often with these publications. Some companies have specialists in those areas that communicate daily with trades.

They place stories, negotiate space, work out marketing campaigns, politic for priority placement (a cover story being a particular choice plum), and otherwise stoke the fires. Once again, their main objective is to convince radio programmers of the immediate desirability of their product.

The single most important information in such publications are the weekly charts. The charts numerically depict the relative sales of specific albums and singles, as the example illustrates. The collective information is particularly useful to determine the relative strength of a company. A star, bullet, triangle or other useful symbol notes a record's upward motion tendencies.

The hypothetical correlation follows this pattern: The greater amount of airplay that is generated, the greater the amount of sales. The greater the amount of sales, the quicker the album moves up the charts. The quicker the move up the charts, the more in demand the music becomes on the radio.

The more in demand the music becomes, the greater the amount of sales generated. And so on, until the market is saturated, and your product is a hit.

When that happens, the publication trumpets your own promotion department to the tip sheet's typesetters. Such visualizations will have the double-pronged action of establishing a winning image about your company, and validate the publication's ability to successfully influence the hit-making process.

Billboard HOT 100

Chart Bound

TITLE—Artist

HOT 100 A-Z—(Publisher-Licensee)

There are a wide variety of charts drawn up to show relative positioning. The most serious of these are those published by major trades and tip sheets based on computerized tallies, which assess a representative cross-country sampling of market segments.

Billboard's end-of-the-book charts award Gold and Platinum certification. The magazine also lists weekly box office top-grossers, Rhythm & Blues action, hot Jazz albums, hot Latin albums and the Easy Listening category, to name a few.

As a projection of tendencies, so important in promoting records, *Billboard* publishes a preliminary mini-chart of records with potential. Ten records a week are noted as 'Bubbling Under'—the top singles and albums, ready to storm the charts as if there's no tomorrow.

Regardless of the chart or style of publication presenting it, bulleted or starred entries always generate the most excitement. The bullet is a sure sign of upward movement, a direct incentive for the promotion department to increase contact with radio stations, and merchandisers to dream up catchy campaigns, which capitalize on the opportunity.

When it happens in this fashion, the interrelationship of each department to the other is underscored. The art department will supply color-separated ads to the advertising department, which coordinates production, and prepares appropriate promo blurbs. Meanwhile, the promotion department is on the phone daily, tracking sales movement and continuing the ongoing process of breaking a record.

If a record is overly frisky (perhaps breaking out in smaller Southern markets quicker than the North), the intelligent national promotion directors would jump on the phone and apprise his or her contacts at the credible trades of this fact.

They will lobby for better positioning, then invest in a full-page ad which graphically depicts the upward movement (usually with the numbered position and a bullet depicted), the radio stations who have added the record to their playlists, and a captioned blurb which succinctly describes the company's elation at having a hit.

Remember: *Image development translates directly into dollars and cents*. Full-page ads are an excellent quickie visualization stimulus in that regard.

While these things are happening, the press relations department is in contact with the feature editor of the trade publications, pitching stories. Such pieces ideally have a personality slant, but mainly function to stimulate radio programmers and other industry functionaries to pay attention to a particular hot act or piece of product.

Press and promotion people also jockey with record reviewers to attain 'single of the week' or 'top album' status which translates into more attention being focused initially on a record.

Besides the charts, the next most significant section of value published in trades are the *playlists*. True to the economy of language in the business, *playlists* are a list of currently played records maintained by each station in the country.

Most trade publications list a combination of albums and singles most frequently played on each reporting station, as well as the names of programmers for the tally.

The significance of a trade or tip sheet publishing summaries is two-fold. On the one hand, there is the effect of stroking radio stations, whom many observers judge to be the most important link in this selling process.

Radio is the single most important outlet for a given company's products—with trade publications being the most effective means to 'middle-man' information and marketing campaigns simultaneously. Radio stations also need the recognition and visibility for survival in their own toughly competitive markets.

On the other hand, *playlisting* disseminates trend information to companies and competition. If Station A—with a great reputation and high numbers in a key market—adds an unknown's record, chances are great that program directors at lesser stations will read about it, and add that record.

The industry releases hundreds of discs monthly, so any trend picking up momentum like that is noteworthy to a promotion department. Record companies draw up marketing campaigns and decide which new artists have the legs to stand on based in part on information provided in a playlist.

Billboard. Singles Radio Action

Playlist Prime Movers • Playlist Top Add Ons • Breakouts

PRIME MOVERS-NATIONAL

TOP ADD ONS-NATIONAL

BREAKOUTS-NATIONAL

Pacific Southwest Region

Pacific Northwest Region

North Central Region

Southwest Region

Besides charts and playlists, trade publications have other features in common. ***Trade*** *magazines* generally follow this format:

1. *A color-separated cover*, usually spotlighting a specific act, or otherwise promoting records.

2. *A news section in the front of the book*, with headlines detailing the latest industry upheavals in catchy detail. Ever since the *Daily Variety* added the word 'boffo' to communicating in English, entertainment trades have developed an intriguing meta-language used as a shorthand description of doings and happenings.

3. *A weekly tally of the industry-wide employment picture*, including who got fired and which executives shuffled to which other companies. In such a volatile business, there is little shame attached to publicizing radical personnel transitions of that sort. *Visibility* is the key, with the parties in question often able to springboard to a new job as a result of their availability becoming known. Firing is an accepted fact of life. Any employee who has been in the business any length of time has felt the lash some time or another.

4. *Feature stories* on chart breaking talent, radio personalities, record company executives, key retailers, and other contributors to the star maker machinery. These are visibility mechanisms —promotion-related—which put both faces and identities to the record grooves. In trade publications, interviews with executives are often more valuable than artist stories based on the information about the business that might flow in a lively exchange.

5. *Editorial commentary*, often in the form of columns and think pieces by senior staff or guest experts like Clive Davis, or other high-level executives respected industry wide.

6. *Weekly columns* of a special nature, usually describing a chart listing.

7. *Marketing campaigns produced on full-blown center-fold inserts.* Usually, these displays pay tribute to a specific artist, focus on production activities in town and country, and otherwise play up the merits of the talents spotlighted. *Coordinated campaigns* involve companies buying ads which congratulate these honorees, thereby stroking a number of business interests.

8. *A radio section.* In radio-oriented magazines, the approach is to offer full coverage of the range of radio doings, with air personalities in key markets the main subjects. Their success formulas and upward job motion are bannered throughout. In general interest trades, the radio section is a subdivision with regional breakouts, pages of playlists and a radio column.

9. *Specialty music sections, with charts.* These include Jazz, Latin, Disco, Country, Rhythm & Blues, and Easy Listening. Columnists summarize weekly activities here also.

10. *A retail section*, that details upcoming marketing campaigns as a stimulus.

11. *A studio section*, detailing current recording activities.

12. *A gossip or geographic section*, replete with 'leaks' from informed sources.

13. *An international section*, which describes via column, feature and chart listings, what is happening in foreign music capitals.

14. *Display advertising*, the most important and money generating element for the publisher in all the trades is *display advertising*. Ads come in all sizes, but the most expensive are custom-prepared with color separations. The separations allow a printer to lay in each layer of color individually as he prints, thereby giving the truest reproduction available on a moderate cost basis. Black and white ads are pro-rated according to the cost of production, size (full page is ideal), and whether the record company of the trade builds it. All the trades circulate a rate card, which depicts standardized pricing.

Tip Sheets are confidential reports sent to program directors all over the country. They offer inside, advance information about newly breaking albums or CDs. There is a wide array of tip sheets, but all follow a similar format. They are worded conventionally, studded with language and flair highly familiar to the boisterous disc jockey.

"Tore the Mutha Down" bannered the issue of Jack Gibson's MELLOW YELLOW pictured here. Even Bill Gavin's sedate REPORT hyperboles its headliners, placing the best of the week's crop into translatable categories ("Smash of the Week," "Artist to Watch," and so forth) on the cover.

With all of the positive media exposure he has received in recent years, Kal Rudman's *Friday Morning Quarterback*, has gained on Gavin's stature. Rudman's appearances on the "Merv Griffin" and "Today" shows, discussing his patented hit recognizing formula in simple terms for middle-class Americans, has extended the influence of FMQ and tip sheets directly into the cultural mainstream.

By and large, tip sheets are small operations. Fewer than a dozen staffers do all the week's work in most cases from writing to charting. Hyperbole in editorial content, particularly *opinionation* which directs readers to airplay a given record is thick, often overwhelmingly so.

Whether they acknowledge it or not, tip sheets perform an independent promotion function in the choices offered to readers. As a result, the charges of susceptibility to record company influence are routinely tossed around in regard to sheets.

JACK THE RAPPER

RADIO, RECORDS & RAP
TELLIN' IT LIKE IT "TIS" IS

THE MOUSE HOUSE POST OFFICE BOX 3027, ORLANDO, FLORIDA 32802, (305)423-2328

*********VOLUME FIVE-ISSUE 218-JUNE 18, 1980*********

TORE THE MUTHA DOWN

CAN'T! Believe my ears, THE RAPPER had a ZOOPER chance to hang into THE COMMODORES latest LP entitled "HEROES" and if this TNT'r don't become DOUBLE platnium, then New Orleans is in the State of Michigan. Yeah! We heard 'em do it LIVE while we were at THE BRE CONFERENCE '80 the other week and was on THE AWARDS NIGHT SHOW that THE RAPPER MC'd. Believe us, THEY blow all WHO attended COMPLETELY out the hotel with all their jams and when they closed out with the gospel rocker "JESUS LOVES", complete with eight suga, sugas, everyone was as limp as six washcloths. You'll get a chance to see 'em for they are starting on 96 one nighters, so watch for THE COMMODORES in or near your town soon. Brother BENNY and Crew ain't jivin' at 'tall. Oh! Virginia, they are SO bad, it's frightenin' . . . "HEROES" . . . that's what they are, and YOU will be too when you cop the LP and then see 'em in person! THE RAPPER speaks NOTHIN' but the TRUTH, all of you know that!**********

• • •

The Rapper's Blazers

SINGLE	ALBUM
"I COME HERE TO PARTY" TFO VENTURE-126	"DON'T LOOK BACK" NATALIE COLE CAPITOL -12079
JAZZ	**BLACK**
"KWICK" KWICK EMI/AMERICA-17025	"MY NERVE'S GONE BAD" NOLAN STRUCK RETTA'S-004;H.A.B. 601-981-4328

• • •

SO HAPPY TO!! Report to all BROTHER SIDNEY MILLER'S BLACK RADIO EXCLUSIVE'S CONFERENCE '80 was a ZOOPER success as the Brothers and Sisters came from near and far and packed the REGENCY HYATT HOUSE out in TINSEL CITY to capacity. The meetings were FULL filling; the social events WERE out of sight and GOOD fellowship flowed like the good ol' Mississippi River. THE RAPPER saw everybody from BILL MANGERS of RCA RECORDS to KARL PARNELL of KATZ, ST. LOUIS, MO., to PAM WELLS of KMJQ in HOUSTON, to REGGIE HENRY of WEXL, NEW ORLEANS to MELVIN MOORE of VENTURE RECORDS to HAL JACKSON of WBLS in THE APPLE to LEON ISSAC KENNEDY, the movie actor to LITTLE ESTHER PHILLIPS, the singer to LEON HAYWOOD the singer to NORMAN THRASHER the Atlanta Billboard man to GREG JOHNSON, the promotion man to JAY JOHNSON of WTLC in Nap Town TO - TO - TO - TO - TO - Oh! They WERE there and if THE RAPPER forgot any names, PLEASE forgive us, for you git OLDER, you can't remember as well (smile). Had a ball M.C.'in' The Awards Night along with DON CORNELIUS of SOUL TRAIN, E. RODNEY JONES, the ol' ex-trumpet player of the SILIAS GREEN from NEW ORLEANS, MINSTREL SHOW and even FLIP WILSON, the hellva comic that could make a rock laff. Our ol' JOCKEY CAP is off to you, BROTHER SIDNEY MILLER, you DO know how to throw a convention and a VERY successful one at that. All THE RAPPER asks is that THE FAMILY AFFAIR is AS BIG. Wouldn't that be nice?!***

The most respected tip sheet is *The Gavin Report*. Bill Gavin ensures his purity by avoiding the dependency of advertising dollars from record companies. He sells by subscription, and has built credibility as the trendsetting entity. Gavin, a former school teacher, utilizes key people to judge records each week. Gavin provides research analyses and a listing of radio reporters in his Correspondent's Corner.

Like the *Friday Morning Quarterback, BRE*, and some of the other radio-sophisticated trade magazines, Gavin breaks his choices into categories: new music appropriate for power rotation (heavy airplay); strong cuts meriting moderate play, and good cuts suitable for less play. There is also a charting of the Top 33 albums receiving airplay at reporting stations.

THE GAVIN REPORT #1
WEEKLY SUMMARY

Headliners

Smash of the Week

LET MY LOVE OPEN THE DOOR – Pete Townshend (Atco)
After 15 years of The Who at the top of the Rock pile, Pete Townshend continues the tradition with a solo effort,
(FYI: It's pronounced "Town-send" the "h" is silent.)

Hot

BOULEVARD – Jackson Browne (Asylum)
Another outstanding songwriter has penned a winner for himself

Top Tip

HOT ROD HEARTS – Robbie Dupree (Elektra)
I'M ALRIGHT – Kenny Loggins (Columbia)
GIVE ME THE NIGHT – George Benson (Warner Brothers)
This trio is ready evidence that the shortage of "hit records" has ended for the time being.

Record to Watch

ONE IN A MILLION – Larry Graham (Warner Brothers)
A clear cross over pattern is developing in a few larger markets.
WYRE (1), WHBQ (2), WQXI (10), WAYS (10), WDRQ (12), WLAC (14), KFMK/FM (16), WXLO (19), 94Q (20), Z93 (21), KHJ (23), KRLA (24), Y100 (25), etc.

Sleeper of the Week

UPSIDE DOWN – Diana Ross (Motown)
Charting in Houston, Los Angeles, New York, Atlanta, New Orleans, Raleigh and Jefferson City, added in Miami, Indianapolis, Monroe, LA, and others.

Top Prospect

ALL OVER THE WORLD – Electric Light Orchestra (MCA)

Top New Airplay

JESSE – Carly Simon (Warner Brothers) Obviously, the blitz is on.

****

The various listings in the following pages offer the correspondents' formats. Each correspondent utilizes whatever research methods are deemed most suitable for the station's needs.

THE GAVIN REPORT
Commentary by Bill Gavin
1981

In a brief phone conversation, Bill Gavin mused about his publication.

We did not create a demand with *The Gavin Report*, we filled a need. We pioneered the procedure of basing all of our information on reports from radio people, rather than from the record business. Right away, that took us out of any obligation or involvement with record people or record promotion.

Each of our four reporters, then, is individually responsible for evaluating what's going on in his market with his particular target audience. Today, with the proliferation of so-called tip sheets, there are dozens of publications around the country using that system. Even the so-called trades—*Billboard, Cashbox* and *Record World*—base about three-fourths of their Top 100 or reports of airplay from radio stations rather than actual sales.

We're the only trade publication that takes no advertising. Not that it *necessarily* influences a trade chart, but it does give us a certain stance of independence. People have commented on it, and have said, "We know you don't take any advertising, so no one can say you're doing the record companies any favors."

We support ourselves by subscriptions. We're the highest priced trade in the business. We charge $220 a year. We have a staff of eleven people, and we just about break-even.

I would hope *The Report* remains as an established publication. It's not just a fly-by-night thing that will disappear when I do. My son will continue on if I decide that I'm too old to keep going. I'm 72 now, and will be taking it a little easier in the years to come.

Earlier in my own career, I was a performer. I did musical comedy, and I was with a male quartet that worked vaudeville and Hollywood motion pictures. Then I went to work in radio in Seattle, Washington, back in 1936 where I broke in at KOMO as an announcer. Then, I came to San Francisco in 1942, and worked in the Office of War Information. I've also worked at NBC.

As far as teaching goes, I'd only taught four years before I went into business. My last year of teaching was in a copper mining town in Utah, and the school district ran out of funds a few months early, which closed down the school and also my job.

When I got back home to Berkeley, I was looking for a job and somebody told me about an audition over at the Fox Theatre. I went over, auditioned, and was hired at $25 a week to sing in the chorus, in the pits. That's when I went into musical comedy, doing the tab version of "Irene."

So actually, my whole background has been music. But the shift to somebody who'd been brought up in the tradition that I came up in, oratorio, the impact of Rock & Roll was a little hard for me to digest. But finally, I managed, and it has been a pleasant experience and an opportunity to grow.

THE VALUE OF TRADE PUBLICATIONS

Commentary by Bill Speed

1981

In his assessment of the whole of trade publications, publisher and journalist Bill Speed compares them to supermarket advertisement.

I see the role that most trades occupy as a common denominator. Everybody perceives of themselves differently, even from the guy who may operate in the same building. With that in mind, you have to think like those who think around you. Like the guy said in *The Godfather*, "Anything is possible." Primarily, what I see my role as, is an information point—a focal point. If you think about it, you can go and try to find it.

Music is what most trades are known for. I try to provide a national overview. Using the analogy of the supermarket, all I'm looking for, basically, is the meat-and-potatoes of what you're looking for. If you like the record and it fits your format, then you might want information about it.

Probably the most important thing I do is to provide information to those who don't have any other access to the type of information that I see, including Federal Communication information and Black ownership communications.

Perhaps a program director has a particular beef that might be institutionalized, such as having to do an air shift at the same time. That's unheard of in most formats. So, if a guy can polarize with another program director, who is doing the same thing, it may give him a better perspective on his particular job.

Based on those variables, I think the most important thing I do is to give those guys a chance to polarize and shop for new music. I think people read trade publications to back sell whatever thought they may have had about something.

In this business, cronies are a very important element of your whole existence. If you're tight with certain people, then you're going to stay ahead of the rest of the pack. For whatever it's worth, people seem to think that if you hang out with certain persons—you'll find out first.

Well, trades are everybody's ego. Because if a guy wants to tell you something, he can't just call you on the phone and tell you, as well as if you read it somewhere. In print, it had a different kind of impact.

Another issue is job opportunities. People are not always very helpful about pointing out job openings, you have to find out somewhere else. Trades are chock full of that information. The best trades should reflect the medium they are speaking for.

BILLBOARD'S RADIO & RECORDS CHARTS

Commentary by Mike Mongiovi

1981

Mike Mongiovi provides a succinct description of Billboard's Radio & Records Charts.

We use the same basic methodology for all the charts, be it Pop, Country, or Rhythm & Blues. Let's take the AOR radio page. AOR stations are FM. They generally add albums and singles occasionally if the artist is hot.

On Tuesday and Wednesday, I make all of the calls to the stations listed in Billboard, asking them for their weekly album adds. We can take up to six adds each week. Many times they have more than six, but we're limited by space limitations. Within the six, there are four starred items—the hottest albums the station is playing each week.

When you ask them for their hot albums, a lot of radio stations are basing their reports on calls to retailers. We take the *key adds* they've reported, and I compile the totals.

In this particular example, the *Urban Cowboy* soundtrack was added on most of the stations all over the country. I'll add those up during the day. *Urban Cowboy* came in number one in the Southwest and Midwest, number three in the Southeast and Northeast regions. After we have all this from the regions, it's just a matter of totaling up the number of adds and stations.

We can go to the boxes across the top of the page. These are the categories the record companies are most concerned with: The Top Add Ons, National Top Requests/Airplay, National, and the National Breakouts. When the record companies get the magazine in their offices, they are immediately interested in what one of their albums is doing.

They open up to the Album Radio Action page. Now, Asylum Records is very happy because in National Breakouts, Billy Squire came in. Breakouts are compiled between adds and Tops. A breakout is the result of combined vigorous airplay and sales throughout the country.

On the other hand, records are added one week, then you may never hear from them. They're added, they play the record, and there's no response, so the public doesn't like it, and that's it.

The main difference between the AOR list and, say, the Top Singles list is small. Top Singles category includes a designation of Key Adds and Prime Movers. Key Adds are denoted by the circles under each station and Prime Movers use stars.

To determine Key Adds, we ask the station to pick two records out of all those they've added to determine the best of this week's picks. Prime Movers are the records that take the biggest upward jump on an individual station's playlist. Again, the basis for rating is phone requests and airplay.

We contact 140 stations for the Top 40 list. It's easy to arrive at the subdivisions. We've divided the country up logically, so that the Pacific Southwest region includes Los Angeles, San Diego, San Bernardino, Bakersfield, Phoenix, Tucson, Albuquerque, and Las Vegas are the cities represented.

It's the same way in the Northwest. We cover San Francisco, Seattle, Portland, and so forth. The Hot Soul Singles chart is important because Rhythm & Blues is the hottest form of music in the country. It's selling tremendously. There are a lot of new and established artists out now. The new artists who are out have, fortunately, hit it at the right time. Now that Disco has become dance music, that category also encompasses Rhythm & Blues.

Regarding 'bullets' and 'stars': When a product has a star or bullet, it gets that star because of airplay and sales. Note the item tagged New Entries. These are songs that we pick up by calling 64 radio stations all across the country. I call 40 of those myself.

We get their playlists and find out what records have been added. We get their entire Singles playlist. We are not interested in albums at this point. When you see new entry symbols, out of the 64 stations, we use the formula of a record having to appear on eight stations to be able to come onto the charts. That can vary, depending on the activity of the other songs. Everything is relative.

Sometimes you have where records are out getting great airplay right off the bat. It's a hundred-position chart. If a song comes on at 90 or above with a New Entry flag, it will not have a star. In this example, we have a song by *War*. It came on at 98, so it has a New Entry symbol, but it doesn't have a star.

That means it had enough stations to come on the charts, but it didn't have enough stations to come on with a star. We bring it on anyway, hoping the fact of it being on the charts, radio stations see it's on the chart and will add the record.

This is what many stations go by. They will go on a record after looking at a *Billboard* chart to see if the record is on yet. If it's not, they will want to see where it debuts and then take it from there.

We are on a computerized system. Everything we do, all the information we take is fed into computers. It enables us to do more extensive research. Before the computer age, adding machines tallied everything, and it would take forever. It tied personnel up and we couldn't do much research during the day.

We use computer-generated sheets to track radio stations. For the week in question, we have listed 170 songs. These include all the songs listed on the charts, plus a lot of songs that have not entered the charts, but record companies have requested that we put them on these sheets. That way we can track them, and when the reports do start coming in, we have it right in front of us.

When we call the stations for the playlists, we speak to their program director. We ask them for the date of the playlist, most often they read all the songs that they have. Most R&B stations have a list of 35 songs. We take the songs by title. If they're playing "Lover's Holiday" we would put a line through it, signifying that they're playing it. And so on down the line, until we get all their songs.

If they're playing a song that isn't on our list, then I'll write it in a different category. Sometimes a song will come on the list and we haven't tracked it because it's still too new. Our magazine may not even have the record from the company yet because often they ship to stations before we get it. We keep track of it, and if there are enough stations to list that song, then it can come on the charts.

We use a point system, which is confidential. But record companies basically know what the points are. There are primary and secondary stations. KDAY in Los Angeles is *evidently* a primary station. It's got big population, and it's a powerful station.

A secondary station would be a smaller station in a smaller city. Maybe it's a day-timer, maybe only 20,000 watts. We have it divided up that way. The printout shows us exactly which stations are reporting on the record we're tracking. Each station is given a certain amount of points, total points and total radio points.

That covers the airplay side, which is only half of how we do the charts. Sales are the other half. Dealers will take their weekly sheets and rate records—both singles and albums—according to their store sales.

We take their top fifteen sellers. Obviously, no single store is selling every single song. There are 170 songs on a given list, and they're only going to rate the top fifteen as Very Good, Good, or Fair, according to how they're doing.

They do the same procedure for LPs. All of the albums are in alphabetical order according to title and label. Again, they rate them according to Very Good, Good, or Fair with a check in corresponding columns.

Each rating carries a certain amount of points. And again, the information is confidential. It's tallied in our computer on a printout.

Each printout has Top 15 points, total sales points, last week's figures, then a grand total. What that means is that a particular song had enough dealers that reported it in their Top 15.

It will get "X" amount of points for being Very Good, and so forth. We have a Grand Total, then there's a comparison: last week's total is also listed. The printout shows what the difference was. Top 15 points are very crucial because a record that's selling in the Top 15 is selling a lot of product. Again, it's the same procedure—total Top 15 points, compared to Top 15 points from last week.

If there's a *minus* from last week, then we let the record companies know that the record is starting to slip in sales. They are very, very concerned because on the basis of airplay and sales, a record can lose its star. Obviously, a record company is concerned with balancing great sales as well as great airplay.

TRADE PUBLICATIONS

TIP SHEETS

JACK THE RAPPER
RADIO, RECORDS & RAP/TELLIN'IT LIKE IT'TIS'IS
© 1981 THE MOUSE HOUSE INC.

THE CONFIDENTIAL REPORT

THE FRIDAY MORNING QUARTERBACK-

impact!

behind the SCENES

The Gavin Report

Mike Mongiovi, guest lecturer from Billboard magazine addressing "The Anatomy of a Record Company" class at California State University, Los Angeles

QUESTIONS FOR REFLECTION

Answer each question with a brief essay.

1. What are significant values of trade publications and tip sheets to the music industry?

2. Trade publications and tip sheets are said to perform a 'gatekeeper' function, providing information that is nowhere else available in one concise form. Do you agree with that assessment?

3. Why are CD/album playlists and charts so important to the business of the industry?

4. Obtain sample copies of each trade magazine. Are their formats congruent with the generalized format described within the chapter? How do they differ from one another?

CHAPTER 5

THE IMPORTANCE OF RADIO IN EXPOSING AN ACT

Now we shall briefly dissect the significance of radio in this process. The diagram depicts a breakdown of listeners' preference by age groups as determined by Arbitron Survey research, which is a leading authority in such matters. The ages surveyed includes one of the most important regions, Los Angeles.

FIGURE VII

LOS ANGELES ARBITRON July 18, 1980

AUDIENCE RESEARCH

The Gavin Report introduces a series of articles by research expert Gary Bond, of which the following is the first:

LOS ANGELES SPRING 1980 ARBITRON

Quarter Hour Share	Error Factor	Cume Rating	Station	Median Age	Quarter Hour Maintenance
7.0%	+1.1	14.2%	KABC	52	40
5.7%	1.0	11.1%	KBIG	50	42
2.1%	0.6	5.2%	KDAY	24	32
3.1%	0.8	10.4%	KFI	30	25
4.2%	0.9	15.2%	KFWB	51	23
2.2%	0.7	8.9%	KHJ	24	20
2.2%	0.7	6.4%	KHTZ	23	28
3.3%	0.8	10.7%	KIIS-FM	24	25
4.8%	1.0	9.9%	KJOI	55	40
4.2%	0.9	10.4%	KLAC	41	33
2.4%	0.7	8.2%	KLOS	22	24
4.9%	1.0	12.4%	KMET	21	32
2.8%	0.7	0.2%	KMPC	50	25
4.8%	1.0	14.9%	KNX	52	26
3.2%	0.8	7.9%	KNX-FM	30	33
2.7%	0.7	7.1%	KOST	50	31
3.8%	0.8	9.7%	KRLA	29	32
3.5%	0.8	10.5%	KRTH	26	27
2.0%	0.6	6.4%	KUTE	24	25

Some of the best news in the Spring LA book is the increased sample size Arbitron used in the market's first Quarterly Measurement report. Arbitron used almost 6,000 diaries to produce the Spring report. That compares to about 3,600 diaries for the Winter report issued a few months ago.

The Spring '80 diary count is 250% above the number of diaries used in the Spring book in 1970. At that time, they had a sample of 1700. The increased sample means that *the numbers you see in this report are more reliable than ever.* That's especially helpful in a market as fragmented as L.A.

Currently Los Angeles has approximately 46 radio stations and counting. With the evolution of the satellite and internet radio, the amount of radio stations will always be on the rise. During the first printing of his book there were very few Urban radio stations. Now with the uncanny work of Radio One founder Cathy Hughes, the Urban radio format is one of the most profitable formats nationwide, yielding a large number of listeners daily.

Los Angeles has three major Urban radio stations—KKBT (100.3 The Beat), KPWR (Power 106) and KHHT (Hot 92 Jamz). That's not counting the Urban stations outside of Los Angeles County, which can be heard while driving through LA.

NEWS AND NEWS/TALK

KABC

KABC is a strong number one. That's typical for a Spring book with Dodgers baseball. Still this is the lowest Spring book KABC has had since 1974, there's a very good reason for that. Typically, the Spring book has been totally (or almost totally) within the baseball season. The change explains why some baseball stations have not been ecstatic supporters of the new Quarterly Measurement approach. Stations are measured in the Cume department.

KNX (1070) AM broadcasts plenty of CBS News Features (KFWB (980 AM, owned by Infinity Broadcasting yielding CNN's "Larry King Live") and KFI (640 AM, owned by Clear Channel) are news radio stations that give KABC a bit of competition on the talk radio front. It is, however, the strong loyalty of KABC listeners that gives the station its dominant Quarter-hour share.

KMET

KMET remains first 18-34 although this is their worst book in over a year. The biggest loss since Winter has been in MEN 18-24. In day parts, the strongest drop was 2pm-Midnight. The station's Cume has remained quite stable. The lower share can be attributed to the audience spending about fifteen percent less time with the station.

KHJ

Here's where the increased sample size really come in handy. Is the KHJ drop real? Is it possible that KHJ's true share for the Spring book is the 3.0 they got in the Winter book? It is possible, but our calculations show the odds are 40 to one against it. That's something we couldn't say with the samples of previous surveys.

KBIG

Booneville's Beautiful Music station is the number one FM stations in the L.A. market. The station is first 25-54 and it has the strongest Quarter-hour Maintenance of any of the major stations. (Next week Gary Bond continues his analysis of the Los Angeles radio audience.)

**All estimates are from the Spring 1980 Los Angeles reports. All estimates are 12 + Monday-Sunday 6AM-Midnight Metro unless other-wise stated. The estimates are subject to limitations stated in the reports.*

Such information is valuable to radio programmers as a barometer of the potential market share they are vying for, since each category represents a particular style of radio format. Even in those days of mixed-media programming and records that crossover from one genre to another, these slices of pie carry heavy economic overtones.

A station's proportional volume of advertising revenue is dependent on the relative size of the slices (format style), and the 'numbers' it registers during each rating period. Therefore, a Black-format station which tallies a 5.8 market share in a region with a total ARB-rated potential of 8 is pulling from a wide variety of listeners.

If there is direct competition in that market, the potential share possibility is further split. Therefore, the instance of a 5.8 market share in an 8 market with various direct competitors is statistical evidence of a station's formidable outreach abilities.

Let's shift gears a bit and talk about the pace and tempo of modern-day radio formats. Regardless of whether the station is AM or FM, Black, album-oriented rock (AOR), or Middle of the Road (MOR), the tempo pattern is similar. Prime morning hours referred to as AM Drive Time, or morning drive, distinguishing it from afternoon peak hours.

Morning drive is the spot where a station's superstar jock gets a chance to shine. The reason? There are more people listening to radios between 6 and 10 a.m. than at any other time of day. T

hat is the time when people are getting up and have clock radios turned on and blasting. "Wake up! Wake up! Wake up!" the jock exhorts. "Get up and go to your job!"

His up-tempo music shakes you into consciousness. He gives the time frequently, and he tells clever jokes that make your brain focus and function.

All these devices create a dependency in listeners to continue relying on an air personality for making their pathway through early-morning life.

That's the formula to the art of *programming*. Simply create a dependency in the minds of listeners regarding what you can offer both informatively and musically, and add a proportional amount of personal savoir-faire and *bingo!* YOU, too, can mesmerize an audience every morning.

Get a sound effect, perhaps a horn or whistle. Do crazy things: Wake up the dead with early morning phone calls, read news headlines aloud from foreign newspapers, or tell corny jokes from a Jock's Joke Book over the air. You're guaranteed 'big numbers.'

That's the function of the morning drive DJ. With apparent subtlety, he/she is selling themselves, their musical choices and all the ads that could possibly be run by you as you begin your day. You might be running as fast as an Olympic champion, managing to dress and primp for work, while also keeping a studious ear tuned to the jock.

You need to stay abreast of the time while fighting freeway traffic, and squeeze the last bit of entertainment in before the thought of the day's work ahead makes you throw up, and the morning jock is there for your pleasure. He's 'rap-o, clap-o', jiving and talking that talk.

Mid-morning—10 a.m. to 2 p.m.—is typically the traditional "housewife time" slot. The emphasis of this time slot is placed on establishing a lower musical profile than in the morning drive.

People are off to work, the office radio is barely audible over the tapping of keystrokes on the computer, or the sound of smooth grooves warms boutiques and bookstores.

The radio personality will more than likely play songs that cater to the ladies smoothly, mixing in topical, women-oriented issues or guest interviews.

The intellectual stretching a station is capable of incorporating into its format happens here. Health and beauty tips, recipes, book reviews, and weight-watching admonitions abound during the brunch time slot.

The traditional housewife is house cleaning, cooking, and busy with personal concerns, therefore, the pace is mild. If a Jazz jock wants to program a John Coltrane record during this time, he would probably go to a Blues ballad.

Using the metaphor of baseball, this is the time of day when a disc jockey digs into his arsenal for curve balls and other off-speed pitches. He may award albums or tickets as listening incentives (I'll give up five Punk Rock albums to the 25th caller from Joplin), or he may have a two-way 'talkback' system set up to communicate with callers. Also note these continual references to "he" are a mere writing convenience.

The proliferation of the female radio personality is overwhelming. Many of them have begun to utilize the brunch time slot as a daily touch point with loyal listeners. The ideal programming approach mixes the best contemporary music available, which is a fusion of the adult sound with mild sophistication (a Marlena Shaw, Webster Lewis, or Sinatra are artist types who come to mind), blended with an awareness of audience.

For the most part, they are not up to bombardment with hard-driving music. A.M. 'up' stations pace down with news talk and information spaced here.

Between 2 and 6 in the afternoon, as this theory of format goes, the majority of you are in your cars, on your way home to the sanctity of the 'crib'…HOW HAS YOUR WORK DAY BEEN? If you have *buzzed* with the craziness your boss forced you to swallow whole without chewing, relax: the afternoon drive time radio personality has to bring out the smooth music for you.

If you're feeling tense about the daily hassles, don't worry, you won't be bothered by incessant announcements of the traffic or time. The programming pitch strokes you in the mode of the setting sun. The second-liveliest radio personality generally occupies this *P.M. drive* slot.

His persona is usually ultra-smooth and articulate, glib, but playing more music. You've listened to voices all day ordering you around beckoning your decisions, or responding with a colorless "no" to an important budget request.

The last thing you'll put up with is a 'chipmunk jock' bombarding your brain. You want music to party home to in peace and comfort. The P.M. drive jock will do his best to accommodate you.

In the golden days of radio, the 6 to 10 p.m. time slot was reserved for dramas and other classic programs. These shows had high visualization content, transporting listeners to the farthest edge of reality each night, from *Amos & Andy*, *Groucho Marx*, and *Superman* to *The Shadow*, *The Lone Ranger* and other all American superheroes and comedians, these programs were the height of entertainment for listeners.

Television now monopolizes the same audience, beginning with the evening news and into prime-time viewing. There is no longer a family listening concept connected with evening radio. Teenagers interested in the latest music, hippest slang and contemporary trends are the prime listeners.

So, the jock who's most effective is also into such things. He is a 'motor-mouth' whose poetic personality fused with popular culture vernacular is the key to successfully reaching his listeners. He 'signatures' the music, getting a priority push with clever voice-overs and custom-produced sound strips. This is also the time of the heaviest phone requests.

All the way around, 6 to 10 p.m. is still primetime for testing the most commercial music product. As the evening progresses into the later hours, the format mellows down. The jock's rap is full of dream fantasy, words of warmth for caressing lovers, titillation for the comfortably alone and shut-in. He soothingly tucks lovers away into slumber land to the best of Benard Ighner, or some funky Jazz fusion.

Female DJs are great favorites in the middle of the night. Let's face it, it's a man's world. Lonely guys want to roll over, toss and turn to the sound of a woman's voice at 3 a.m. Jazz and Blues are a very effective counterpoint in the early, murky moods that move you.

So now the question arises: What is the significance of this format breakdown to selling records?

That's easy, we're glad you asked. From the record company's standpoint, every item referred to has some significance. After a record is released, the company has to figure out a variety of radio-related questions.

What formats will it immediately fit into? What regions will readily give it airplay? What time of day is best to break it in? (If the record is a ballad) How many ballads are already on the playlist? Will the record merit inclusion in a high (or heavy) rotation?

If such questions are not asked as prior action and effective marketing plan formulated from the process, a promotion team can waste needless energy soliciting airplay on a *stiff*.

Such action can prove to be fatal, especially when your promotion man is carrying a *smash* hit with him on his next trip into the station. Without airplay, there is no consistent way to be competitive big numbers-wise in today's market. It's the rare group these days that sells Gold or Platinum without radio.

Placement in a 'heavy' or 'power' rotation ensures frequent enough airplay to engender ongoing sales interest. It's as simple as that. Most records added to a station's weekly-changing playlist start at a low rotation.

With heavy requests and favorable sales tallies, the most successful product moves up in rotation week by week. Finally, in power rotation, a tune may be played a dozen times a day—including twice an hour during evenings.

A company knows they have a surefire hit when a record gets simultaneous airplay as you quickly pan across the radio dial and hear the tune playing at the same time on a wide variety of formats.

THE IMPORTANCE OF TELEVISION EXPOSURE

Commentary by Don Cornelius

1981

Soul Train is a case in point...

By now, *Soul Train* is unquestionably the most successful Black-oriented television program in history. It has enjoyed over a dozen years' run in syndication week-by-week.

Soul Train offers a formula montage of entertainment, which includes the *Soul Train* dancers and gyrating teenage guests, the patented *Soul Train* line with its gauntlet-like effect, the dazzling visual display of the stage design, the lit-up logo, and the ebullient personality of the host Don Cornelius or other exceptional celebrity personalities are always holding things together.

Discounting the occasional appearances of Black acts on the *Carson show, Merv*, or Jazz Fusion used as background on news programs, *Soul Train* is 'it' as an outlet for the majority of R&B and accessible fusion acts on the tube. Resultantly, *Soul Train* has been able to sustain itself for the wide variety of A-list talents who have graced its air.

And, Cornelius has been prudent enough to form creative alliances with innovative people in the music industry—Dick Griffey in the *Soul Train* Records partnership, and the use of *MFSB* and the *Three Degrees* to record that now-classic theme song.

Cornelius has also made significant acknowledgements of trends, giving television exposure to *Donald Byrd* and Jazz Fusion early on, and incorporating the *Dramatics*, smash talents like the *O'Jays, Teddy Pendergrass* and *Chaka Khan* as part of the unofficial *Soul Train* 'family.'

Every time one of these artists had a hit record, they were seen on the show. So were *Herb Alpert, Elton John*, *David Bowie*, and the *Doobie Brothers* when crossover action into the Black market was warranted.

Cornelius described his motivation for creating *Soul Train* as cracking a color barrier in television, where "Almost every decision-maker you see is White." In this pioneering effort, he began with a $400 investment and limited access to television airtime in his Chicago hometown.

He based *Soul Train* on the judgment that "Blacks are collectively better at dance and popular music than anyone in the world." His main idea was "To create a show that did not imitate *American Bandstand* other than in format. Once it works, it belongs to all of us. Basically, the format is age-old, but *Soul Train* has given it a unique character."

He assessed the value of *Soul Train*: "For most Black artists, it is the only outlet to television—the main power medium—in America. It provides an outlet for artists to use television who do not ordinarily have that opportunity readily available to them.

If it weren't for *Soul Train*, most Black artists would have nowhere to go. *Soul Train* is on the mind of that kid who goes into the studio aiming for his first hit record."

As to the all-important question of whether *Soul Train* breaks acts, Cornelius was candid. "We're a contributor, but that one hour a week is just a miniscule amount of exposure time, radio is still the king. Our main advantage is taking an artist a good way beyond the normal radio audience."

Cornelius added, "Many people in the industry are convinced the show can make a record a hit. But, we are not in the selling business. We only give what our audience wants, and we can help expose a record after it has crossed a certain level.

There is a graduation of levels of exposure for a record, and *Soul Train* is a level up from FM radio. However, many people may see something in the show that does not exist."

Soul Train is primarily aimed at a Black audience though public response of Whites has been generally favorable. The most prominent have been the attempt by Dick Clark to create a competitive, Black-hosted *American Bandstand* spinoff. The other was the public comment made by Fred Astaire that he has been a fan of the show since its inception. That was a big deal.

The fact is, given the relative population distribution of the country, a Black-oriented show still draws a predominately White audience if aired on national television. Cornelius has publicly defended *Soul Train's* Black orientation as analogous to a show like "Hee Haw" catering to Whites.

Cornelius further provided a thumbnail criterion for artists who appear on his program. "We provide visual exposure for acts who have achieved a certain status which makes them attractive to the spotlight.

We don't take this for granted, because the continued success of acts has contributed to *Soul Train's* credibility. *MFSB* was launched with the *Soul Train* theme, but the record sold on its own."

Cornelius described *Soul Train's* future as 'unlimited.' "Black music is the base, a continuous flow of Black creativity in the same way that Pop music feeds *American Bandstand* and has kept it on the air for 30 years.

If you understand and do the job correctly, you'll be around. My responsibility is creating the best damn show I can, because somebody needs to do this even if Black music goes away.

The most precious feeling an act receives is to be recognized on the street as 'so-and-so.' Once on *Soul Train,* six to ten million people have seen you. Television is a great personalizer.

Whether you like it or not, people call you by your first name when they see you on the street, because they'll recognize you from *Soul Train*."

PROMOTION MANAGER CHECKLIST
A 12-POINT PROGRAM

The following is a sample summary of a record promotion handbook.

1. *Service of all key stations in your marketing area*
Whether your market has four or six significant stations, they must be serviced, and your efforts must be sincere for exposure on all these stations. Remember, promotion must include all formats: MOR, GM, Country Progressive, R&B, and Top 40. The need to cover all such stations that have an effect on the entertainment buyer is apparent—impact comes from frequency of exposure, and only by covering the total marketing area can you reach the total population with your music message.

2. *Radio Service*
Servicing all stations noted in point one is done basically through three channels:
(a) factory mailing service
(b) your own mailing service
(c) your physical delivery of sample product

In order to be proficient in servicing your area, you therefore, must know which stations receive product directly from the factory, and your internal mailing lists must be updated to maximize the impact on all important stations in your distributing areas, it goes without saying that your physical contact with these same important stations on regular frequency will remain the most important facet of service.

3. *Contact with all station personnel*
Do you know all of the key personnel at all radio stations you service? Moreover, do they know your product? Do they receive separate service if required? Are you able to get concentration on your production through this personal contact?

Your play will increase if there is a personal relationship with all personnel who actually perform mic-side.

4. *R&B stations*

A separate note is made as part of the twelve-point check program only because a reminder may be necessary that music is the blending of various cultures to form something extraordinarily unique. The regular service of other formats is as important as Black stations for accomplishing complex exposure. Cross-fertilization of product through cross-fertilization of radio formats is a required tactic. And the job is incomplete without topflight, all format representation.

5. *Country format stations*

The same holds true for Country as for R&B stations. Country music is great business. Of equal importance is the starting point of exposure and popularity through Country formats, to be spread to other formats, principally MOR and Top 40.

6. *Use of national charts, tip sheets, and factory literature*

Do you digest this information? Do you carry it with you? Do you use it to build your knowledge for a more authentic and believable approach to promotion? We remind you that the most knowledgeable promotion manager wins more battles, and that the more believable you are through this information, the better your performance will be.

7. *Reporting Stations*

Do you know who the reporting stations are throughout your entire marketing area? Reporting stations include all type formats, and the stimulation of all reporting stations to the respective tip sheets and national trade magazines will create total exposure and enhance the end result—sales. If your efforts produce exposure of product, the next step then, of course, is to let everyone know about it through reporting this activity, primarily from the radio stations to the trade-at-large.

8. *Reporting store and your relationship*

Knowledge of accounts that report sales activity to local radio and/or national publications is one of the key points of total promotion. You have not completed your promotion activity until all such reporting accounts have been contacted by you, made aware of your product and activity, stimulated into purchasing and displaying the product, listing the product on their mailers, and above all, working with these reporting accounts to the extent of asking for and receiving reports on your product to the outlets mentioned.

In today's market, the album has to receive this kind of attention as did the traditional single record. Therefore, reporting stores and one-stops must be a part of your regular weekly itinerary.

9. *Communication with home office*
A key point in a 12-point program, of course, is communication. How can your efforts be meaningful if your activity is not made known as it relates to a total national picture? Communication verbally to Home Office national promotion must be a minimum of two times a week, with extra calls whenever anything significant happens, on the spot. This cross relationship of *immediacy* provides the momentum for overall national impact through knowledge, as provided by each local region.

10. *Communication—branch and branch personnel*
Another key point in a 12-point program is the quality of the communication from you, the promotion manager, to *all* branch personnel. You must take the responsibility of seeing to it that the branch manager, branch sales manager, order desk and branch salesman are aware of all album and single airplay so that they support you with product to the accounts. It's more true today than ever before that the product must be available if you are to realize a sale and a continuing buildup of impact on a key piece of product, "Out of sight, out of mind," is a truism for a recording today at the account level.

11. *Creative promotion*
One of the elements that make up a true 12-point program is creating a promotion—creating a scheme that will cause heavy attention to your product. There must be a regular flow of mailers to your radio stations and also to the branch listing of accounts. In order to isolate a given piece of product from the mass of product, other creative techniques must be worked out, such as wire campaigns, gimmick gifts, station contests. *Remember, the more creative you are, the more awareness there will be of the product being promoted.*

12. Publicity—artist relations
Finally, a 12-point program would not be complete without the following:

(a) A review of all publicity materials supplied from your publicity department and usage of this material. The more you know about the artist and/or the product, the more believable you will be, and, as a result, the more impact you will create on the product. Actually, use publicity by showing it to the various people you contact.

(b) Become active in the area of publicity. Be in touch on a regular basis with all record reviewers and feature writers. Obtain the printed work on a product you promote.

(c) On artist relations—prepare well for an artist visiting your area. The well prepared and interested face you show the artist will help cement the relationship with that artist, which in turn creates a strong image of the Company wherever that artist travels.

Your best spokespersons coast to coast are a happy group of artists who in turn tell other artists and related industry people of the awareness and preparedness of the Company.

FORTY-ONE REASONS NOT TO PLAY A RECORD

We're Not Playing Your CD Because:

1. IT'S TOO NEW
2. IT'S TOO OLD
3. IT'S TOO HARD
4. IT'S TOO SOFT
5. IT'S TOO BLACK
6. IT'S TOO WHITE
7. IT'S TOO TEEN
8. IT'S TOO COMMERCIAL
9. IT'S NOT OUR SOUND
10. THAT SOUND ISN'T MAKING IT ANYMORE
11. IT SOUNDS LIKE 1987
12. I LIKE IT, BUT THEY DON'T
13. THEY LIKE IT, BUT I DON'T
14. THEY'VE BEEN COLD
15. THEIR LAST ONE WAS A STIFF
16. IT DOESN'T SOUND LIKE THEM
17. I'LL DO WHAT I CAN FOR IT
18. IT'S GOOD, BUT WE HAVE A HUNDRED GOOD RECORDS
19. AFTER A WHILE, THEY ALL SOUND THE SAME
20. IT'S NOT HIGH ENOUGH ON THE CHARTS
21. WE'VE PLAYED THE OTHER VERSION
22. IT'S GOOD BUT WE ALREADY HAVE A NEW PAUL SIMON, JOHN LENNON, CAROLE KING, AND THREE DOG NIGHT THIS WEEK
23. IS IT HAPPENING ANYWHERE?
24. THAT STATION PLAYS ANYTHING, WHO ELSE DO YOU HAVE?
25. IT'S A HIT, BUT WE'RE GOING TO WAIT
26. CAN'T HEAR THE VOCALS
27. THE VOCALS ARE TOO STRONG
28. GREAT LYRICS, WEAK PRODUCTION
29. GREAT PRODUCTION, WEAK LYRICS
30. SOUNDS TOO MUCH LIKE
    (a) ROD STEWART
    (b) CAROL KING
    (c) STEVIE WONDER
    (d) MICHAEL JACKSON

(e) CROSBY, STILLS & NASH
(f) BREAD

31. THE GAVIN CONFIDENTIAL SAYS IT'S NOT HAPPENING
32. SOUNDS TOO MUCH LIKE THEIR LAST RECORD
33. WHY DID THEY CHANGE THEIR SOUND?
34. I DON'T CARE IF IT IS 5 WITH A BULLET, IT'S HYPE
35. IT'LL SELL WITHOUT US
36. IT'S TOO LONG
37. WE DIDN'T HAVE ROOM THIS WEEK
38. THE TRADES MEAN NOTHING
39. BUT THOSE ARE BLUE COLLAR MARKETS
40. SCREW _____________ (Fill in the Blank)
    GAVIN, RECORD WORLD, RUDMAN, RANDAL, BILLBOARD, BRE, RUES, MUSIC CONNECTION
41. I REPORT TO _____________ (Fill in the Blank)
    GAVIN, RECORD WORLD, RUDMAN, R-3, BRE, BILLBOARD

Too often, radio personalities have found out they've been dealing with guys who they thought were operating from a friendship basis, only to realize they were actually dealing with a piece of vinyl.

THE VALUE OF PERSONAL RELATIONSHIPS
Commentary by Jimmy Bee
1981

Independent record promoter Jimmy Bee stresses the value of personal relationships.

Here's the way I do business, I'm going to meet and greet you simply because I intend on doing business with you since you're at the radio level, and I'm in the promotion/marketing end. First of all, we should establish a relationship as people. If we don't establish that relationship first—show respect for one another—then we won't have anything going anyway.

You've got to remember this: If your friendship is only based on a piece of vinyl, then we really don't have a friendship. That means, as long as you have a job, then we're cool. The minute you get fired, you don't hear from me.

As a second consideration, I'm a true community man. *SEPIA Magazine* did an eight-page story on me. So, it's on the record that I will not support or represent any record company, whether Black or White owned, that will not support the Black community. If they can't do it, then I don't need their money. Different people have different principles. I found that mine are the best. They work for me.

You cannot always wait until you need something to get in touch with these people. For example, I was in Atlanta, Georgia, for the JACK THE RAPPER CONVENTION, and we were doing a fashion show with Melba Moore. But, the main objective was to do a thing with Maynard Jackson (Senator Herman Talmadge was running for re-election, and Maynard was trying to stop him, so he needed support).

One year, I co-hosted a Christmas party with the Mayor's office for 500 children. I missed my Honorary Degree with the East Bay Skills Center because I was out of town. But, my involvement is basically different than most record cats. I don't come on with that bullshit. I'm not plastic, so you can't see through me. You've got to be real. You've got to be honest. You've got to have high credibility.

If you own record stores and the only time you see Jimmy Bee is when I need something, how are you gonna feel? It's not cool. Are you gonna say, "This guy is just like all those others." When he wants something, then I hear from him.

When you're on the road, you get out there and do your job first. *Then* you play if you want to play, because it's business. Black music is the biggest thing happening in the music industry. Blacks are the last hired, the first fired. Yet, you don't have any big-named recording artists speaking out against this. Don't you know if a big-name artist spoke up that shit would cease?

Here's more insight into the significance of personal relation-ships. If you're working for a company, guys will do anything to get a record played. Why? Because they tell you to go out there and tell the jocks that you've *got* to have the record. That's bullshit.

You can't go to the veterans in this business and bullshit them. They know better. If a record is a hit record, you have all your facts together. If the record is a work record, then you say, "Hey man, I think this record's hit, but it's a work record.

If it's a record that you feel will sell mediocre, then you say, "I don't believe this is a hit, but if it gets a certain amount of exposure, the record will sell enough units to help establish this act." That way, the next record you come with will happen out of the box.

You can't go to the veterans in this business and hype and bullshit them. They'll see right through all of that. They'll disrespect you, and then you'll really be out in the cold.

THE IMPORTANCE OF A QUALITY PRODUCT

Commentary by Jan Barnes

1981

Veteran promotion executive Jan Barnes stresses the quality of product as an aide in placing records.

You've got to be able to deal with Program Directors on the basis of being a professional and knowing your product. Additionally, you've got to keep records of what is happening retail-wise, what's happening radio-wise, nationally, regionally and locally.

Honesty is the key. Avoid hype, because you'll find that major radio stations do a lot of research. If you're not professional working your product, you'll also find that you may get jammed somewhere down the road with your records. Follow through is very important, as is the professionalism involved in your job.

The quality of the product is the number one thing. The way the business is going today, there is a lot of good new product from the many new artists, as well as old established ones. With things especially tight right now, you're only as good as the product.

THE RELATIONSHIP BETWEEN INDUSTRY SEGMENTS

Commentary by Bob Law

1981

Programmer Bob Law notes the close relationship between industry segments.

Record companies and radio stations have a very close relationship. Companies need radio stations to help sell their product and radio stations need companies to get the product. It really ought to be called 'The Radio-Record Industry.'

The relationship is so close that it ought to be viewed as one world—one industry. It's a partnership. Ideally, each should serve each other's interests, which is promoting artists. For example: We put on a series of free concerts around the city and record companies help us by supplying artists.

It's not benevolence that is behind doing this, it's an opportunity to showcase new artists, or artists with new products. It allows us to create an event, and so works in our interest. Everything we do is a partnership. We get as much out of it as the record companies, and vice-versa.

THE RELATIONSHIP BETWEEN RADIO STATIONS AND RECORD COMPANIES

Commentary by Reg Henry

1981

Programmer Reg Henry comments about the relationship of radio stations and record companies.

It is the innate function of a radio station to expose the products of a record company to the marketplace, and to give truthful feedback on the potential of that record. The sales may be slow on a record, but requests may be heavy.

Honest feedback from a station will give a company insight on whether to stay with the product or to abandon ship. Unless it is a piece of product from a super group with a string of successful hits, or unless it is a piece of product that you have gone on because of surrounding airplay—more or less forced on, as they say—most product that I put on starts in a light rotation.

How long it stays there depends on the initial response during the course of the week, from both sales—which are dependent on the amount of stock available in the market—and phone requests, which entails the announcer's feedback to programming. We also monitor the other stations in the market to find out just what they're doing with the piece of product.

CULTURAL FACTORS INFLUENCING RADIO FORMATS

Commentary by Al Ramirez

1981

Programmer/Engineer Al Ramirez discusses the cultural factors influencing radio formats, visualizing the relationship between stations and companies as less than a love affair.

Programming philosophy really has to change with the market place, depending on the city and region you're in. There are many examples of radio station formats that work beautifully in New York, but don't work in Los Angeles.

There's the example of the ABC Programming whiz Rick Sklar, who tried to implement the successful WABC format in San Francisco. His reasoning was that San Francisco is the West Coast version of New York. They installed the format at KSFX, with all the jingles, IDs, all done in New York.

It was a miserable failure because it was not geared for San Francisco's tastes and lifestyle. Every city is unique in that regard. A programmer who develops that formula will probably be successful where the format is successful, whatever city that might happen to be. If he goes into another city and tries to force that formula, chances are it wouldn't work.

I speak from experience. A station I was programming in St. Louis was being consulted from Houston: Many of the things that were successful in Houston, they felt would also be successful in St. Louis. It was my contention that was absolutely incorrect.

One big reason for this, of course, is the tremendous difference between Houston and St. Louis. At the time, there was a depressed job market, and the city was also declining in growth.

In Houston, they couldn't build skyscrapers fast enough. So, the paces of the cities were different, and the ethnic makeup between

Houston and St. Louis was also different. Houston was a large Hispanic market, and St. Louis was not.

The Houston format looked incorrect to me, so I decided to resign my position rather than institute a lot of these changes. Of course, they were instituted after I left, and since then the ratings have not been what they thought they would be.

Ethnicity, or the lack of it, is the single most important thing a programmer has to take into account. A Black radio station in Washington, D.C., would have a higher percentage of the general population being Black than a Black radio station in Minneapolis/St. Paul.

Here in Los Angeles, there's a sizeable Black market. However, there is a larger Hispanic market than the Black market, then you've pigeonholed yourself as far as available income from advertisers is concerned.

If you have a mixture of audiences, such as Hispanic, Black and White audiences, or Asians, you increase your revenue potential, as well as your ratings. A higher percentage of the total population would be listening to you then, or at least available to you.

Regarding radio stations and record companies, I think they both hate to be dependent on each other, but they are. Radio stations look for new product from the record companies to help maintain their formats, and record companies have a selfish motive working with radio stations.

There is definitely a motive behind it, and that motive is profit potential. If a radio station plays a record, it is, in essence, free advertising for the particular record, which increases the possibility of sales. Obviously, record companies want radio stations to play as many of their particular records as possible.

However, I think the situation has gotten to the point where several record companies try to dictate programming policy, including the kinds of records that companies do play by their singles release scheduling.

I wish I had a dollar for each time that a promotion person has said, "I need *you* to get a bigger radio station on my record." Which didn't take into consideration the needs of my particular radio station, but the fact that the promotion person stands to get a more important radio station on the record if I go on it.

I'm speaking about records that are correct for a station's particular image. The most easily definable example is the Disco record as opposed to the non-Disco Black record—a mainstream R&B record.

My particular station's philosophy is to point away from Disco; we maintain a low Disco profile. In doing that, you don't neglect playing hit records, whether they're Disco or otherwise. However, you do not break a record that is not within your particular format or philosophy. By that, I would not program a Disco record in early release unless I was sure it had potential beyond a Disco audience.

Most record companies don't look at it that way, of course. They want you to go on the record because they need it, because it is *their priority*. There have been many times when record promoters have told me, after I've added a particular record even of their own label, "Oh, you went on the wrong record."

It's their initial reaction because they're under heavy pressure from their bosses to play what their bosses decide are important records to the company, regardless of whether it's good or not for any particular radio station.

That's something I object to, and always have. I've always listened to every record I could and considered them equally to weigh how it fits within our sound. I believe that a radio station has to maintain a certain level of independence from a record company.

Most record companies lobby very hard for specific records, and it's been a tried and true method for them. Just recently there's been very big hypes that record companies have built up and stations followed suit.

In a most recent situation, we received a lot of pressure from people who'd say to us, "A lot of radio stations are on this record, why aren't you guys on it?" Honestly, I would say, "I just don't believe it's a hit record."

Time proved me correct, and a lot of those radio stations had to drop the record eventually because it wasn't happening. The public at large didn't like the record.

Many companies lose track of what's going on in the street at the grassroots level. Most A&R decisions are made in ivory towers in New York or Los Angeles. Do you know what I do? As a programmer, I go into large parking lots and walk among the cars to see what frequencies the car radios are tuned in to.

It gives me an indication of what people are listening to. Several years ago, I sat at a Jim Dandy Fried Chicken stand on Crenshaw Boulevard for over three hours, listening to the music on the teenager's radios.

There was this kid with a portable radio, who was listening between KGFJ and KDAY. This guy had it perfect. He had a little twist of the dial down to a science. He knew exactly how far to twist so he'd land at KGFJ and vice versa.

It was an education in itself, listening to what records and under what circumstances this kid would change stations. It is things like that which record companies have lost sight of, in my opinion.

Radio, generally, has been a little more responsive to the needs of the listening public. We communicate with them more on a one-to-one basis via request lines. Disc jockeys are always out doing promotional things at local clubs—talking to people.

A&R department people don't do too much of that same thing. If you allow a record company to, in effect, program your radio station with their product, you're serving their needs. You're not necessarily serving yours.

There are several examples of how this is shown in cold, hard ratings. Two radio stations in Los Angeles tend to play a lot of new product, a lot of untested product from record companies. However, they are generally the lowest on the totem pole as far as Arbitron ratings are concerned.

In New York, the exact opposite is true, WBLS is the number one radio station. However, the marketplace tolerates it—almost *demands it* if they're the number one station. So again, what works in New York may not necessarily work in L.A. Los Angeles is a very slow-responding market, musically.

People generally want to hear what they are familiar with first, rather than music they have never heard before. Programmers who are most sensitive to the changes in urban differences—city-to-city—that all intermingle for cumulative effect will ultimately become the most flexible and the most successful.

There are so many variables that correlate to specific urban factors. The greater the population density—as it is in the East—the more familiarity of people who know what everybody else is doing, and when that happens, it effects radio listening and music buying habits.

On the other hand, privacy is a very big thing in Los Angeles, and buying tends to be more individualistic. In other cities, there are heavy ethnic concentrations for blocks and blocks of all Polish or Croation people. Little Italy and Chinatown in Los Angeles is nothing like Chinatown in San Francisco. It's not as significant or centralized.

The Black population in Los Angeles is not as centralized as some people think either. There are pockets within the Black population in Orange County, Pacoima, Monrovia, Pasadena, and Altadena as well as up in both the Northern parts of the San Fernando and San Gabriel Valley areas.

In a market this size, the way it has evolved as far as population layout is concerned, it's going to be very hard for one station to be very dominant over everyone else. Everyone will have his or her share of the market, and it will be very tight.

While in a city like St. Louis, there's one station that's incredibly dominant, KMOX. In Minneapolis, it's WKDO and KDKA in Pittsburgh. Those stations are monstrosities. Everyone listens to them and they virtually control what people think in that city.

There's no station in Los Angeles like that, and, primarily, it's because of the actual size of the city and the diversity of the different peoples that live here.

If you compare the population of New York City and Los Angeles, they're close as far as numbers are concerned. However, Los Angeles' population is spread out over a wider physical area. That, of course, is reflected in population density figures.

One other observation about record companies is that they release far more pieces of product than the market can actively support. The chances that a radio station can play all of the releases by a company are slim. CBS releases as many as ten or fifteen pieces a week—new records.

The chances are diminished for all of them being played. If you multiply that by the number of record companies that are out there —the four or five major companies—that's a lot of product each week that is not making it.

So, what do they do? They take losses on that product. To me, that's like blood-letting. You are saying in effect, "Let me cure the cut by letting the bad blood out and weaken you more."

That's a bad business ploy. I think that record companies have too many executives making decisions in this manner without knowing what the hell the marketplace will tolerate, and then put pressure on the promotion people in the front trenches. They're often executed to cover the executives' shortsightedness.

THE FUTURE OF BLACK MUSIC IN THE INDUSTRY

Commentary by Don Mizell

1981

A veteran executive in radio and records, Don Mizell commented about the future of the Black music industry.

In the future, radio and records could become less mutually dependent with the proliferation of the new technology, cable and low power television, microwave relay, computer digital printout systems, the rest. These technologies threaten radio and records, and threaten to sever the relationship. But it also provides the seed of communication and mutual benefit.

The reason that it threatens them is this: If you can get the music directly from satellite or punch it up and pay a rental fee on your computer or home entertainment system, the music doesn't have to come in a record form. It does not necessarily have to be bought. It can be rented and, furthermore, does not have to come over the radio for the first level of exposure.

That doesn't mean that the music business will go away, but the record business might. It also doesn't mean that radio is going away, however Black radio primarily as a means of distributing Black music may go away. So, these businesses will have to adapt in order to survive—to diverge in the way they interrelate and in the configuration that their product is offered. That doesn't necessarily spell the death of records on or of Black radio.

What it's going to require is anticipating common ways of developing new forms of cooperation, or they may just go their own merry way. The challenge for the record business is to keep coming up with good music and putting it into configurations that are competitive.

For Black radio, the problem is continuing to expand in all markets, and how to define and refine the definition of itself as information services systems (which may or may not include music).

Some say, "Well, it's always been that way, and it will always be that way. This is an issue that is questionable. There may come a time when the listener may have more control over the choices they will expose themselves to prior to making any purchases or rental.

Then the question becomes: What need is there for Black radio to perform that function? The challenge to Black radio is to figure out how to be continually creative and innovative, while still being an integral part of the people's lives, which it always has been.

I think in that sense, it's going to have to really change the concept of itself from simply playing music—which the record company creates—to providing a whole range of information and entertainment that is hard to get by any other means. Its greatest strength has been as the primary information alternative for the community that is available all day and everywhere. Television cannot go into the car. Radio can follow people, daily.

Because radio is so fragmented and specialized in contrast to the more general market orientation of television, it can reflect the community a bit more strongly. It has had that leg up on television. It can be more about the community than television, given radio's economics. *And*, it has the versatility to go where you go, which television can't do as well.

KEY TOP 40
SINGLES AIRPLAY STATUS

Artist / Title

BB		CB		RW		R&R	
TW	LW	TW	LW	TW	LW	TW	LW

DISTRICT I	
New York	WABC (rr1,bb6,cb,rw)
New York	WXLO (rr1,rw,cb,g)
New York	WNBC
New York	WHLI-FM
Boston	WRKO (bb6,rr1,rw,cb,g)
Boston	WBZ (bb4,rr3)
Boston	WVBF (bb2,rw,g)
Providence	WPRO (bb2,rw,cb,g,rr2)
Boston	WACO (g)
Providence	JB105 (g)
Portland	WJBQ (cb,rw,g,rr3)
Manchester	WFEA (g)
Bangor	WGUY (rr3,rw,cb,g)
Dover	WTSN (rr3,g)
Hyannis	WCOD (g)
Portsmouth	WHEB (g)
Bath	WIGY (g)
Philadelphia	WFIL (bb6,rw,cb,rr1,g)
Philadelphia	WZZO (bb4,cb)
Philadelphia	WIFI (bb2,rw,rr2,cb,g)
Scranton	WARM (g)
Easton	WEEX (g)
Allentown	WAEB (cb,g)
Wilmington	WAMS (g)
Waynesboro	WEEO (rr3,g)
Atlantic City	WMID (g)
York	Q106 (WQXA) (g)
Harrisburg	WKBO (g)
Reading	WRAW (g)
Washington	WPGC (bb6,rr1,rw,cb)
Baltimore	WCAO (bb4,rr1,rw)
Richmond	WLEE (bb2,cb,g)
Annapolis	WYRE (bb1,rr,g)
Baltimore	WLPL (bb1,cb)
Norfolk	WGH (bb1,g)
Richmond	WRVQ (Q94) (rr2,cb,g)
Baltimore	WFBR (cb,g)
Parkersburg	WZYQ (g)
Norfolk	WNOR (cb,g)
Washington	WINX (g)
Hartford	WDRC (bb4,rr2,rw,cb,g)
Troy	WTRY (bb2,rr2,cb)
Albany	WPTR (bb2,cb)
New Haven	WAVZ (rr2,rw,cb,g)
Bridgeport	WICC (rr2,rw,cb,g)
New Haven	WFIF (g)
Waterbury	WOOW (g)
Albany	3WD (g)
Danbury	WINE (g)
Hartford	WTIC (rr3)
Buffalo	WKBW (bb4,rr1,rw,cb)
Rochester	WBBF (bb1,rr2,cb,rw,g)

Syracuse	WOLF (rr2,cb,g)
Buffalo	WYSL (cb,g,bb2)
Buffalo	WPHD (r)
Utica	WTLB (cb,g)
DISTRICT II	
Cleveland	WGCL (bb4,rr1,rw,cb)
Pittsburgh	WKTQ (13Q)(bb4,rr1,rw,cb,g)
Pittsburgh	WPEZ (bb4,rr1,rw,cb,g)
Erie	WRIE (bb2,rr3,rw)
Akron	WCUE (bb1,rw,cb,g)
Erie	WJET (bb1,rw,cb)
Canton	WINW (rr2,g)
Pittsburg	WKKX (rr2,g)
Wheeling	WKWK (cb,g)
Johnstown	WCRO (cb,g)
Canton	WOIO (g)
Youngstown	WHOT (g)
Cleveland	WZZP (g)
Youngstown	Y-103 (g)
Alliance	WFAH (g)
Altoona	WFBG (g)
Detroit	CKLW (bb6,rr1,rw,cb,g)
Detroit	WDRQ (rr1,rw,cb,g)
Grand Rapids	WGRD (bb2,rr3)
Grand Rapids	WZZM (bb2,rr3,cb,g)
Flint	WTAC (bb1,g)
Saginaw	WKNX (rr3,g)
Detroit	WXYZ (g)
Muskegon	WTRU (rr3,g)
Travers City	WCCW (g)
Kalamazoo	WKMI (g)
Bay City	WHNN (g)
Jackson	WIBM (g)
Saginaw	WSAM (g)
Claire	WRNN (g)
Detroit	WCAR
Cincinnati	WSAI (bb4,rr1,rw,cb)
Cincinnati	WKRQ (bb2,rr1,rw,cb)
Columbus	WCOL (bb4,rr2,rw,cb,g)
Louisville	WAKY (bb4,rr2,rw,cb)
Indianapolis	WNDE (bb2,rr3,rw,cb,g)
Columbus	WNCI (rr2,cb,g)
Indianapolis	WIFE (rr2,rw,cb,g)
Lexington	WVLK (rr3)
Dayton	WING (cb,g)
Louisville	WKLO (cb,g)
Evansville	WGBF (rr3,g)
South Bend	WRBR (g)
Terre Haute	WBOW (g)
Hamilton	WMOH (g)
Alliance	WFAH (g)
Chicago	WLS (bb6,rr1,rw,cb,g)
Milwaukee	WOKY (bb4,rr1,rw,cb,g)
Milwaukee	WZUU (bb2,rr1,rw,cb,g)
Chicago	WMET (rr2,rw,cb)

Madison	WISM (g)
Freeport	WACI (rr3,cb,g)
Peoria	WIRL (cb)
Rockford	WROK (rr3,cb,g)
Stevens Point	WSPT (cb,g)
Wausau	WRIG (g)
Wausau	WIFC (g)
Appleton	WYNE (g)
Appleton	WKAU (rr3,g)
Two Rivers	WOTC (g)
Lafayette	WAZY (g)
Neenah	WNAM (g)
Minneapolis	KDWB (bb4,rr1,rw,cb,g)
Minneapolis	KSTP (bb4,rr1,rw)
Minneapolis	KDWB (bb2,rr3,cb)
Omaha	WOW (rr3,rw,g)
Rapid City	KKLS (bb1,rr3,rw,cb,g)
Omaha	KOIL (bb3)
Des Moines	KIOA (bb2,rr3,cb,g)
Des Moines	KGGO (g)
Cedar Rapids	KCRG (g)
Devenport	KSTT (cb,g)
Dubuque	WDBQ (cb,g)
Mason City	KRIB (g)
Waterloo	KWWL (g)
Souix City	KWSL (g)
Ottumwa	KLEE (g)
Rapid City	KTOQ (rr3,g)
Duluth	WEBC (cb,g)
Duluth	WAKX (rr3)
Lincoln	KLMS (g)
Grand Forks	KKXL (rr3,rw,cb,g)
St. Cloud	WJON (rr3,cb,g)
Rochester	KWEB (g)
Bismarck	KFYR (rr3,cb,rw,g)
Morehead	KVOX (rw,cb,rr3)
Grand Forks	KNOX (g)
Eau Claire	WEAQ (rr3,rw,cb)
Souix Falls	KISD (g)
Huron	KOKX (g)
Minot	KKOA (g,rr3)
Thief River	KTRF (g)
Aberdene	KSDN (g)
St. Louis	KSLQ (bb4,rr1,rw,cb,g)
St. Louis	KXOK (bb4,rw,cb)
Kansas City	WHB (bb4)
Kansas City	KBEQ (rr3,rw,cb,g)
Wichita	KLEO (rr3,rw,cb,g)
Topeka	KEWI (rr3,rw,cb,g)
Jackson	KJAS (g)
Wichita	KEYN (g)
Cape Girardeau	KGMO (g)
Columbia	KTGR (g)
Manhattan	KMKF (g)
Junction City	KJCK (g)
Lawrence	KLWN (g)
Joplin	KFSB (g)
Salina	KSKG (g)
St. Louis	KIRL (g)

DISTRICT III	
Miami	WQAM (bb4,rw,cb)
Ft. Lauderdale	Y-100 (bb2,rr1,rw,cb,gl)
Tampa	WRBQ(Q105)(bb2,rr2)
Miami	WMJX (96X) (rr1,cb,gl)
Jacksonville	WAPE (bb1,rr2,cb)
Orlando	WBJW(BJ105)(bb1,rr2,cb,gl)
Tallahassee	WGLF (rr3,rw,cb,gl)
Lakeland	WQPD (bb1,rw)
Jacksonville	WIVY (rr3)
Orlando	WLOF (rr3,gl)
Sarasota	WYND (bb1,rr3)
Daytona	WMFJ (cb,gl)
Cocoa Beach	WRKT (gl)
Cocoa Beach	CK101 (rr3,rw,gl)
Ft. Meyers	WLEQ (gl)
W. Palm Beach	WIRK-AM (rr3)
Tampa	WLCY (rr3,cb,gl)
Ft. Meyers	WMYR (gl)
Tallahassee	WONS (gl)
Atlanta	WQXI (bb4,rr2,rw,cb,gl)
Atlanta	WZGC(Z93)(bb4,rr1,rw,cb,gl)
Augusta	WBBQ (bb4,rr2,rw,cb,gl)
Birmingham	WERC-AM(bb4,rr2,rw,cb,gl)
Birmingham	WSGN (bb4,rr2,rw,cb,gl)
Montgomery	WHHY (bb4,rr3,rw,cb,gl)
Marietta	WFOM (bb2,rr3,rw,cb,gl)
Savannah	WSGA (bb2,rr2,rw,cb,gl)
Vadalia	WTCQ(98Q) (rr2,rw,cb,gl)
Augusta	WAUG (rw,cb,gl)
Gainesville	WFOX (gl)
Athens	WRFC (rr3,rw,cb,gl)
Columbus	WCGQ (rr3,gl)
Savannah	WSGF (gl)
Gainesville	WDUN (gl)
Warner Robbins	WRBN (gl)
Albany	WALG (gl)
Carrolton	WPPI (gl)
Carrolton	WSTR (gl)
Athens	WAGQ (gl)
Atlanta	WQXI-FM (gl)
Mobile	WABB (rw,cb)
Huntsville	WAAY (rr3,rw)
Pensacola	WBSR (rw,cb,gl)
Panama City	WDLP (gl)
Ft. Walton	WNUE (gl)
Florence	WBCF (gl)
Florence	WQLT (gl)
Gadsden	WQEN (gl)
Birmingham	WKXX (cb,rw,gl)
Guntersville	WGSV (rw,cb,gl)
Huntsville	WVOV (gl)
Charlotte	WAYS (bb4,rr2,cb)
Raleigh	WKIX (bb2,rr2,rw,cb)
Fayetteville	WFLB (rw,cb,rr2)
Spartanburg	WORD (bb1,rw,cb)
Winston-Salem	WTOB (bb1)
Columbia	WCOS (gl)
Charleston	WTMA (bb1,gl)
Winston-Salem	WAIR (rr3,rw,cb,gl)
Asheville	WISE (rr3,gl)
Reidsville	WFRC (gl)
Shelby	WOHS (gl)
Wilmington	WGNI (gl)
Kingstree	WKSP (gl)
Anderson	WANS (rr3,gl)
Memphis	WHBQ (bb4,rr1,rw,cb,gl)
Nashville	WMAK (bb4,rr2,rw,cb,gl)
Nashville	WLAC (bb4,rr2,rw,cb)
Little Rock	KAAY (bb1,rr2,rw,cb,gl)
Chattanooga	WFLI (rr2,rw,cb,gl)
Chattanooga	WGOW (bb3)
Nashville	WBYQ (92Q) (rr3,gl)
Knoxville	WRJZ (rw,g,cb)
Little Rock	Z-98 (gl)
Bowling Green	WBGN (bb1,cb,gl)
Pine Bluff	KOTN (cb,gl)
Paduka	WDXR (gl)
DISTRICT IV	
Dallas	KLIF (bb4,rr1,rw,cb)
Ft. Worth	KFJZ (bb4,rr2,rw,cb,gl)
[illegible]llas	KNUS-FM (bb4,rr2,rw,cb)
[illegible]reveport	KEEL (bb4,rr2,cb,gl)
Oklahoma City	WKY (bb4,rr2,cb,gl)
Tulsa	KAKC (bb2,rr2,rw,cb,gl)
Oklahoma City	KOMA (bb2,cb)
Tulsa	KELI (bb2,cb)
El Paso	KINT (bb2,cb,rr2,gl)
El Paso	KELP
El Paso	KEROK
Lubbock	KLBK (gl)
Lubbock	KSEL (gl)
Monroe	KNOE (g,rw,cb)
Odessa	KRIG (gl)
Longview	KLUE (rw,gl)
Marshall	KMHT (gl)
Midland	KCRS (g,cb)
Shreveport	KROK (gl)
Temple	KTEM (gl)
Killeen	KIXS (gl)
Houston	KILT (bb4,rw,cb,gl)
Houston	KRBE (bb4,rr1,rw,cb,gl)
Houston	KRLY-FM (gl)
Houston	KAUM-FM (gl)
Beaumont	KAYC (rr3,gl)
San Antonio	KTSA (gl)
Austin	KNOW (gl)
McAllen	KRIO (gl)
Corpus Christi	KEYS (gl)
Victoria	KVIC (gl)
Galveston	KILE (gl)
Laredo	KLAR (gl)
San Angelo	KGKL (gl)
San Antonio	K-Z100 (gl)
Bryan	KTAM (gl)
Austin	KHFI (rr2,rw)
Beaumont	KWIC (gl)
Corpus Christi	KRYS (gl)
New Orleans	WTIX (bb4,rw,cb,gl)
New Orleans	WNOE (rr2,rw,cb,gl)
Baton Rouge	WIBR (gl)
Lafayette	KVOL (g,cb)
Gulfport	WROA (gl)
Jackson	WJDX (rr2,rw,cb,gl)
Lake Charles	KAOK (gl)
New Iberia	KANE (gl)
Abbeville	KROF (gl)
Lake Charles	KLOU (gl)
Los Angeles	KHJ (bb4,rr1,rw,cb,gl)
San Diego	KCBQ (bb4,rr1,rw,cb,gl)
Phoenix	KRIZ (bb4,rr2,rw,cb,gl)
Anaheim	KEZY (bb2,rr2,rw,gl)
San Bernardino	KFXM (bb1,rr2,rw,gl)
San Diego	B-100 (rr2,rw,cb,gl)
Los Angeles	K-100 (rr2,rw,g,cb)
Los Angeles	KTNQ(10Q)(rw,rr2,cb,bb1,gl)
Bakersfield	KERN (rr2,rw,cb,gl)
Los Angeles	KHS-FM (rr2,rw)
Los Angeles	KFI (g,Rock)
Santa Barbara	KIST
Whittier	KRHC (gl)
San Luis Obispo	KSLY (rr3,rw,cb,gl)
San Luis Obispo	KATY (gl)
Bakersfield	KAFY (gl)
Oxnard	KACY (cb,gl)
San Bernardino	KOLA (gl)
Santa Maria	KSEE (gl)
Phoenix	KRUX (gl)
Tucson	KTKT (rr2,g,rw)
Las Vegas	KENO (bb1,cb,gl)
Arcata	KATA (gl)
Los Angeles	KRTH (rr)
San Francisco	KFRC (bb4,rr1,rw,cb,gl)
San Francisco	KYA (bb4,rw,gl)
Fresno	KYNO (bb1,rr2,rw,gl)
Modesto	KLIV (bb1,rr2,cb)
Sacramento	KNDE (bb1,rr2,cb,gl)
Stockton	KJOY (bb,rr3,gl)
Sacramento	KROY (g,rr2,bb,cb)
Salinas	KDON (rr2,rw,gl)
Modesto	KFIV (gl)
Stockton	KSTN (gl)
Reno	KCBN (rr3,gl)
Livermore	KKIQ (gl)
Seattle	KJR (bb4,rr1,rw,cb,gl)
Seattle	KING (bb4,rr2,rw)
Portland	KGW (bb4,rw,cb)
Spokane	KJRB (rr2,rw,cb,gl)
Tacoma	KTAC (bb,g,cb,rw,rr3)
Spokane	KREM (gl)
Salem	KBZY (gl)
Portland	KPAM (rr3,cb,gl)
Lewiston	KRLC (gl)
Eugene	KBDF (g,cb)
Medford	KYJC (gl)
Tri Cities	KALE (gl)
Boise	KFXD (rr3,gl)
Boise	KIVZ (gl)
Lewiston	KOZE (gl)
Moscow	KRPL (gl)
Bellingham	KPUG (gl)
Denver	KTLK (bb4,rr1,rw,cb)
Salt Lake City	KCPX (bb4,rr2,rw,cb)
Denver	KXKX (rr1,rw,cb)
Denver	KIMN (rr2,cb,gl)
Salt Lake City	KRSP (bb2,rr2,cb,gl)
Albuquerque	KQEO (bb1,rr2)
Albuquerque	KRKE (rr3,cb,gl)
Pueblo	KDZA (rr3,gl)
Great Falls	KQDI (rr3,gl)
Missoula	KYLT (gl)
Roswell	KBCQ (gl)
Roswell	KBIM (rr3,gl)
Billings	KOOK (gl)
Cheyenne	KRAE
Casper	KATI (gl)
Colorado Sprgs.	KYSN (rr3)
Great Falls	KEIN (gl)
Bozeman	KBOZ (gl)

R&B LPS AIRPLAY STATUS

Date

Artist / Title

BB		CB		RW	
TW	LW	TW	LW	TW	LW

DISTRICT I			
NEW YORK	WBLS-FM		
NEW YORK	WLIB		
NEW YORK	WKTU		
NEW YORK	WRVR-FM		
NEW YORK	WWRL		
BOSTON	WILD		
Brookline	WBOS		
BUFFALO	WBLK		
Amherst	WUFO		
Rochester	WDKX		
HARTFORD	WKND		
New Haven	WYBC-FM		
PHILADELPHIA	WDAS		
Philadelphia	WDAS-FM		
Philadelphia	WHAT		
Philadelphia	WCAU		
Atlantic City	WUSS-FM		
Newark	WNJR		
Trenton	WTNJ		
WASHINGTON	WOL		
Washington	WOOK-FM		
Washington	WKYS		
Washington	WHUR-FM		
Arlington	WEAM		
BALTIMORE	WEBB		
Baltimore	WSID		
Baltimore	WWIN		
Richmond	WANT		
Baltimore	WEAA		
Baltimore	WCAO		
Richmond	WKIE		
Lynchburgh	WJJS-FM		
Baltimore	WXYV-FM		
Highland Springs	WENZ		
Norfolk	WOWI-FM		
Norfolk	WRAP		
Annapolis	WANN		
Roanoke	WTOY		

DISTRICT II			
CINCINNATI	WCIN		
Dayton	WDAO		
Louisville	WLOU		
Columbus	WVKO		
Gary	WLTH		
St. Mathews	WSTM		
Ft. Wayne	WCMX-FM		
CLEVELAND	WABQ		
Cleveland	WJMO		
Cleveland	WLTY		
Canton	WHBC		
Akron	WAKR		
Toledo	WKLR-FM		
Pittsburgh	WAMO		
Youngstown	WGFT		
DETROIT	WJLB		
Detroit	WGPR-FM		
Detroit	WJZZ-FM		
Detroit	WCAR		
Lansing	WKAR		
Flint	WAMM		
Saginaw	WWWS		
Inkster	WCHB		
Grand Rapids	WKWM		
CHICAGO	WVON		
Chicago	WGCI-FM		
Chicago	WJPC		
Chi. Hts.	WMPP		
Gary	WWCA		
Harvey	WBEE		
Indianapolis	WTLC-FM		
Milwaukee	WNOV		
Oak Park	WBMX-FM		
West Allis	WAWA		
ST. LOUIS	KATZ		
St. Louis	KKSS		
E. St. Louis	WESL		
Kansas City	KPRS		
Kansas City	KPRT		
Omaha, Neb.	KOWH		
Jefferson City	KLUM		

DISTRICT III			
ATLANTA	WIGO		
Atlanta	WVEE-FM		
Atlanta	WAOK		
Americius	WIPE		
Thomasville	WTUF		
Manchester	WFDR		
Savannah	WEAS-FM		
Savannah	WSOK		
Albany	WJIZ		
Columbus	WOKS		
Columbus	WFXE		
Macon	WDOO		
Macon	WIBB		
Valdosta	WGOV		
Dawson	WDWD		
Augusta	WROW		
Augusta	WTHB		
ALABAMA	WYLS		
Mobile	WGOK		
Mobile	WBLX		
Montgomery	WXVI		
Birmingham	WATV		
Birmingham	WBUL		
Birmingham	WENN-FM		
Birmingham	WJLD		
Tuscaloosa	WTUG		
Tuskegee	WBIL		
Selma	WTQX		
Huntsville	WEUP		
TENNESSEE			
Memphis	WHRK-FM		
Memphis	WLOK		
Memphis	WDIA		
Berry	WVOL		
Nashville	WMAK		
Nashville	WLAC		
Knoxville	WJBE		
Chattanooga	WNOO		
Jackson	WDXI		
LITTLE ROCK	KOKY		
Pine Bluff	KCAT		
Texacana	KADO-FM		
SOUTH & NORTH CAROLINA			
Greensville	WHYZ		
Florence	WYNN		
Columbia	WOIC		
Charleston	WPAL		
St. George	WQIZ		

DISTRICT III (Cont.)			
Bennettsville	WBSC		
Goldsboro	WBRN		
St. Mathews	WKQI		
St. Mathews	WQKI		
Charleston	WPXI		
Beaufort	WSIB		
Bullins	WCIG		
Sumter	WWDM		
Chapel Hill	WRBX		
Winston Salem	WAAA		
Durham	WSRC		
Fayetteville	WIDU		
Chadbourn	WVOE		
Greensboro	WEAL		
Greensboro	WQMG-FM		
Charlotte	WGIV		
Wilmington	WWIL		
Goldsboro	WOKN		
Raleigh	WLLE		
Wilson	WGTM		
MISSISSIPPI			
Jackson	WKXI-FM		
Jackson	WOKJ		
Laurel	WNSL-FM		
Gulfport	WTAM-FM		
Jackson	WJMI-FM		
Meridian	WQIC		
Meridian	WTNK		
Greenville	WESY		
Lebanon	WBAD		
Yazzo	WYAZ		
Hattiesburg	WORV		
FLORIDA			
Jacksonville	WERD		
Jacksonville	WPDQ		
Miami	WEDR-FM		
Ft. Lauderdale	WCKO-FM		
Ft. Lauderdale	WRBD		
Miami	WMBM		
Tampa	WTMP		
Pensacola	WBOP		
Pensacola	WTKX-FM		
Orlando	WORL		
Winter Green	WOKB		
Lakeland	WWAB		
Ft. Lauderdale	WSDO		

DISTRICT IV			
TYLER, TEXAS	KZEY		
Forth Worth	KNOK		
Forth Worth	KNOK-FM		
Dallas	KKDA-FM		
Dallas	KKDA		
San Antonio	KAPE		
Beaumont	KJET		
Houston	KYOK		
Houston	KXYZ		
Clear Lake	KMJQ-FM		
Galveston	KGBC		
OKLA CITY	KAEZ		
Okla City	KFJL		
BASTROP, LA	KTRY		
W. Monroe	KYEA-FM		
Shreveport	KOKA		
Baton Rouge	WXOK		
New Orleans	WBOK		
New Orleans	WXEL-FM		
New Orleans	WNNR		
New Orleans	WYLD-FM		
New Orleans	WYLD		
Natchez	WNAT		
LOS ANGELES	KDAY		
Los Angeles	KKTT		
Los Angeles	KACE		
Los Angeles	KJLH		
Los Angeles	KBCA		
Los Angeles	KUTE		
Alameda	KJAZ		
Lemoore	KOAD		
San Diego	XHRM		
Bakersfield	KSGY		
Las Vegas	KVOV		
Las Vegas	KCEP		
Phoenix	KXTC		
SAN FRAN	KDIA		
San Francisco	KSOL-FM		
San Francisco	KRE		
San Francisco	KSFX		
Sacramento	KPOP		
Fresno	KLIP		
Seaside	KZEN		
SEATTLE	KYAC		
Seattle	KTOY		
DENVER	KDKO		
Denver	KADX		

L-R Chuck Offuitt – Promotion Rep., Billy Paul – Artist,
Frankie Crocker – Program Director WBLS

Don Cornelius interviewing Johnny Nash on *Soul Train*

REALITY IN RETROSPECTION

Dr. Don Mizell

2017

In 1981 Dr. Don Mizell contributed commentary to the first edition of this book that is listed under Chapter 5 "Producers". He discussed the future of the music business, which, from a retrospective review between 1981 and 2017, has virtually come to pass. I asked Dr. Mizell to revisit his chapter and explain to us how he was able to conceive of such dramatic changes in the future of the music industry that, to most of us, might have sounded like science fiction.

Westbrooks:

Dr. Mizell, as you know, we wrote that book some years ago. As a matter of fact, it was in 1981, and it was titled The Anatomy of a Record Company: How to survive the Record Business. We primarily used it as a textbook at the university where I was teaching at the time. It went on to become an in-demand book at a lot of the colleges and universities. I have gotten so many calls to reissue this book that I finally made the decision to do so. And in so doing, going through the first book I was just astounded by your commentary. I could not believe how in 1981 you were so on point about the status of the music business and the future of the music business. Describe your thought processes at that particular time.

Mizell:

Leave it up to you, Dr. Logan Westbrooks, to ask me a question that I have difficulty answering. And I usually don't have difficulty answering any questions that I'm asked. The reality is that I don't remember even writing it. When you called and reminded me of it, it was startling to me because I didn't remember. I didn't know that I even knew this. Since then I've had a real journey back into the inner recesses of my mind to see what I was thinking and where it came from, because when you first asked me, I had no idea. I found it very disturbing, I was like "Well, maybe I'm an imposter," (laughter) "and I'm not really who I say I am, or I've lost my mind, or this is like a deep dream."

I had a lot of questions as to why I don't remember even doing this. But I must have said it. It's there in the book. So, I'm glad that I had an opportunity since then to reflect on it, and over time, I've been able to kind of piece together what I think was going on in my head. It's kind of complicated and nuanced.

Essentially, the bottom line is that I have always been interested in the future, since I was a kid liking science fiction and "Flash Gordon." I was interested in tomorrow and what's coming later. Some of that had to do with being from the South where the past represented oppression, restriction, and setbacks for Black folks. And the future represented new possibilities and liberation.

Except that in the White man's version of the future, there were no Negroes. So, I clearly was off my rocker, because I was putting myself into a future that they had already eliminated me from.

But that did not stop me because I always just felt that tomorrow things would get better by and by. Progress. That's the existential context of my early interest in the future.

Then I went to college and got the opportunity to be able to start reflecting in a much more disciplined way about the evolution of societies and cultures. In my senior year, I was about 21. That was about ten years before the article in question.

I kind of got a very good grasp of my understanding of how social change works. Fundamentally, it was that technology is the driver of social change, and that technology is going to have more and more of an impact over time.

The effect that it has on social change is that it accelerates the rate of social change. That's why it took a long time from TV to computers, but it didn't take that long to move to the next level of change to the Internet.

As we go into the future—as we all have seen now—change is driven by technology, and it has much more of a disruptive impact because it happens faster and more fundamentally. It has a tendency to uproot and overthrow whatever the structures are, the status quo, and how things are set up.

Typically, social structures last a long time if there isn't a great rate of technological change. In other words, technological change drives social change. It is not the only driver, but it is one of the most fundamental, and it certainly is the most fundamental for the rate of social change.

I already had that Big Idea in my mind for ten years, and I was monitoring that as I went along in my studies in general and well before I got into the record business. I went to law school, I went to the American Film Institute, and I was just really monitoring it over all.

Then in 1977, I had the great fortune to start a label imprint at Elektra. I was supposed to start a Jazz label, but Joe Smith wanted this to be a division that would be able to get Jazz on R&B/Black radio. Now old school Jazz would not be able to do that because it was already being viewed as passé.

You had all this commercial Jazz happening, but people were not giving it respect as an art form. There was crossover Jazz, and they spoke about it in terms of its commercial appeal. But I thought that it had an intrinsic value beyond its commercial bona fides as an art form. And one night I dreamed up the notion of calling it Jazz Fusion.

There was already Jazz Rock Fusion as a term that existed, Jazz Rock, Soul Jazz existed, and so did crossover Jazz and something they would call fusion Jazz. Not fusion as a form of Jazz but Jazz that is a form of fusion.

So, what I came up with was Jazz Fusion, that fusion music was a scientific concept that the whole is larger than the sum of its parts. Whatever goes into it, there is something that comes out of it that is greater than just the constituent elements. Scientists are trying to create fusion energy, but nature already has.

When I came up with the term Jazz Fusion, I didn't want the music to be defined in commercial terms. I also wanted to define it in a way where it would embrace the future because Jazz is an adventurous art form and had been open ended in its past innovations, but it had stopped doing that. It had become ossified with certain conventions.

The spirit of Jazz was always exploratory and improvisational, and I wanted to reflect that. That didn't mean going backwards, that actually meant moving forward. Fusion would be a musical way that we could still talk about the Jazz element but as more than just Jazz in that it incorporates other genres as musical concepts.

I dreamed up the name Jazz Fusion and pushed it out there into the media and market. Lo and behold, it became a commonly used generic industry term. It defined a music that had already been happening for ten years—circa *Bitches Brew*. Then Jazz Fusion became a Grammy category in 1979. Wow!

I coined the term Jazz Fusion as my way of trying to project the future of the music, where it would incorporate more and more the disparate elements of all genres and cultures from around the world into a fresh and vibrant style of Jazz as a subset of fusion, and not vice versa.

That's kind of what happened with me in relation to the music creatively, before I got to thinking about the impact of innovations in digital technology. I was looking at the future of music, not in the business. What we're seeing now is that a lot of my projection was actually accurate.

The Jazz Fusion category exists still, so I created a Grammy category before I actually won the Best Album Grammy in 2005 for Ray Charles' *Genius Loves Company*. In 1979 the Academy came to me and asked me to be on the first Jazz Fusion committee because I was the first person to coin the term in 1977.

My label went under, though, in 1980 because the Disco tsunami wiped out a lot of Rock & Roll, R&B, and Jazz Fusion releases.

Which brings me to your question. Stevie Wonder was the biggest artist in the world at that time. (This was before *Thriller*, Michael Jackson's mega seller in 1984). I was recommended to Stevie (the owner of KJLH radio) by Rod McGrew who was then running KJLH.

Rod wanted to go work with Barry White. He was tired of radio after a decade, so he suggested me, and Stevie hired me. Suddenly I am in charge of a small progressive radio station in L.A. The competition is brutal. There are four Black-owned competitors—KGFJ, KACE, KDAY, and KUTE.

I had to figure out how to beat the competition. I had to anticipate the future much more clearly, and that was the framework I began operating out of when you and Dr. Lance Williams (co-author of *The Anatomy of the Record Company*) came to talk to me.

I had to project the future. That meant breaking with the conventional wisdom in order to survive. Because if I looked at what everybody did, there was no way that I was going to beat them. We were dividing up a small pie, which was Metro L.A., and I could not even broadcast into the valley (Suburban L.A.).

I thought I'd better try and come up with a competitive advantage going forward that would be to do "what they're **not doing**, think what they're **not thinking** and see what they're **not seeing** about the future."

What did that mean in terms of your question about the record industry? Well, I had already come from the record industry with my Jazz Fusion imprint. I had already established an industry standard, future-oriented term for Jazzy progressive music. Now I'm running a Jazzy progressive Black music radio station. I started reading future oriented music broadcasting stuff and just started thinking about it.

Here's the industry backdrop story. In the history of the music business, the driver of growth was always change in the consumer product platforms. We started out with 78s, then we went to 33 rpm LP albums, to 8 tracks, and then audiocassettes. The year 1981 (the time of my essay) was before CDs hit the market, which is kind of amazing. We were still playing LPs at the station.

The driver of the change was that the industry was always trying to find ways to deliver the product in a way that the customer would have greater fidelity with flexibility in how consumers experienced it because that was likely to grow the business in a way that increased profitability. Put the consumer in greater control of their listening experience, and they would get more involved with it. Enjoy it more. Spend more time and money.

What would be next—even more affordability or flexibility with greater fidelity and sound than we already had? Maybe. That's what we would be looking for. Okay, hopefully, but there are always what we call unintended consequences in any type of change that you seek or pursue.

The engineers were looking for ways to improve the consumer experience—for example, the cassette tape was a better version of the 8-track tape experience because it was smaller, more portable, better sound. And some players possibly would let you play a specific track and repeat it. But ALL the CD players allowed you to play a selectable track, repeat it, etc. You didn't have to rewind. All you had to do was click on whatever the desired track, and voila! People loved that.

I knew the CD digital platform was the key marker of coming change. What digital does is basically this: Digital was the platform that flattened everything audio signals to a reduction pattern of zeros and ones, which paradoxically, allows you to then be able to re-deploy that form of music—audio sound of information—across a broader range of platforms. What digital does, for example, is to allow you to play it on a computer, a CD player, augment it with visuals on a DVD, and shoot a digital movie. Because everything is converted to zeros and ones signals, with digital you can come back in a lot of other formats.

What would be the net effect? More control in the hands of both the producer and the consumer of their experience. That is the impending outcome, and that will trigger disruptive changes in often unintended and unforeseeable ways. Convenience, versatility, access, control, etc.—those are the key drivers of the technological changes pursued.

If that is what is going to be happening, then that means that what I said in my article would (be happening). I did not know all the ramifications then, but I did know that there would be unintended consequences, and that the disruptions of the normal paradigm that we'd been operating under for well over 20 or 30 years could or would go out the door moving forward. Like, "Why do I have to buy the thing?" "You don't. You can rent it." and "Why can't I rent that (referring to a record)? I can rent a car, I can rent a TV, I can subscribe to pay or cable TV. Why not a record or a channel?" You can. Soon.

Some of this came from logical extrapolations from what I knew were the technological forces at work in general driving change in society, and, in particular, media business. I applied my intellect in thinking carefully about the ramifications to the radio and records paradigm because I had to. I had to win. And we did.

Westbrooks:
What information did you have that helped with the analysis of the ultimate shift in the music industry?

Mizell:
Well, all the above provided the intellectual scaffolding for my analysis. I was actually studying Arbitron and how they were working with information technology to measure the listening audience. It led me to critique Arbitron's rating methodology.

If Arbitron is measuring ratings based upon statistically sound sampling rates in order to extrapolate a credible rating, it is still not what is actually going on. But it is in a range of statistical plausibility. Because you can't measure any better than that with the technology used to measure listening habits, people take that measurement as reliably valuable and are willing to pay for it.

The rating does not reflect exactly what's going on, it's just a reliably derived extrapolation. If I give listening measurement diaries to listeners in certain areas, their listening patterns might be reasonably considered a projection of many more people within a certain common psycho-graphic range. It is not actually the exact reality, but it is the statistically acceptable reality.

Arbitron was not measuring Black audiences the same way as it measured White audiences. I basically wrote and published a critique of their methodology as statistically invalid and forced them to agree that it was really unfair to Black audiences and the radio stations that served them. Apples to apples.

That concept created a major shift in ratings because once they had to use the same methodology for all audiences, suddenly their statistical extrapolations showed that Black radio was actually way more popular than their ratings had suggested. KJLH exploded to the top of the adult Urban market around that time.

I think that was a direct response to the article that I wrote and published in BRE Magazine (Black Radio Exclusive) about the statistical fallibility of comparative ratings methodology between Black radio and White radio. When the Black stations exploded to the top, suddenly they didn't want to call them Black anymore. We couldn't be Black and be the winner. Now we had to be Urban. Ha! Why can't we be Black anymore?

This was after the Black pride revolution. Then the next problem with that is when they become Urban. Well we ain't Black and the next thing you know, they got lost in their own thinking and then here come these other stations and they are like, 'We need Black music, but we're going to out-Black you without being Black.' The next thing you know, they fall down the rabbit hole and lose their clout.

What I'm saying to you about my thinking and my research is that I had a certain worldview and certain principles that I was using to interpret and project into the future. The particular issue of what I came up with about record companies and the music industry was in the context of a larger perspective that I had been developing, contemplating and researching for ten years before I was in college.

I was very clear. I knew that CDs were coming, but they hadn't come yet. But cable had just hit. It was not big yet, though, and Blacks were not on MTV yet, but cable disrupted the broadcast business, too, through television. Then here comes BET (Black Entertainment Television).

All these things had a way of changing how you think about how to break a record. Then when cable comes along, now you've got MTV, and now the record company can make videos. They provide free programming through these channels that play these videos, and that's a tremendous driver of profits.

Suddenly, how artists look and move is way more important than just how they sing. If you look good and can dance but you can't sing, you now have digital technology in the studio where you can adjust the voices. That changed the whole game. I mean if you're ugly and can't dance, then you're in trouble. The fact that you can really sing doesn't mean anything. It might mean something, but we've got digital vocal tuners and we can dumb down the whole thing and people don't know what to think or like. It's like if they still hear some great singing, and it scares them.

It's intimidating—a problem. Not for every single person, but what I'm saying is that all these digital technological innovations are disrupters, and they automatically will reap the meltdown of how things have gone. What you want to look at to project future impacts are the things that are the drivers of the technological change.

What things are going to enhance the convenience, the choice, the flexibility of use to put in the hands of the consumer and also improve their entertainment experience through listening or seeing or whatever. Everything else that happens will flow from that, and some of that may not be knowable. You just have to guesstimate through the pathway emerging that some people call the law of unintended consequences.

Westbrooks:
Why do you think that the labels were so slow to respond to the technological changes?

Mizell:
I think that they were like anybody. If I have my foot on your neck, why would I let off of it? So that you can jump up and kill me? (Laughter) You must think I'm stupid, and why would you think that when I've got all the money and the guns? (More laughter) I'm gonna keep my foot on your neck as long as I possibly can because my gun is cocked right on your head, so don't make any false moves. Just kidding, but you get my drift.

The moguls realized that with CDs they could re-sell their whole catalog inventory and not have to pay to re-record anything—just remaster it if they wanted to. That was pure profit to the bottom line because there's no cost to record the stuff. All you have to do is re-package it on a CD. Digitize it. It made them look more successful than they were.

The business was always fueled by new artists and new hits, but this was the first time they made big money from catalog. And what happened was that they got complacent—drunk on drinking their own Kool-Aid hype—like they are really doing their job well. But they actually are not, they are just pimping the past. Pressing old wine in new bottles, as it were.

What happens is that the people who really know how to pick talent and make hits, who really know how to make a great record, play an instrument and sing well became dispensable, considered an unnecessary cost and unreliable profit center. They were cut back and dwindled. That's part of what made being an actual musician obsolete, and A&R people also became obsolete.

So much money came in during the mid-to-late 1980s when CDs came in just from milking those catalogs. The industry managed to bamboozle Wall Street and make them think that we were really kicking ass, when all they were doing was pimping the past. And they fattened up the balance sheet cow to sell it to the Wall

Street suits who basically were rubes with too much money from all the financial wheeler dealer tricked up bullpucky shenanigans.

All the cats who really knew how to do the business—who built the business—sold out to the bean counter knuckleheads who knew nothing and cashed out before the business, as we knew it, collapsed like a house of cards.

When the suits got hold of it, everyone had bought CDs of their old collection. They weren't hip to the new music and were not buying like before. In 1990 everybody who really knew how to do this business (the legendary record execs and producers), they had all sold out and got their money and went home and hid behind closed gates and walls.

The suits bet that the CD was going to keep going strong. They were wrong. You need to know how to make a good record, hype it. The people who knew how to do it have run off with too much money, leaving the suits holding the bag trying to figure out how to get their money back.

So, what do we do? We start hacking budgets and cutting back. First up: the Black music departments. That was the beginning of the end of the golden age of the music biz, especially Black music.

CDs—digital technology—killed the record business as we knew it. It was a double-edged sword. By now the artists don't sing as well, and they don't have to. The rappers can't even sing at all, and they don't have to. And guys that can play are few and far between because they aren't needed. All of this contributed to the dumbing down of the creative musicality that drove the industry.

In the meantime, the Back stations, which are no longer Black—they are called Urban—are holding on for dear life now because when they became Urban, then the rest of America wasn't accepting their identity because they didn't have the Black stigma.

Then in 1996 President Bill Clinton deregulated the broadcast ownership policy where a company could only own one station and one newspaper in a city. Now you can own everything in the town. Well, that killed Black minority ownership, which had been one of the key drivers to the innovative creativity in Black radio, which, in turn, really helped facilitate the creativity in the music because you could get your stuff played at Black-owned outlets.

All of this worked against the creativity, which was always the driver of what made the music business blossom. Black radio—and radio in general—was the door through which this was exposed because they were the voice of the community.

I'm saying that this did not have to happen the way it went down, but it was a curious confluence of the people who really had built the industry cashing out that left the industry to suits who really didn't understand that you could not just buy a hit record.

You can make a hit record a bigger record if you have money behind it, but you cannot make a stiff a hit record, no matter how much money you put behind it. You'd just get tons of returns, but you cannot market the heck out of a bad record and make it a hit record. And you need to know how to tell.

Now, if you have a good-looking artist that can dance and you manufacture them, you can run up the pole with it. But if it's not really happening, then it won't stick. If it is, it might stick. If you get it to stick long enough, it can possibly explode to another level—a quantum leap. In the meantime, you won't have money to do anything with any of the other creative artists who need nurturing and so forth.

The main thing is that the record industry got complacent when they found pure profit in the early CD era and had a ten-year run making a ton of money without having to produce a new generation of great artists with great new music. I'm not saying that there were no great artists that came out. What I am saying is that the record business actually got on CDs, though they resisted in the beginning.

They embraced it when they saw that it was going to bring a tremendous amount of money to the bottom line without cost, and they didn't have to pay the artist the royalties that they did under the original contract. The way that they interpreted it, they just made a lot of money.

They convinced Wall Street that it was going to continue, and they sold out for a premium and Wall Street was left holding the bag. Then came all these foreigners, and all these lawyers and accountants who didn't know crap about the creative process; which is what always drove the record business—talent and creativity. It had stopped being a creative business.

Now it's lawyers, and accountants, and MBAs. That is why they got caught flat footed, but the people who made the record business huge didn't get caught flat footed, they got paid. And left. Those who got caught flat footed were the rubes who bought it and over paid.

Westbrooks:
What do you foresee about the future of streaming for content creators, and specifically for independent artists?

Mizell:
Streaming is definitely going to come on stronger, but I don't think that these artists are going to get paid properly. It's just like back with CDs in the beginning, the artists got paid less royalties on CDs sold than they had been getting on records sold—and for dubious reasons.

That's the same thing that's happening with streaming. They may get paid even less than with CDs, because with CDs, those were records that had been big sellers already, from established artists. With streaming, a lot of artists are people they don't know, so they don't even have any leverage.

However, if the artists band together and their lawyers don't sell them out, they can make them pay more properly what they are supposed to get; which is what should be a formula that is the functional equivalent as if they were selling the product and/or an ASCAP/BMI type performance royalty. I don't know what the number or the formula is, but it is knowable.

Westbrooks:
So, it's rather bleak for the independent artist then?

Mizell:
It's bleak if you stay in the slot that they have designed for you to stay in. I think artists and their reps need to really just open up their head and think expansively about it in a creative way, where they understand that they can use music to make money, but the sale of music itself might not be where they earn most of their money.

I think the current smart formula now is: "You have to have exposure. Then monetize." People have to first hear the music, and they have to like it. They also have to identify it with the artist. If you can aggregate that and database it, then that can be monetized.

It's not so much about selling the album, it's about people becoming so aware of you and they also like your stuff (they identify with your musical artistry and artistic persona), and they want to be a part of your fan base aggregation. And their friends.

That is a psycho-graphic group that can be monetized, meaning that there are sources of revenue that will pay you to access your fan group following, and that's how you're going to make money.

So, it might be a bit bleak and it might not. It all depends on how you play the hand you're dealt. You've got to have some sharp people with you. You've got to make some fabulous music that people like, but you need to play a game where you don't see 'not selling the music' as failure. Today the success of the music is the foundation for making money from related and derivative activities.

If it's getting out there, and people like it and you have a way to identify who they are, how to reach them and where they are, then you can monetize that by letting other people sell them other stuff and you getting paid from what they buy or go do. You will get a piece of that automatically.

So, in the future, I wouldn't just sell the right to have a corporate sponsor get at them. I would sell them that and also make sure that the artist would get a percentage of whatever they make going forward, and more if the company continues to profit more off of your audience.

You have a stake in their success, and vice versa, so they are not just getting it. At the same time, you've got to be careful. You don't want to have a stake in some slimy low life product or shady company because that could kill your audience appeal, and then you won't have anything.

You've got to watch it. It's complicated, like life. But it can and will be done. Do your homework. Put together your team. Make a plan with a sound strategy. Execute.

QUESTIONS FOR REFLECTION

Answer each numbered question with a brief essay.

1. Why are the 'numbers' of a radio station so important in its overall operating scheme?

2. Describe the types of interaction between radio stations and record companies. Both the text and responses from the informed sources indicate wide disparity as to the specific interrelationship.

3. How does a record company help to maintain a radio station's survival? What is the company's stake in that process?

4. Conversely, what is the radio station's value to companies? What is a station's stake in the hit-making process? Why would good radio action on a record breaking in a 'secondary' market be of prime value?

5. Describe the record promotion person's role in this process.

CHAPTER 6

MUSIC FOR THE PEOPLE
The Influence of Hip Hop Culture on the Music Industry

Perhaps the most lucrative and the most innovative genre of music that's single-handedly managed to maintain the record industry's multi-billion dollar status is Rap.

In the history of music, the influences of African and African American culture have taken music to new and exciting heights. While not always being embraced by the masses, Black cultural aesthetics have always been prevalent in American music. Today, Rap music has revolutionized every part of all culture.

What is Rap?

At best, Rap is best defined as one of the four elements of Hip Hop culture in which syncopated rhymes are spoken to and over beats of music. Often the rhymes are rapped free style (spontaneous and from the heart) or pre-written. Ideally, the rhymes have definitive meaning reflecting the present lifestyle and circumstances of the rapper.

It's neither fantasy or frivolous and encompasses the emotion and feelings experienced by the rapper. More often than not, audiences view it as the most powerful art form within the genre of music, because of its sheer ability to speak directly to members of Hip Hop culture.

Simply put, it's the resurgence of African Oral Tradition in the vein of the *griot*, or storyteller, who also would 'rap' to villages of people to an African beat.

The difference is that now that the cultural art form of Rap has been embraced and mimicked by mainstream culture, it has been argued as being colorless, when its roots are the direct offspring of African culture and traditions.

The other three elements of Hip Hop culture are: *deejaying, graffiti*, and *dancing* (at the time of Hip Hop's inception, the culture encompassed break dancing, now it is called Hip Hop dancing).

While these three elements are a part of Hip Hop culture, contemporary society revels in the success that Rap has brought to record companies, therefore, the other elements are not of interest in the stronghold that Rap has on record companies.

Rap is the meat and potatoes of Hip Hop culture, which was once, at its beginning, the movement behind ghetto life as seen through the eyes of urban Black and urban youth, not the b-boys, the b-girls, and deejays who attempt to emulate the message behind the movement.

Now seen as a colorless culture, due to the infiltration of non-Black rappers and R&B singers, Hip Hop culture is a wave in which music media (print, television and online) is constantly riding all the way to the bank.

As a brief history, Rap music evolved in the 1970s in New York City by Jamaican emcee DJ Herc. In previous chapters, we have detailed the influence that music magazines such as *Jack the Rapper, Billboard, BRE*, and *Cashbox* have had on record sales for record companies.

In this chapter, we will discuss the significant influence that Hip Hop cultures—with particular emphasis on Rap music—has had on the rate of success for record companies. There are several different types of Rap music: (a) hard core (b) gangster (c) commercial (d) underground (e) rock rap, and (f) political.

The hard core Rap includes Rap music in the vein of groups such as Mobb Deep and Black Moon. Music in this category most often details murderous activities. The gangster Rap category includes music from groups such as E40, NWA, and Ice T.

This particular category glorifies ghetto life, and often violent activities in all of these categories. One such artist that fits this description is the multi-Platinum artist Tupac Shakur.

The next category is underground Rap, which includes artists such as Mos Def. The next category is Rock Rap, which includes artists such as Kid Rock, Korn, and Limp Bisket.

The final category of Rap music is political Rap, which can be summed up as Rap music that makes a socio-political statement. This category includes music from artists such as Talib Kweli, KRS-1, Mos Def, Public Enemy, and Tupac.

A most significant aspect of a Hip Hop artist is not only to sell numerous amounts of records, but also to reach masses of people on a global scale and transcend the realms of the typical Hip Hop artist into a music legend.

Tupac managed to do this in a short period of time. As the only Rap artist to ever take a political and social stance to the degree in which activists Malcolm X and the Black Panthers did, Shakur used his music as a platform to unify Black men worldwide.

His music was further used as a vehicle for giving the world a socially charged message. Despite his many run-ins with the authorities and civil rights leaders, Shakur could indeed be revered as the Malcolm X of Generation X, and had the ability to make people believe in something significant.

Unfortunately, as with many socially conscious individuals, it seemed as if Shakur was so far ahead of his time that his lyrical messages may have struck fear in some, and his life was tragically taken in a violent way in September 1996.

In his memory, MTV Films has released a film titled *Tupac Resurrection*, due in theaters in November 2003. Since his death, there have been many copycats of the Shakur style, but there has yet to be a Rap artist who actually walked with the people and promoted socio-political consciousness through their music.

Many would dare to compare rapper Eminem to Tupac. However, their comparisons are in vain, for Eminem is more of a commercial rapper with adept lyrical skills, whose music has no real impact on promoting change and recycling the Black dollar within the Black community.

Arguably, many would suggest that slain rapper Notorious BIG (aka Biggie Smalls), had an impact on the Rap world. However, it was not for his ability to promote Black consciousness, but for his Rap style and for his alliance with Bad Boy Entertainment.

Best remembered for his riff with rapper Tupac Shakur, and battle rhymes that spawned a media frenzy which led to an East Coast versus West Coast Rap beef, the life of this rapper was also tragically taken less than six months after Tupac Shakur was slain.

Amazingly, the two had no idea of the amount of power in which they possessed over their fans, because to this day both are still highly revered and have murals painted in their memory.

Apparently, in several interviews Shakur mentioned that there was no such thing as an East Coast versus West Coast Rap beef, because he was originally from the East Coast and simply sought to unify Black men worldwide.

In other interviews such as the *Vibe* exclusive on Tupac, he mentioned that his issue was with the urban record label, Bad Boy Entertainment, and their artist Notorious BIG only. The power of music is insurmountable, and the fan loyalty goes beyond that of the record company.

Clearly, in this tragic situation two Rap moguls were murdered over battle rapping against each other. I'm sure it goes deeper than that, however, only three entities know the real deal. Tupac, BIG, and, of course, the higher power.

Rap and Radio: The Urban Format

Not only has Rap music become the battleground for record companies, it's become a battleground for radio as well. In the early 80s a woman by the name of Catherine Hughes started a company that would become a multi-million dollar radio operating empire targeting African American listeners nationwide.

The name of the company is Radio One, Inc., the year was 1980. Hughes founded the company in Washington, D.C., operating only a 1,000-watt station. Since its inception, the company has expanded to 66 stations with formats ranging from Gospel to Adult Contemporary to Urban (or Hip Hop).

For nearly a generation, Hughes has enjoyed being in the forefront of the Hip Hop revolution in music, often debuting hit and chart topping Urban artists first on one of her radio stations.

Needless to say, it was not long before mega radio operating giant Clear Channel Communications, Inc., took notice of Hughes string of successes and waged a counter attack against her in many of her strong markets.

As we stated in the beginning chapters of this book, the music industry is a numbers game that translates into dollars and cents. Rap music is a money magnet. The more that listen to it, the more money is generated and advertisers are more willing to support it, which inevitably means more money for the record company…and that's a plus.

In 2002 alone, Radio One raked in $151 million due to its broadcast of Rap music. This was $28 million increase over its $123 million profit in 2001.

So, it is fair to say that Rap music has been good to Radio One, Inc. It has a distinct advantage over Clear Channel, Inc., in that it had a head start in developing radio personalities who are strongly connected in their markets as well as its long-known credibility amongst listeners for keeping an ear to the street staying on top of the latest Hip Hop trends, providing significant leverage over Clear Channel Communications, Inc.

At any rate, in radio as in the contemporary record company, it is not unusual for companies to look to Rap music and Hip Hop culture to boost margins.

THE LEGACY OF HIP HOP MUSIC:
The Genre and the People Who Make it Happen
Commentary by Davey D
1985

Davey D is a Hip Hop researcher/journalist whose work on Hip Hop culture has spanned nearly 20 years. This excerpt was quoted with his permission.

Rap became popular because it offered unlimited challenges. There were no real set rules, except to be original and to rhyme on time to the beat of music. Anything was possible. The ultimate goal was to be perceived as being 'def' (good by one's peers). And the fact that the praises and positive affirmation a rapper received were on par with any other urban hero (a sports star, a tough guy, a comedian, etc.) was another drawing card.

Additionally, because of its inclusive aspects, Rap allowed one to accurately and efficiently inject their personality into the music. If you were laid back, you could rap at a slow pace. If you were hyperactive or a type A, you could rap at a faster pace. No two people rapped the same, even when reciting the same rhyme. There were, and still are, many people who try to emulate someone's style, but even that was indicative of a particular personality.

Rap continues to be popular among today's urban youth for the same reasons it was a draw in the early days: It is still an accessible form of self-expression that is capable of eliciting positive affirmation from one's peers.

Because Rap has evolved to become such a big business, it has given many the false illusions of being a quick escape from the harshness of inner city life. There are many kids out there under the belief that all they need to do is write a few 'fresh' (good) rhymes and they're off to the good life.

Throughout history, music originating from America's Black communities has always had an accompanying subculture reflective of the political, social and economic conditions of the time. Rap is no different. Hip Hop is the culture from which Rap emerged. Initially, it consisted of four main elements; graffiti art, break dancing, deejays (cuttin' and scratching) and emceeing (rapping).

Hip Hop is a lifestyle with its own language, style of dress, music and mindset that is continuously evolving. Nowadays, because break dancing and graffiti aren't as prominent, the words 'Rap' and 'Hip Hop' have been used interchangeably. However, it should be noted that all aspects of Hip Hop culture still exist. They've just evolved onto new levels.

Hip Hop continues to be a direct response to an older generation's rejection of the values and needs of young people. Initially, all of Hip Hop's major facets were forms of self-expression. The driving force behind all these activities was people's desire to be seen and heard. Hip Hop came about because of some major format changes that took place within Black radio during the early 70s.

Prior to Hip Hop, Black radio stations played an important role in the community by being a musical and cultural preserver or griot (storyteller). It reflected the customs and values of the day in particular communities. It set the tone and created the climate for which people governed their lives, as this was a primary source of information and enjoyment.

This was particularly true for young people. Interestingly enough, the importance of Black radio and the role deejays played within the African American community has been the topic of numerous speeches from some very prominent individuals. For example, in August of '67, Martin Luther King, Jr., addressed the Association of Television and Radio Broadcasters.

Here he delivered an eloquent speech in which he let it be known that Black radio deejays played an intricate part in helping keep the Civil Rights Movement alive.

He noted that while television and newspapers were popular and often times more effective mediums, they rarely language themselves so that Black folks could relate to them. He basically said Black folks were checking the radio as their primary source of information.

In August of 1980 Minister Farrakhan echoed those thoughts when he addressed a body of Black radio deejays and programmers at the Jack the Rapper Convention. He warned them to be careful about what they let get on the airwaves because of its impact.

He got deep and spoke about radio stations being instruments of mind control and how big companies were going out of their way to hire 'undignified,' 'foul,' and 'dirty' deejays who were no longer being conveyers of good information to the community.

To paraphrase him, Farrakhan noted that there was a fear of a dignified deejay coming on the airwaves and spreading that dignity to the people he reached. Hence, the role radio was playing was beginning to shift. Black radio deejays were moving away from being the griots. Black radio was no longer languaging itself so that both a young and older generation could define and hear themselves reflected in this medium.

Author Nelson George talks extensively about this in his book *The Death of Rhythm and Blues*. He documented how N.Y.'s Black radio stations began to position themselves so they would appeal to a more affluent, older, and to a large degree, White audience. He pointed out how young people found themselves being excluded, especially when bubble gum and Europeanized versions of Disco music began to hit the air waves.

To many, this style of music lacked soul, and, to a large degree, sounded too formulated and mechanical. In a recent interview, Hip Hop pioneer Afrika Bambaataa spoke at length how New York began to lose its connection with Funk music during this time. He noted that established Rock acts doing generic sounding Disco tunes found a home on Black radio.

Acts like Rod Stewart and the Rolling Stones were cited as examples. Meanwhile, Black artists like James Brown and George Clinton were, for the most part, unheard on the airwaves. Even the Gospel like soulful Disco as defined by the 'Philly Sound' found itself losing ground.

While the stereotype depicted a lot of long-haired suburban White kids yelling the infamous slogan 'Disco sucks,' there were large numbers of young inner city brothers and sisters who were in perfect agreement. With all this happening, a void was created and Hip Hop filled it.

QUESTIONS FOR REFLECTION

Answer each numbered question with a brief essay.

1. What is Hip Hop culture, and why is it dominating the airwaves?

2. Who started Radio One, and why is it an important outlet for Rap music?

3. How many different styles of Rap music are there, and what is the relevance to contemporary music?

4. Explain how Rap music has changed the face of the record industry.

CHAPTER 7

THE RESIDUAL SUCCESS OF GOSPEL MUSIC AND ITS STRONGHOLD ON THE MUSIC INDUSTRY

It is the Urban format fused with Christian values music genre in which many thought would never succeed. Gospel music has indeed superseded the expectations of the music industry.

At one time, it was stigmatized as a genre which catered to the Black cultural value system. Now, the genre is one which falls under the bigger hub genre of Christian music.

From Gospel-centric rappers to traditional choral style melodies, one thing is for sure, Gospel music is where it's at. "Gospel's landscape is changing," says Crystal Rose Records CEO Brian Spears. Not only is there a steady increase in sales, but the marketing strategy towards consumers is also evolving within the genre. Two of the most highly recognized Gospel labels are EMI Gospel and Verity Records, but with the rise of the independent record CEO, the two aforementioned labels are facing more com-petition than they bargained for.

Gone are the days of 2002 when commercial Gospel recording artists in the vein of Kirk Franklin dominated the charts. Currently, it is the underdog labels of the genre which continuously thrive regardless of sales.

Tried and true, the Gospel genre has remained resilient in its endeavors within the music industry. As of 2002, the top ten performing labels in Gospel were the following: Gospo-Centric, Verity Records, Elektra, EMI Gospel, Epic, Malaco, AIR, Blackberry, Wellspring, and World Wide Gospel.

So how do they do it? Lisa Collins, CEO of Eye on Gospel Publications has an explanation that is easy to follow.

GETTING YOUR RECORD CHARTED

Commentary by Lisa Collins
©2003 Eye on Gospel Publications
(now called Gospel Roundup)

You don't have to be a major label or even be on one to have your record show up on Billboard's Top Gospel Albums Chart. All your product needs is a bar code so that when it is sold, it will register on SoundScan, which is the mechanism used by Billboard to monitor sales.

While it takes the sale of approximately 6,000 units to chart on Billboard's Top 200 Chart, the number of units you must sell in order to show up on the Gospel charts is much less.

While Billboard's Top Gospel Album Chart is based on data from SoundScan, placement on Billboard's Top Contemporary Chart is based on airplay on contemporary Christian stations, as well as the availability and sales of products at Christian bookstores. Here sales are monitored by Christian Scan, which is managed by the Christian Music Trade Association.

QUESTIONS FOR REFLECTION

Answer each numbered question with a brief essay.

1. Is it necessary to be on a major label in order to get on the Billboard's Top Gospel Albums Chart?

2. Why is having a bar code important?

3. Explain why smaller independent labels are dominating Gospel music.

CHAPTER 8

THE PRODUCERS

As a distinct role, the producer's job is relatively new in the business. In creating a hit record, there are no set rules to go by. In short, a hit record results from the hard work and chemistry of the people involved.

The legacy of great hits over the years showcases people who are innovative enough to break through standardized clichés to develop something that is unique. Those who have been consistently and creatively distinctive have carved out a most viable niche for themselves. Achievements of such magnitude are the direct result of identifying one's potential audience and thoroughly entertaining them.

The producer is at the forefront of the rigorous search for a precisely unique sound. In today's sophisticated method of recording, drawing from a pool of resources including a vast collection of talent, is where the producer becomes the focal point. Producers pull all these elements together and decides who will be the arranger, studio musicians, and the lyricists.

The most creative producers thrive on a particular musical concept that marks much of their work. For example, some producers are masters of using strings, others are extremely lyric-conscious, while others may stress the value of pain-staking retakes until a song is 'perfect.'

Each producer utilizes different work styles, and most today are musicians, who have struck Gold or Platinum, or they are journeymen session talents who have managed to graduate to the next level of responsibility. Often, the most successful producers act alone, as with a George Martin or Freddie Perren. But, so many successful productions nowadays are team efforts.

Thom Bell and Linda Creed, Kenneth Gamble and Leon Huff, Nile Rodgers and Bernard Edwards, Nicholas Ashford and Valerie Simpson, and James Mtume and Reggie Lucas are each noted for a given range of effects, which characteristically stamp the cream of today's commercial music.

Usually, producers are writers. One writes lyrics and the other the music for most of an album. If tunes are contributed from an outside source, one producer may act as an arranger, while the other may play multiple instruments and vocals, bringing new music possibilities to life.

There are thousands of reasons for creative match-ups. For instance, some people can write beautiful lyrics, but can't measure a large enough picture frame to put the words into. Some take on a partner as a buffer to the outside world during recording.

Other producers can't live and/or work without each other. So much attention is focused on the producing end of music these days, everyone with halfway decent ears has a favorite, do you?

The producer's role is between the most exciting of all creative functions in the music-making process. It parallels the intensity of the film director, even though it lacks that craft's rigidly enforced entry standards. There is no music producer's union equivalent to a Director's Guild with its measured steps of time-based apprenticeship.

The prerequisite for entry into music production is simply the opportunity. The producer, as creative administrator, may not even read music. Rather, he shrewdly surrounds himself with the musical and layman ingredients to shore up any lack in his expertise.

He selects appropriate material. He decides who will play on which sessions. The producer is combination psychiatrist, parent, domineering SOB and loving colleague when the given need arises. He rides herd on studio sessions as if his life depends on it

Amidst the current 'up' trend in the production business, top producers earn top dollar sums of $15,000 to $25,000 plus a percentage of the ultimate month and a half worth of work. Representing the company, an Executive Producer is a liaison between the business of managing the deal and creativity of generating the artistic effort.

Executive Producers are, invariably, in a ranking position at the distribution company. Or, they are managers who are overseeing their client's interest to completion.

An exemplary Executive Producer may be Larkin Arnold. In his days as head of Capitol Records' Black Record Division, Arnold signed and oversaw production activities of a slew of chart makers from MAZE to NATALIE COLE.

Moving over to Arista, Arnold signed and developed a number of acts, which profited from his active participation, including GQ and HIROSHIMA.

Arnold has a keen sense of the means to finely integrate business and art. As creative administrator, the producer is in a fiscal position. He is the direct overseer of the nurturing process, which begets a record company's main commodity, which is its albums and singles.

In these days of manufactured sounds derived via over-dubbing and electronic effects, the multifaceted producer is more valuable than many of the inveterate one-shot groups that he is producing. So, the producer's job has evolved tremendously over the years.

In the earliest days of recording, when acetate cylinders and piano wire were *de rigueur* items at sessions, 'producers' were often music enthusiasts and talent scouts who did little more than advise a singer where to point their voices, then flicked on a switch.

Have you ever heard any recorded outtakes of producers—artist exchanges from the 'olden days'? Musicians and producers had many vehement, antagonistic relationships during the golden era of Jazz and Blues.

The classic encounter is captured on "Bummer Road," a recording by Sonny Boy Williamson II (Willie 'Rice' Miller) on Chess Records #1536. Over the course of a dozen takes of the same tune, "Little Village," Sonny Boy and producer Leonard Chess curse each other jokingly, and verbally joust amidst the creative overtone.

True, the natural adversarial relationship was present there. Chess owned the label Sonny Boy was signed to. The session outtakes reveal him flexing his control and power in an arrogant way.

He abruptly stops the tape in the middle of the first take as Sonny and his band are into a deep wail, a righteous tiff. Sonny curses him, his family, heritage, everything. In the dual role of owner (business) and the producer (creative), Chess exerted control on all significant fronts.

In this particular session, he changed the title of Sonny Boy's song, the tempo and Sonny Boy's harmonica soloing space. Sonny Boy reacted vigorously, but indirectly, bouncing his hostility off other musicians and improvising obscene lyrics into a new take.

Chess maintained firm control, stopping the tape immediately on such occasions. He maximized control over the situation by critiquing progress of the tune, largely ignoring Williamson's barbs.

Each important R&B trend has been marked by the influence of producers. Willie Mitchell relied heavily on the repertoire of musical knowledge acquired in and around his native Memphis for his seminal trendsetting work with Al Green.

Willie produced classic hits like "Love & Happiness," "Look What You've Done to Me," and "I'm Still in Love with You" on an eight-track tube amp specially rebuilt to accommodate the qualities of Green and the other Hi Records acts.

Memphis has been such a fertile developing ground for all styles of contemporary music that Stax had no corner on talent with Green as the foundation. Hi Records was consistently and proportionally competitive in the early 70s. Mitchell was ever so Jazz conscious in his arrangements, one of the first modernists to reintroduce horn breaks into Soul music.

Likewise, producers and teams like Berry Gordy, Holland-Dozier-Holland, and Barrett Strong were instrumental during Motown's early years. The lead of steam built up by the Detroit based Indie in the 1960s was out of a desire to build an independent Black judgment, with great hits the fuel for the fire.

Two basic producer classifications were developed early on, and have remained as models for establishing business relationships. Staff producers work directly for a company with artists signed to that label.

Willie Dixon was a staff producer at Chess Records' during its latter years, and in that role worked directly with the same artists whose bands he graced as a bassist during the heyday of electric Blues 20 years prior.

Holland-Dozier-Holland personified the producer's multiple abilities in 60s Motown Soul. By contrast, Tom Wilson was an underrated Black producer who shaped the subtlety of Bob Dylan's sound in the 60s.

The other type is the independent producer, who has acquired a name for himself and hires out freelance to a variety of projects. Richard Perry is an example of an independent producer who pyramided into a giant score, ultimately establishing Planet Records. Over the years, he has run the Indies gamut, from TINY TIM to the POINTER SISTERS.

Another category inching its way into being is the independent, which freelances within a given company. Nile Rodgers and Bernard Edwards are examples of this type: They became major selling artist/producers with CHIC and have had the opportunity to produce artists of their choosing. Hence, Rodgers/Edwards touched, visualized the careers of SISTER SLEDGE with "We Are Family."

Narada Michael Walden, and Earth, Wind & Fire's Verdine White and Larry Dunn, likewise have branched out, producing material for acts signed to a parent label as a bonus for good efforts themselves.

The ratio of female producers is astonishingly rare. The Linda Creeds and Carole Kings are exceptional for their perseverance. There are a few female artists who produce themselves, including Carla Bley, Roberta Flack, Joni Mitchell and Judy Collins.

Victoria Spivey owned her own label, Betty Carter likewise, and Mitchell, Linda Ronstandt, Dolly Parton or Loretta Lynn have enough clout to establish their own custom labels.

But, the dearth of women producers is staggering, in light of the ever-present need for the kind of sensitivity exerted by women in other roles—singers, instrumentalists, and in creative jobs in other media.

Rachel Elkins' role in producing the song "Switched in Bach" is an illustration of the irony of the music business. Elkins was Goddard Lieberson's secretary at CBS, and came up with an idea to produce a contemporary sounding album of selections of Johan Sebastian Bach. Elkins was given a deal which included a high royalty rate. Folks thought they would just let her fool around a bit.

The work was the first CBS classical album utilizing a synthesizer, and it ultimately became one of the biggest sellers of all times. Walter Carlos (now Wendy Carlos via a sex change), who recorded the album, won a Grammy—not to mention a special place in Rachel's heart. She became a millionaire practically overnight.

Roberta Flack's work as a self-producing artist has been note-worthy for the progressive growth in depth and direction. Flack has gone from a sugary sweet sound in her 1975 album "Feel Like Making Love," to a full range of colors and dimensions over time. Her style currently is collaborative. She jointly produced her first efforts of the 1980s with Eric Mercury, as well as duets with the late Donny Hathaway on many of its best moments.

Such pairings recall earlier work with Gene McDaniels and Les McCann. As with many self-producers, her style is an outgrowth of a need for more creative self-control. In that sense, she isn't a 'pure producer,' pursuing that trade full time. But her recently produced efforts show how far she is advancing.

Flack told Los Angeles Times writer Dennis Hunt, "A White male artist who is starting out as a producer wouldn't have such a hard time. He would get much more support…there are no great women producers because they have such a hard time getting started.

A Black woman has an even tougher time getting started. A lot of the men don't think you're serious or capable, so they don't give you much help or support. You just have to do it without them."

Roberta Flack is a rare exception to the usual situation facing females. She's been afforded the opportunity for one simple reason: her records sell large amounts, which gives her a better negotiating position with the company. The more she sells, the more power she exerts.

Even so, Flack had to convince high-level executives at Atlantic of her production competence throughout the past decade and a half. Each opportunity presented a unique set of pressing conditions.

Freddie Perren is an example of the journeyman, 'pure producer' who capitalized on his feel for the public's need. Over the past decade, the Howard University graduate has worked with a variety of Motown acts, and Yvonne Elliman, Minnie Ripperton, Tavares and the Sylvers, earning a solid track record in the process.

When Disco broke as big as it did, Perren jumped in with a magic touch. He and partner Dino Ferakis quickly assaulted the charts with memorable hits by GLORIA GAYNOR ("I Will Survive", "Yo Vivine"), and PEACHES AND HERB (The entire 2 Hot! album).

In an interview with Billboard's Jim McCullaugh, Perren identified himself as a producer who is able to be conscious of both singles and albums. He noted his success as derived from a combination of factors, including great familiarity with the medium, the time put in at his craft, a certain style of 'street sense' which affects his decision-making abilities as to his styles and material choices, and the 'formula' aspect of his production.

Regarding the latter, Perren observed, "There are certain things I do look for when I listen to what I believe will be the final mix. I may listen to it seven or eight times, then I zero in on things. I want to be consistent from beginning to end. Sometimes when you listen to it all together, it may sound hot, but then you have to pick it apart. I can usually do that.

I sensed the SYLVERS' "Hot Line" would be a smash. Perren has become successful enough to establish his own label, MVP RECORDS, an outgrowth of the production company he started as an umbrella for his varied writing, arranging, and creative activities. Not bad for a guy who doesn't read music.

Norman Connors is actively administrating. He's laying ground rules for the afternoon overdubbing, alternately observing and talking through the oversized phone console. His mood is medium-cool, laid back but never out of control. Though others in the booth are more verbal and exude an air of importance, he's clearly the forceful presence.

The nearly completed status of the current project behooves him to be a sensitized observer, filtering out extraneous musical elements harmful to a final recorded gem. Connors listens a lot, allowing assistants to critique the current status of the artist's tape that he's producing.

Seated behind him is another 'find'—blind keyboardist Ellis Hall, Boston-based and styled in the Ray Charles mold. Ellis is peppery, fire-voiced sort of guy consumed by dedication to his music. That feeling surfaces immediately as he overdubs an ARP synthesizer format. As the layering goes on, Ellis runs down a note-by-note breakdown of the sequence.

It's a great opportunity to observe the versatility of the ARP as well as the dimensions of a 32-track board. The layering takes the form of dubbing figures and single-chord runs over parts needing more sweetening and harmony.

The work-up helps flesh out the track, as Ellis adds more lead riffs and vamps, higher octave dub-ins and brief synthesizer breaks. The tape thus augmented, the sweetened tune is played back and it's tough in this form, very heavy on the bass.

Rhythm guitar sounds like it was fretted with a biker's chain. Drumming emphasizes lots of triplet, Jazz-voiced percussion, with the sound of a hi-hat articulating, and bass bridging back to a keyboard section.

At the end of the 3:57 playback, Connors is satisfied. "This is a tune you can all be pleased with," he notes. Next, Hall prepares to dub a low-end (bass line) synthesizer part. A new tape is rewound on the console, a rough-cut funk set.

As the recording progresses, Kendun Recorders resembles a party. Band members and crew listen to the playback and rock. The chords Ellis that rehearses are heavy metal, funk laden, and just plain old stone to the bone Funkadelic.

On the tape, the rhythm guitar player takes off on an Al McKay style loping rhythm run over the bassist's funky flaming. It has a strong feel for the bass style popularized by Byron Miller on George Duke's best mid-tempo music. The play back is jammin' and kickin', as Ellis dubs synthesizer parallel to the bassline to sound like a unison back-to-back statement.

Ellis's road manager asks Norman if he has heard the ideas for the horn line. Ellis remarks, "The horn line is gonna knock you from here to Mississippi." Another guy remarks aloud, "But, I don't want to go that far." Silently, I estimated the distance from Burbank to Mississippi as 2,299 miles and agree with him.

On the next tune, Ellis dubs another low-end synthesizer line full of fat bass notes over the second verse. He uses both hands in the arcing call and response motion. Left hand (bass) and right hand (rhythm) are once again played a full octave lower than the melody, filling to the bass drum pulse, "Makes you wanna get up and dance," exclaims an onlooker.

The line is continued in successive takes. Ellis starts in midline and ends abruptly. "It's just a quick line to support the drummer," he voices to no one in particular. The road manager tells Ellis the track is too cluttered with riffs. "I think it sounds better when you play 'dot-dot-dot," he observes, simulating a synthesizer rhythm. The passage is short but difficult, and it requires tremendous concentration.

The mood in the studio changes accordingly, from one of festivity to a respect for the rigorous agony of creation. Ellis is up for it, ready to make a head-on assault. After more discussion and suggestions, the process continues. Ellis vamps a taste, tries to get "that straight up funky" but anxiety definitely shows through. He decides to skip the low-end part and work on the clavinet line.

While the keyboardist makes his way from the control booth into the studio, Norman inquires about logistics, and the availability of the studio for the next day's sessions. Judging from the nature of his questions and the undertone of urgency communicated while listening, he's ready for a windup fairly soon.

Viewed from the control booth, Studio A is a large area. In the shadowy darkness of its unlit spaces with band instruments set up in various corners, it has an ominous cast. There are lots of places for a bogeyman (or a boogie-man, even!) to hide.

The clavinet track progresses well. It's being mixed into another rhythm part heavy on bass, with drum and guitar also effective. Finally, after a particularly steamy bridge, Ellis quits. Pleased, he says, "CBS look out!" A band member adds, leaving the booth, "If marketing don't dig it, they can go to the market."

Framed by rows of vending machines dispensing practically everything from beer to candy in an adjacent lounge, Norman talked later about his career. He first rose to prominence in the early 1970s as Pharoah Sanders' drummer, then began recording (and producing) himself fairly quickly. His bands began receiving attention as a showcase for talents like Dee Dee Bridgewater, Jean Carne, Michael Henderson, Phyllis Hyman, Elinor Mills, and newest vocalist, Adaritha.

Connors described his evolution, "I think it was just a natural thing. I've been into all kinds of music. I was right on top of it when people like Stanley Clarke, Chick Corea and the Mahavishmu Orchestra broke out.

Fusion—I was right there when they made the change to that particular form. So, all that was a part of my education, environment and experience, too, along with the more avant-garde esoteric styles of Pharaoh and Archie Shepp, which is really out of the John Coltrane school. That's where the majority of my experience has been in that area of music.

"But at the same time, I've always had a particular ear and taste for R&B music. I kept it to myself when I was into the Jazz thing. No matter how deep-rooted I was in my type of Jazz playing, I was always fascinated by the Stylistics and Delfonics music.

I had all the early Temptations records. I was attracted to pretty melodies and the lyric quality of a song, regardless of who sings it or what group plays it."

Connors' present role as a producer is nevertheless quite a contrast from his earliest drum experience. The stereotyped image of drummers bags them as bashers, without a feel for the subtleties of arranging and melodic composition.

"Not so," says Connors, "my concepts were more related to horns and vocals. I was a drummer, but I thought more like a horn player. I appreciate the romance of the song."

To the query as to his attitude during productions, Connors commented, "With the guy you just saw, I can just lay back. He's over-dubbing and he knows exactly what he's doing. There's no problem. On solos, I'm a little different. If a guy takes a creative solo, then I really have to be on top of that. All those tracks you heard, I had to lay to get that.

It's like building a house. I'm like the engineer. You design the foundation and you make sure it's built. The foundation is built now. I've got what I want in the rhythm, so now it's time to let the keyboard player fill where he can because he's a genius, so it's no problem. I have a master concept and they have a concept, so it's like a marriage. It's there, but it needs an administrator."

THE EXECUTIVE PRODUCER
Commentary by Dave Cavanaugh
1981

Dave Cavanaugh helped pioneer the modern concept of the Executive Producer.

The executive producer's role is one of total involvement. The producer and executive producer collaborate, as far as the artist is concerned, as far as the repertoire is concerned, the cover, liner, the mastering, pressing and so on. You work in covering all areas connected with the creative end of the finished product you intend to release.

An executive producer may also produce. In my case, I produced a lot of product and had a lot of other producers report to me. Those other producers had the responsibility to adhere to budgets, to clear the initial cost, then finish as close to budget as possible.

I've worked with a range of artists over the last 30 years, from Frank Sinatra, Dean Martin, Kay Starr, Nancy Wilson, Dakota Station to Rock & Roll acts, such as the Original 5 Keys, to George Shearing and big bands like Billy May, Glen Gray, Woody Herman and Les Brown.

I started at Capitol Records as a producer. After a while they assigned other producers to me because I was handling more artists than I could physically manage. I was working 12-14 hours a day, seven days a week. So, they added other producers.

I'd come up with concepts, repertoire and such, then meet with artists and the associate producer, while getting the project underway. Wherever possible, I'd attend some of the recording sessions. It's a matter of responsibility, and I was fortunate enough to have some good producers working for me. Some, you could leave completely on their own, some you had to work more closely with.

SUCCESS AS AN EXECUTIVE PRODUCER

Commentary by Larkin Arnold

1981

Larkin Arnold, the epitome of a successful A&R Executive, discusses his successes and the executive producer's role.

I don't really know if there's a formula to acquire a creative taste, as opposed to it being more or less innate within the individual. I cannot think of any procedure that I followed that helped me attain the success that I've had.

Through my training as an attorney, I realized that God has given everyone certain talents. Some can sing, others can dance, and some can even play football. And, there are those whom He has given the talent to recognize talent in people. I think, perhaps, that's the talent he's given me.

My main criterion is that something has got to be pleasing to me. I've got to see something in the artist or the act, that given time, money, and experience will allow it to blossom into what is latently within.

So, I've been fortunate to pick certain acts out of the hundreds that I review. Fortunately, some of them have encountered success. It takes basic, hard work. You've got to look at a lot of acts, listen to a lot of tapes to be able to really differentiate the quality from the mediocre.

I was fortunate to grow up at a time when I was very heavily influenced by Motown and its quality presentation of acts. In some ways, I tried to remember the class that Berry tried to bring when he projected our people. I do the same thing in a more updated fashion.

Motown was a great influence on my life. If I think of anybody in the Black music era, Motown had to have affected them. The label had almost all the Black stars. They were taking kids out of the ghetto, and spending time and money to give them special choreographers, dress designers, a lot of things, which coming from a disadvantaged background, our people didn't have access to. Motown was careful to be interested in the grooming of their artists, and not just in their ability to sing.

In selecting talent, it's basic things that tell me when things are not going to happen. I am a very critical person by nature. For an act or artist to be able to survive my criticism and still maintain an interest for me, then there must be something there. I attempt to maintain high standards when I sign acts. Ninety-nine percent of them do not measure up, so the ones that do meet the standards, I guess are the ones that I'm left with.

My experience in the Capitol legal department helped me to really understand the workings of a record company—all the various departments, how they interacted with one another, the people involved and the respective amounts of authority and responsibility that they have. It was part of our job in the legal department to outline a flow chart for areas of responsibility within the company. So, I knew who, what, where and when. That was a big asset.

A lot of people at the time didn't think that Capitol, which was basically a Rock and Country label, would be able to penetrate the Black music market. They had not been very successful marketing the music of the streets. I guess it was a combination of luck, timing, and making my interest known.

Before I released any records, I spent time within the company putting the machinery together to be able to deliver it. I studied various reports from our field people as to ways to go about it, incorporating some of my own ideas and having an organization (Capitol) that would be able to deliver the record once we got the talent.

I negotiate from a business standpoint with regards to the act. I know from prior experiences about how much we can hope to sell if everything works right—or conversely, if it doesn't. I try to negotiate a deal that we'll make some profit on, regardless of the act.

The acts I signed while at Arista weren't exact copies of other acts I've been involved with, but there's no act that I've signed over at Arista that I would not have signed at Capitol had I been there. I think it was a process of more time, more exposure, looking where the market was going, trying to anticipate the void that would be there and have something there for it. I don't think that I've made a philosophical change in my approach to the business.

Likewise, the acts that I signed over at Capitol I would sign over at Arista. I tried to find talented people, regardless of what areas of the country they are in, or what type of music they perform. Whether it's a HIROSHIMA, GQ, MAZE or NATALIE COLE, if they're talented people, and I think the public might appreciate them I try to help see that their talent is exposed.

I tend to give the public a lot more credit than my contemporaries in this business do. I think they are willing to accept something new and different if it's quality. It doesn't necessarily have to be a repetition of what has gone before.

I thought HIROSHIMA was bringing something new and unique to the music field, and that they had something to say, something to contribute. I thought when properly presented, people would be receptive to it. The success that they've had on their first album has more than borne this out. I look forward to them growing, and affecting many more people in the future.

It's difficult to make a general statement with regards to the role of executive producer because it varies from project to project, depending on the artist involved and the producer involved.

My role with regards to a self-contained band like Frankie (MAZE) who writes, produces and sings his own material, is less perhaps than working with a NATALIE COLE or PHYLLIS HYMAN —vocal interpreters.

Where you have an artist who's not a producer, I think the key role within the executive producer's function is to marry them with the right producer, whose work lends itself to the right public presentation. Often overlooked is the issue of compatible personalities. Some producers are stronger minded than others and some artists are more opinionated, stubborn people together because there's very little give and take.

To use the old cliché, "If the vibes are not right, it more or less comes through on the record." You have to take into consideration not only their technical talents as a producer, but also whether their personality will mesh with the artist you're signing.

In most instances, the producer and the artist don't know each other until they meet in my room. In those cases, you have to hope that you've picked the right person—talent-wise and personality-wise—so when they're in the studio with these people anywhere from six to ten hours a night for four to five weeks, they can get along, and we can come out with something that's very good.

After that, it's basically the selection of the songs to be recorded. You need an objective person in the executive role to intercede between artist and producer, and to keep the project moving as a commercial venture.

Neither one is allowed to trip out, so that the songs he's written—he thinks are all great—and likewise with the producer who has a differing opinion. Somebody just needs to be there and say, "Listen, I can understand and appreciate both of you, but from a business standpoint, I think we should go with this one and so forth."

That's where most executive producers' functions stop. I follow it all the way down to the selection of the cover, the sequencing of the songs on the album—so that I'm able to project the image that I have in mind, after talking with the artist and finding out where he wants to go, so that we're able to project it correctly to the people.

Sometimes you can have an album of music that perhaps may be very soft, sensual and romantic. If you have not communicated with the art department, you may come out with a cover that is very hard and brutal and has no relationship to what the people will hear once they buy the package. I try to make certain that we are in sync all the way down to the posters and everything, to present to the public just exactly what it is that we're trying to sell.

You've got to have the machinery to be able to deliver the product. Fortunately, my position enables me to oversee that all the way down to the number of records we're going to put in a particular store, or ship on a release. I'm grateful to the people I've worked with giving me the leeway, authority, and, of course, responsibility to make these things happen.

It's a lot of fun to be able to sit in a room in the South Bronx and hear something, and visualize exactly what you want to do with it, have it all come to pass, and hear your music all around the world—when you saw them before anyone else did. I never sign an artist until I have an image, an outline, and a program for that particular artist.

I've got to see the act, and if I like the act, then I just think about them. In thinking more and more things that need to be done, who I need to get, who will be going to shoot the picture, or how I need the pose for the cover, are all factors.

A TASTE OF HONEY was a classic example of the whole thing. I saw them at a club and there were four in the group. At the time, I really didn't think two girls and two guys would create that much of a stir. So, I concentrated on the two women. I put only them on the cover.

Then, I'd seen a group over in Europe, Baccarat, two women in evening gowns, so I wanted them in evening gowns. Really dressed up nice, yet with their instruments to show that they did play. When you picked it up, you got an idea of what you're about to hear.

As it happened, the act won best new artist awards in 1978, Grammys, Platinum selling. It was very, very gratifying. Most people are unable to visualize their dreams and then put them in motion. That's what I'm able to do in this job.

Producers Gary Kline & Kip Cohen

Producers Thom Bell and Linda Creed
Promotion Manager – Armond McKissick

L-R, Leon Huff—Producer, Logan H. Westbrooks, Kenny Gamble—Producer

QUESTIONS FOR REFLECTION

Answer each numbered question with a brief essay.

1. Describe the evolution of the producer's role. How has modern technology helped facilitate change?

2. In what ways might a producer be characterized as a 'creative administrator'?

3. Describe the ideal relationship between a producer and executive producer.

4. What are some of the obstacles faced by a would-be producer breaking in? How would you overcome such challenges for maximum success?

5. Fantasize that you have achieved the opportunity to produce an act with hit potential. Plot out the project in as much detail as you can.

CHAPTER 9

CHUCK BROWN

Go-Go: The Creation of a Music Genre

2017

Chuck Brown was a man determined to leave his mark on the music world, and he did just that. He's credited with creating Go-Go music, his signature style established in the Washington, D.C., area. Go-Go is deeply rooted in Funk, Soul, Latin rhythms, African percussions and call and response—perfect for dancing.

When I heard "Bustin' Loose", I signed Chuck right away to my newly-formed label—Source Records. I knew immediately that it would be a hit. In fact, it became his first Gold record and the first Gold Record for Source Records. It stayed atop the Billboard Charts for 4 weeks.

"Bustin' Loose" was used on the soundtrack for the 2005 movie *The Honeymooners*, in a commercial for Chips Ahoy cookies. "Hot in Herre" was used in a commercial for Bud Light. "Bustin' Loose" has been sampled by Hip Hop artists, most notably Nelly's "Hot in Herre", which attained astronomical success. From 2008-15, the Washington Nationals played it after every home run they hit. "Bustin' Loose" is the essential Go-Go song.

Brown used his deep, melodic voice to show his softer side when he sang romantic love songs. He released a duet album of love songs with singer Eva Cassidy called *The Other Side*. But bringing the funk was his mainstay, and he always delivered incredibly hot live performances.

Later, as an elder in the music world, rather than become obscure and irrelevant, Brown became a beloved idol to new generations of musicians and music lovers. By any measure, he left an enduring legacy on Funk music through Go-Go music.

Called the "Godfather of Go-Go", Brown was, indeed, a father figure to a generation of musicians. He encouraged them to take their musicianship seriously and to always excel rather than just get by. Drummer Ricardo "Sugarfoot" Wellman took Brown's message to heart.

Wellman was a no-nonsense guy who always strove for perfection. He was such an extraordinary drummer that other drummers would come to his shows to find out what he was doing. He was so fast with his right foot that he could do double kicks and triples that were unbelievable to other drummers. Wellman was considered an innovator in funk music, but his style transcended into Jazz and Latin music. He went on to play with Carlos Santana and Miles Davis. In 2013, Wellman was inducted into the Go-Go Radio's Hall of Fame.

Brown also encouraged Go-Go musicians to continue to create new music and not just rely on cover tunes. In 2016, four years after his death, the Chuck Brown Band released a new tribute song to him titled "Show Me Love", which was performed at the first "Go-Go Music Day" in Washington, D.C. The event was established for Go-Go bands to release and perform their new music.

In 2006 Brown was awarded a Lifetime Heritage Fellowship by the National Endowment for the Arts. In 2007 he was recognized by the National Visionary Leadership Project, joining the ranks of Ray Charles, Quincy Jones, B.B. King, and Eartha Kitt. There's a street named Chuck Brown Way in D.C. and a park called Chuck Brown Memorial Park.

He deserves every accolade he's received, and I'm proud of the role I played in putting him on a national stage and helping to establish his worldwide reputation with Go-Go. Not bad for a man that just wanted to make good music and establish his own sound.

The link between the 70s "Bustin' Loose" and "Hot in Herre" in 2002 was the inspiration for the book "The Anatomy of the Music Industry," to explore how the industry has transitioned from the old to the new model.

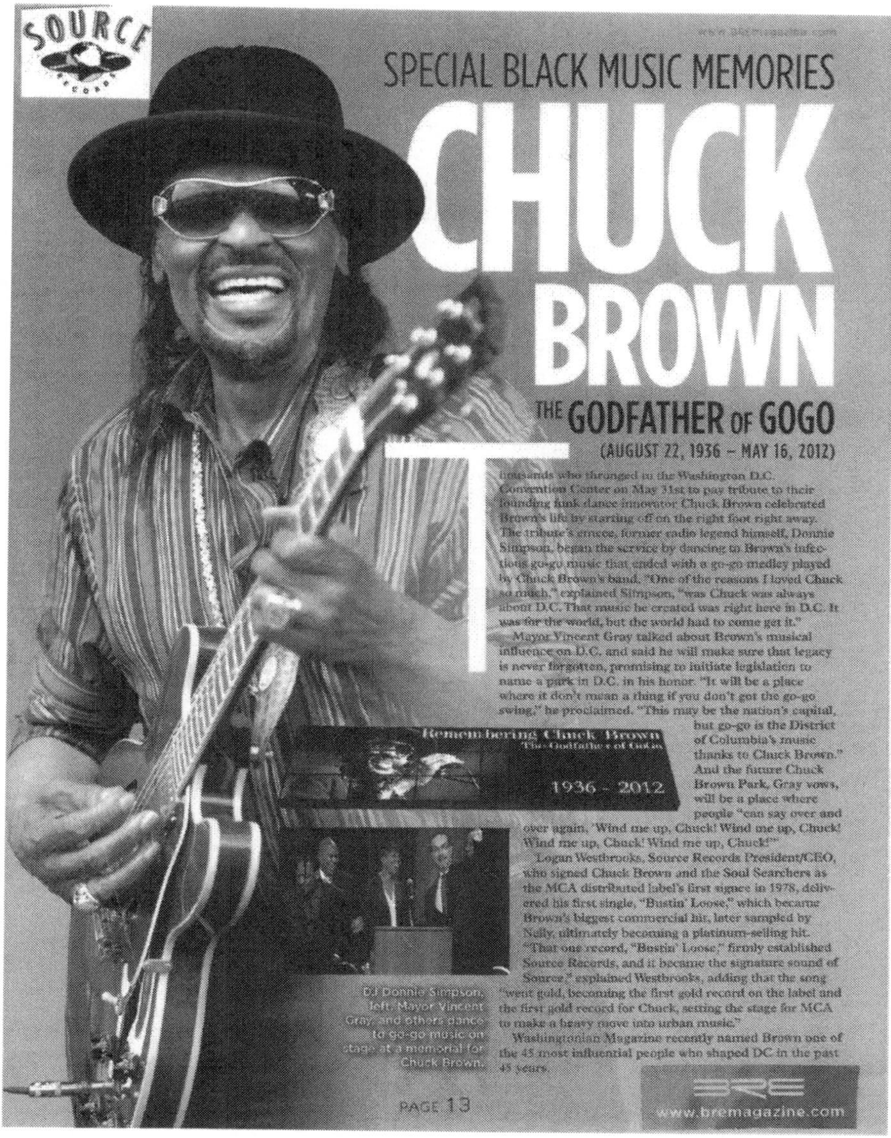

SPECIAL BLACK MUSIC MEMORIES

CHUCK BROWN

THE GODFATHER OF GOGO

(AUGUST 22, 1936 – MAY 16, 2012)

Thousands who thronged in the Washington D.C. Convention Center on May 31st to pay tribute to their founding funk dance innovator Chuck Brown celebrated Brown's life by starting off on the right foot right away. The tribute's emcee, former radio legend himself, Donnie Simpson, began the service by dancing to Brown's infectious go-go music that ended with a go-go medley played by Chuck Brown's band. "One of the reasons I loved Chuck so much," explained Simpson, "was Chuck was always about D.C. That music he created was right here in D.C. It was for the world, but the world had to come get it."

Mayor Vincent Gray talked about Brown's musical influence on D.C. and said he will make sure that legacy is never forgotten, promising to initiate legislation to name a park in D.C. in his honor. "It will be a place where it don't mean a thing if you don't got the go-go swing," he proclaimed. "This may be the nation's capital, but go-go is the District of Columbia's music thanks to Chuck Brown." And the future Chuck Brown Park, Gray vows, will be a place where people "can say over and over again, 'Wind me up, Chuck! Wind me up, Chuck! Wind me up, Chuck! Wind me up, Chuck!'"

Logan Westbrooks, Source Records President/CEO, who signed Chuck Brown and the Soul Searchers as the MCA distributed label's first signee in 1978, delivered his first single, "Bustin' Loose," which became Brown's biggest commercial hit, later sampled by Nelly, ultimately becoming a platinum-selling hit. "That one record, "Bustin' Loose," firmly established Source Records, and it became the signature sound of Source," explained Westbrooks, adding that the song "went gold, becoming the first gold record on the label and the first gold record for Chuck, setting the stage for MCA to make a heavy move into urban music."

Washingtonian Magazine recently named Brown one of the 45 most influential people who shaped DC in the past 45 years.

1936 - 2012

DJ Donnie Simpson, left, Mayor Vincent Gray, and others dance to go-go music on stage at a memorial for Chuck Brown.

PAGE 13

www.bremagazine.com

ONCE A HIT ALWAYS A HIT

How one song busted loose on the charts throughout the years

2017

The year was 1981 and Chuck Brown's "Bustin' Loose" topped the Billboard charts. Could it have been the bass line that made it a hit? Or was it simple timing that kept it burning up the airwaves, for as the old saying goes: *"Success happens when opportunity meets preparation."*

During that time the rights to the song belonged in part to Chuck Brown of the Soul Searchers as well as to the label in which he was signed, Source Records. Protected under Ascent Music, a BMI publishing company owned by author Logan H. Westbrooks, the song was hardly expected to remain a hit for two decades.

The basic objective of this chapter is to indicate that if a song was a hit in 1981, it will most likely be a hit in 2002. Such is the case with "Bustin' Loose." In 2002 Rap superstar Nelly in association with Hip Hop producers the Neptunes remade the song and called it "Hot in Herre"—an up-tempo Hip Hop dance groove.

As was the case in 1981 with "Bustin' Loose," "Hot in Herre" soon became the official party song of the year. The relevance here is that the ingredients that make up a hit song never change. You need a solid groove, fused with a hip hook and you've got a hit chart-topping song.

If you keep it simple, you can't go wrong. Chuck Brown's hook was simple: "I feel like bustin' loose…bustin' loose," as was Nelly's "It's getting' hot in here, so take off all your clothes. I'm getting' so hot I wanna take my clothes off." Both songs seem to follow the same theme. Keep it simple.

"Hot in Herre" soon became the official party song of the year in 2002 (as was "Bustin' Loose" in 1981) in addition to being named BMI's song of the year. The relevance here is once a song is a hit, it will always be a hit no matter who samples it or redoes it.

Nowadays, the art of sampling ensures the skeletal format of the original song remains the same. Once again, for the sake of illustration, "Bustin' Loose" and "Hot in Herre" will be referenced.

More often than not, hit track masters such as the Neptunes will usually sit in a studio and listen to hundreds of classic songs in search of the right groove to fit the artist in which they are producing. In this case, since the artist was Nelly, they had the task of finding the perfect groove to match his mellow yet Hip Hop 'party on' style. Once they came across "Bustin' Loose," there was something about the song that made them recognize they had a hit on their hands.

In short, if it ain't broke, don't fix it. So, after finding the groove, the next step was to contact the copyright owners and propose a deal whereby all parties involved would be in agreement. This is where things can get a little tricky because "Bustin' Loose" was written by Chuck Brown, so he retained 100% of the writer's rights to the song.

However, the publishing was owned by Source Records' Ascent Music Publishing. Therefore, regarding the new song "Hot in Herre," there were new writers, including Nelly and the Neptunes as well as the original song owners Chuck Brown and Ascent Music Publishing. To clarify this even further, it is important to note that Ascent Music retains ownership of the original copyrights to "Bustin' Loose."

THE SOURCE RECORDS STORY 2017

One of my friends in the music industry had worked very hard and created a successful television show. That friend was Don Cornelius and that show was *Soul Train*. He was ready to branch out and establish a record label called *Soul Train* Records. He asked me to join him and his partner Dick Griffey.

I thought it was a fabulous idea, and in 1976 I resigned from CBS International and relocated to the West Coast to help him launch the label. I became Vice President of Marketing.

Running a record label consumed more time than Don imagined, so he decided to fold *Soul Train* Records and concentrate only on the *Soul Train* TV show. Griffey went on to re-form *Soul Train* Records into Solar Records and took the *Soul Train* Records artists with him to Solar.

When I relocated to the West Coast, I also got into real estate. After *Soul Train* Records, I delved more heavily into real estate and devoted all my energies to acquiring rental property, which included apartment buildings and office buildings. My first prized acquisition was when we acquired Crenshaw Square on Crenshaw Boulevard in Los Angeles.

In 1978 I received a phone call from my very good friend and former assistant at CBS Records, Marnie Tattersall, who was now an executive at MCA New Ventures. She informed me that MCA New Ventures had monies available under a program called MESBIC (Minority Enterprise Small Business Investment Corporation). MESBIC was looking for new ventures to partner with in the music business.

Tattersall told me that they had received numerous proposals from interested individuals, but none of them had the expertise that I had. She suggested I seriously consider putting a proposal together to submit for consideration. After several meetings with Marnie and meeting the head of MCA New Ventures, Norbert Simmons, I decided to give it a try.

I assembled a team and started working on the proposal to present to MCA. I also solicited the staff of MCA New Ventures to assist with the numbers. The process took about six months to complete. Ultimately, I secured financing with MCA New Ventures, and a manufacturing and distribution deal with MCA Records.

While all this was going on, I was teaching a course at California State University called "The Anatomy of a Record Company," so I decided to ask my students to suggest a name for the record label. The name they all agreed on was Source Records. The name was available, and we secured the rights to that name.

I found a two-story office building on the corner of 5th Avenue and Washington Boulevard. There was a neighborhood community agency on the first floor, a rehearsal hall and a recording studio, office space, and ample parking.

My wife and I made an offer on the building and it was accepted. It was ideal because the rehearsal hall and recording studio was under lease, and we could move into the second-floor office space immediately.

With financing in place, we refurbished and remodeled the space, and put together a small, hardworking and dedicated staff:

Initial Staff
Ralph Bates – V.P. Marketing/Sales
John McCray – V.P. Promotion
Michael Williams – A&R
Holly Pruitt – Press & Publicity
Jaunese Allen – Executive Assistant & Office Manager
Alexandria Poe – Secretary
Ken Jackson – Controller
George Glasco – In-house Attorney
John Mason of Mason & Sloan Law Firm
Payson Wolff – Consulting Attorney

After the label was up and running, we brought in the following staff:
Marnie Tattersall – V.P. of Business Affairs

Mable John – Publishing
Janie Bradford – Publishing
Beverly Douthet – Publishing (intern)
William Earl Hicks – Promotion Manager
Marlon McNichols – Promotion Manager

I had made phone calls and put the word out that I was looking for artists to sign and master tapes to purchase. A producer named James Purdy in Washington sent me a tape on an artist that he had produced. The song was "Bustin' Loose" and the artist was Chuck Brown & the Soul Searchers.

I instantly liked the song and the beat, so I decided to play the tape for my class and see how they liked it. They loved it, and I quickly decided to acquire that tape, sign the group and prepare it for the first release to launch the label. The single was a master purchase, and I also immediately went to work producing the album.

All of this was happening in the latter part of the last quarter of the year, and I knew from a marketing and airplay possibility that we could secure airplay and have our record in place at the major stations by the first of the year. This would give us a jump on our competition for airplay.

The strategy was successful, and "Bustin' Loose" hit the airwaves as planned. We had a showcase at the Whiskey nightclub in Los Angeles on Sunset Strip. We invited and brought in all the tastemakers throughout the country, which was all a part of the overall marketing plan. We also taped the *Soul Train* show. In 1979 "Bustin' Loose" skyrocketed to #1 and held that spot for four weeks on the Billboard R&B Charts as it went Gold.

Chuck Brown was an integral part of Source Records history and a key component in the evolution of Urban music. Source Records further acknowledges members of the Soul Searchers band. They were LeRon Young (guitar), John Buchanan (trombone and keys) Leroy Fleming (sax and flute), Don Tillery (trumpet), Jerry Wilder (bass), Curtis Johnson (organ), Gregory Gerran (percussion), Ricardo Wellman (drums), and Skip Fennell (keyboards).

At the same time, I continued soliciting master tapes and looking for other artists to sign. I was co-managing a Sam & Dave type act group called the Valentine Brothers that I was considering signing. One of my partners brought in a female act, and my neighbor Ralph Johnson—the drummer for Earth, Wind & Fire—had a group that his brother played in that was being considered.

The company's basic product philosophy was to make very selective master purchases on product that had been thoroughly researched, and in most instances, test-marketed with actual commitments from major program directors for airplay.

This was in keeping with the decision to deal only with the current sounds of contemporary music. Source Records sought to sign, on a very limited basis, only commercially viable artists, producers, and product from the hundreds of opportunities available.

After the dramatic success in breaking Chuck Brown & the Soul Searchers, there was excitement from established and new Black artists interested in signing with Source. Harold Melvin & the Blue Notes signed with Source and released *The Blue Album* in 1980.

Two songs that charted from that album are "Prayin'" and "Tonight" featuring Sharon Paige. Chuck Brown's next release was "Sticks and Stones" and was produced by Wayne Henderson of the Crusaders.

The Source Records artist roster included:

- Chuck Brown & the Soul Searchers:
- Harold Melvin & the Blue Notes
  featuring Sharon Paige on "Tonight's the Night
- Smash (DeBarge Brothers)
- Valentine Brothers
- Opus 7
- Lee Moore
- Rose Banks
- Travis Biggs
- Flakes

- Jeri-Q
- Mabel John (no releases)

Chuck Brown & the Soul Searchers had sold more than seven million records in his career, including one Gold album and two Gold singles. In 1979 "Bustin' Loose" also garnered six Cashbox Magazine awards including (1) Top New Male Vocalist for a single (2) Top New Male Vocalist for an album (3) Top Male Vocalist for Black Contemporary Single (4) Top New Male Vocalist for Black Contemporary Single (5) Top Male Vocalist for Black Contemporary Album and (6) Top New Male Vocalist for Black Contemporary Album.

Smash is a solid group of extremely talented musicians with an explosive sound of R&B, Funk, and Soul. All members play multiple instruments and sing, led by Bobby DeBarge's impressive falsetto. Members are Bobby DeBarge (vocals, Fender Rhodes), Tommy DeBarge (vocals, bass), Greg Williams (vocals, trumpet, B-3 organ, Fender Rhodes), Stanley Hood (soprano sax, alto sax), Stanley Brown (vocals, lead guitar, rhythm guitar), Arnett Hayes (B-3 organ, clavinet, Fender Rhodes), Darnell Wyrick (tenor sax, soprano sax, flute, percussions)

Harold Melvin & the Blue Notes with Sharon Paige. The Blue Notes had sold more than 17 million records during their career, with one Platinum album, three Gold albums, and four Gold singles. They were one of the early proponents of the Philadelphia Sound and were one of the first million-selling artists for Philadelphia International Records. Sharon Paige had been featured on three Gold albums.

Opus 7. Collectively, the members of Opus 7 all played and co-produced songs for various artists that sold more than 25 million records. They were a semi-established group, well known in the southern region of the country.

Rose Banks. Also known as Sister Rose, she had previously sold millions of records as a key member of Sly & the Family Stone. She is the sister of Sly Stone.

Travis Biggs. Had been a featured musician on four Platinum and three Gold albums for Isaac Hayes. His Source Record album showcased all his musical abilities on violin and keys.

SOURCE RECORDS CATALOG

Artist	Album Titles	Release Date
Chuck Brown & the Soul Searchers	Bustin' Loose	01/19/1979
Valentine Brothers	The Valentine Brothers	01/19/1979
Smash	Smash	03/16/1979
Travis Biggs	Solar Funk	07/06/1979
Opus 7	Thoughts	10/19/1979
Harold Melvin & the Blue Notes featuring Sharon Paige	The Blue Album	1980
Chuck Brown & the Soul Searchers	Chuck Brown & the Soul Searchers	06/06/1980

Artist	Extended Version Titles	Release Date
Chuck Brown & the Soul Searchers	Bustin' Loose Pt. 1 & Pt. 2	11/20/1978
Chuck Brown & the Soul Searchers	Game Seven / If it Ain't Funky	04/06/1979
Valentine Brothers	Sound of Music / I'm in Love	11/20/1978
Flakes	Miss Fine Lover / Instrumental	03/12/1979
Lee Moore	Reaching Out for Your Love / Instrumental	07/20/1979
Harold Melvin & the Blue Notes	Prayin' / Your Love is Taking Me on a Journey	11/16/1979
Jeri-Q	Who's Taking You Home / It's the Law	11/02/1979
Sharon Paige with Harold Melvin & the Blue Notes	Tonight's the Night / Your Love is Taking Me On a Journey	01/18/1980

Artist	Single Titles	Release Date
Chuck Brown & the Soul Searchers	Bustin' Loose	11/06/1978
Valentine Brothers	Sound of Music / I'm in Love	11/06/1978
Chuck Brown & the Soul Searchers	Game Seven / If it Ain't Funky	04/06/1979
Valentine Brothers	We Belong Together / Let Me Be the One	03/23/1979
Flakes	Miss Fine Lover / Dance Don't Cha Wanna	03/02/1979
Lee Moore	Reach' Out (For Your Love) Pt. 1 & Pt. 2	07/20/1979
Opus 7	Bussle / Hit and Run	09/14/1979
Harold Melvin & the Blue Notes	Prayin' / Instrumental	11/16/1979
Jeri-Q	Who's Taking You Home / It's the Law	11/02/1979
Sharon Paige with Harold Melvin & the Blue Notes	Tonight's the Night / Your Love Is Taking Me on a Journey	02/01/1980
Opus 7	The Way Yu Move Me / Hey Big Brother	01/11/1980
Rose Banks	Papa, Daddy Dear / Papa, Daddy Dear (Stone's Fusion)	03/28/1980
Chuck Brown & the Soul Searchers	Sticks & Stones / Pt. 1 & Pt. 2	04/04/1980

Within our first year of operation, we grossed over three million dollars. That was quite a feat for a new startup. Source Records was manufactured and distributed for retail in the United States and Canada by MCA Records—one of the five major record distributors in the industry. Internationally, Source was distributed by EMI/Liberty/UA Records and K-TEL.

Source also had two subsidiary music publishing companies—Ascent Music, Inc. (BMI) and Aroma Music, Inc. (ASCAP). They are still housed and operating in the original Source Records headquarters, which is still intact and fully functional.

CHUCK BROWN AND THE SOUL SEARCHERS
BUSTIN' LOOSE
FOR PROMOTION ONLY

CHUCK BROWN AND THE SOUL SEARCHERS

EXTRA
Source Records
Final Edition
Disco Invasion
SOURCE RECORDS:
'We Don't Scare Talent Away'
EXTENDED VERSION
Candid Comments
Making More Music Than
The Body Can Stand
THE WEST COAST SCENE
SOURCE
MCA RECORDS

Harold Melvin And The Blue Notes · The Blue Album
HAROLD MELVIN
and the BLUE NOTES
Featuring Sharon Paige

SOURCE
RECORDS
FIFTH AVE
1902
Thank you Black Radio!

THE LIVING LEGENDS
FOUNDATION, INC
VANGUARD AWARD
PRESENTED TO
LOGAN WESTBROOKS
FOR BEING A TRAILBLAZER ON THE FRONT LINES.
OPENING DOORS FOR BLACK ARTISTS AND EXECUTIVES THROUGH DIPLOMACY AND INTEGRITY:
FOR YOUR GENEROSITY AS A HUMANITARIAN, GIVING BACK AND PAYING IT FORWARD.
ALL WHO WORK IN BLACK MUSIC AT MAJOR RECORD LABELS STAND ON YOUR SHOULDERS.
OCTOBER 9, 2015

QUESTIONS FOR REFLECTION

Answer each question with a brief essay.

1. Explain what makes a style of music a genre.
2. How is a musical legacy established?
3. What are some qualities of a song that can give it an enduring appeal?
4. What major label was Source Records partnered with?

CHAPTER 10

DISTRIBUTION
Custom Labels – Associated Labels
1981

Prior to distribution, the record company has invested thousands of dollars in the product, and must now seek a return on its investment. Success or failure here is directly linked to a label's very destiny.

Distribution is the most important element in the selling process. This is the means of getting the product into the market place and consumer exposure. Distribution, sales and marketing go hand-in-hand. If the means for distribution is inadequate, sales will likewise suffer. The first requirement of any company is to quickly establish a distribution deal for their product.

Historically, the record business has seen a tremendous range of ways that records get distributed. Many lesser-known artists press their own records and sell them at concerts. The Grateful Dead have distributed through mail order, as do some independent specialty record stores internationally.

Then there are the classic examples from earlier days of the Blues and R&B era, when small companies were owned by men who traveled across the country distributing records out of the back of their cars.

On these journeys, there was a great opportunity to scout talent, interact with local radio personalities and otherwise, test the musical temperature in various regions. Such tactics are inappropriate today.

There are two types of distribution styles that currently work: major label distribution and independent distribution. In both types the distributing company collects money from record sales for the small company and charges a fee for circulating its product.

Independent distribution is by far the more difficult route to pursue for profit, but getting a major label deal is a rough prospect unless you are already *Certified Platinum* coming in. Independent distribution entails a record company with music to sell, and making separate distribution deals with separate entities in various regions.

On the West Coast alone, eight different independent distributors are working the key markets your product needs to be placed in. Smaller labels frequently end up with 20 to 25 deals with independent distributors.

There are many other pitfalls involved in working with the independent distribution network. Shall we name a few? A distributor may take unproven product, sell it, and refuse to pay the company of origination. The case of Butterfly Records is a good example.

Over a year's time Butterfly grossed $12 million, distributed by independents. But, the company had little luck collecting because, as a new outlet, distributors adopted a wait and see attitude as to the company's longevity.

"I'll sit on it," was the strategy, waiting for further contact by the company of origination. But, if a small company goes out of business for whatever reasons, the distributor feels he has direct access to profits from the half million, or whatever the future is, in units sold.

Can a small label recoup revenues in such instances? Of course, however, such labels generally operate on a shoe string budget, unable to sue 20 to 25 distributors. And, they are in business to promote and produce records, not to sue and fatten a lawyer's pocket. Butterfly ultimately went the route of major distribution.

On the other hand, you may wonder how such unscrupulous independent distributors are able to flourish. Every label that is unattached to a major label or needing distribution help is fair game. The history of relationships between independent labels and independent distributors has a similar ring as in most capitalist businesses.

Personal dynamics are a key, as is the relative power on each side. The *fabric* of the music business is based on independent distribution, especially in the natively American genres of Pop, Folk, Blues, R&B, Jazz, and Soul. Each deal carries a certain personalization.

Motown is a lone surviving major independent, relying heavily on independent distribution. Its greatest asset is the *juice* which the operation generates industry-wide. Its image as a hit generator, and the longevity of business relationships helps out in dealings with various distributors.

And nobody messes with Motown's money because they'll be deprived of upcoming hits—sure sources of revenue. Why kill the whole goose by being a *Simon Legree* on the short end?

But few small independents have clout like Motown in conflict resolution. The invariable situation is as follows: a company achieves another hit. Meanwhile, the company needs to develop a continuous mechanism of generating hits—everything from paying public relations people to reimbursing a vinyl manufacturer.

Consequently, a cash flow problem surfaces and the label is suddenly in over its head. Major label distribution is an umbrella operation. Fifteen to 20 subsidiaries are set up all over the country as regional offices.

These local facilities service the entire area in a wide array of ways, from merchandising campaigns to direct wholesale sales. Label distribution is coordinated through a specific division or holding company organized solely for this purpose.

The advantages of major label distribution are obvious and logical. An artist is in the mainstream of the merchandising system when a major label is working his album. If he and/or his custom label occupy a high enough position in the parent company's pecking order, his music is placed in highly visible prominent places with large promotion campaigns organized in support.

Because of the corporate overtones, the distribution effort is single-minded, it is swift, and then it is oriented toward maximizing success.

CUSTOM LABELS

Custom Labels, custom labels…exactly what is a custom label? The concept has a particular history that has been periodically touched on throughout the text. In today's market, custom labels are proving to be the most viable outlet for entrepreneurs and artists with an independent bent.

The concept of custom labels is as old as the business itself. Moreover, the operating principle is as old as prevailing relationships between smaller and larger entities in life. Each needs the other for a panorama of reasons: survival, support and continued new material are among the most significant.

The first custom labels in Blues and Jazz of the 1920s were called 'race labels.' The first products were called 'race records,' with artists as diverse as Ethel Waters and Blind Lemon Jefferson mic-side doing the picking, key-tinkling and warbling. These works were classified as such, both because of racism's need for such distinctions and the recognition that such separation has market value.

Such labels included RCA-distributed Bluebird, Arto, Black Swann, and Solo Art. Black Swan exploited its 'uniqueness' with this catchy slogan: "The only genuine colored record. Others are only passing." In this way, the massive Black buying public could identify its own artists and readily support a growing medium.

With the crushing effects of the Depression hastening one company after another to jettison 'race product,' the term became 'specialty labels,' with Jazz, Folk, and electric Blues ultimately added as viable fare. Specialty labels became the backbone of the nurturing Black music industry after World War Two.

The most well established specialty labels became major independents as the industry grew and became more institutionalized. Chess and Vee Jay became significant leaders in the Blues-based genre, while Atlantic took hold in hard R&B and vocal Jazz forms. Regardless of their size and impact, most specialty labels were distributed independently.

In the early 60s and 70s, the increased clout of numerous artists and personal managers inaugurated the contemporary custom label relationship. Prototypes included the Beatles' short lived run with Apple (*they* broke up, *it* was in chaos); the Rolling Stones' self-named label and Led Zeppelin's Swan Song.

Each case points up a unique approach. Thoughts of Apple conjure up the latter Beatles' years, when impresario Allen Klein made them the same amount of money in *seven months* as they'd generated for *seven previous years*.

Apple had the potential of being a small label operation, which neatly offered its artists a conducive vehicle for survival in a control-oriented business. Distributed by Capitol, the effort was launched a few years ahead of its time.

Rolling Stones Records was one of those neat plums which Mick and the boys negotiated when their American deal with London Records (British Decca) expired in the early 1970s.

Atlantic was in the process of consolidation as part of Warners' corporate scheme, so they were readily amenable to a deal that provided the group with more creative control, and a guaranteed advance bankroll to run their own ship, provided the music stayed commercial.

The Stones have responded by staying together, keeping their corporate business surprisingly tight and closed-mouthed, and producing the most bankable music of their careers. Encroaching middle age will do that.

The Swan Song deal transferred Led Zeppelin's product trademark from Atlantic to its own custom mode. There was no change in distributor. In the matter of transference, the group assumed complete artistic control. Their custom label deal was a tangible acknowledgement of the Zep's abilities to sell multiple platinum units, and the leverage power such numbers brings to subsequent bargaining.

There are no guidelines for such machinations. Often, headlines—making custom label deals have intriguing twists. Others are simple, concise, straightforward business matters. The most *political* custom label deals involve an entity's positioning move, vis-à-vis another. Usually big bucks are the stakes in high-pressure situations.

CBS' relationship with Philadelphia International Records (PIR) is an example of a successful custom-major label relationship. CBS was in need of an already established first-class production organization whose work it could distribute.

The operators of the label, Kenneth Gamble and Leon Huff, needed a first-class distributor for its state-of-the-art product. So, they sold CBS on the idea of circulating music by the O'Jays, Harold Melvin & the Blue Notes, the Three Degrees and others.

They knew they had the ability to cut hit records, but lacked finances to promote and distribute the music nationally. CBS made the deal with PIR, and, accordingly, the custom label provides finished artist tapes, which are then pressed into records, manufactured and distributed by CBS.

CBS then collects the monies for sale of the records and takes its portions off the top. It is then PIR's responsibility to pay appropriate royalty fees to its contracted artists in amounts previously negotiated.

All of the labels these days have a slew of custom labels. TSOP (The Sound of Philadelphia) is a custom label of a custom label, Philadelphia International. Motown has had a number of custom labels over the years with Tamla and Gordy being key parts of the success story from the beginning.

Nowadays, custom labels emanate from all reaches of the industry. Most are artist-generated, solid umbrellas for the varied production interests of a given super group or producer. Others, like BID Records or Source Records, the *home base* entity of this discussion, are products of the legitimate aspirations of experienced executives who have mastered the ability to make money-selling records.

CUSTOM LABEL OPERATIONS
Commentary by Hillery Johnson
1981

Veteran executive Hillery Johnson, founder-president of Hilltak Records, described key nuances of a custom label operation.

The advantage of a custom label is being free from corporate red tape, all the restrictions that occur in a corporate situation. The advantage is that decisions to be made can be made rapidly. You, as a label entrepreneur, live or die by your decision, as opposed to living or dying by someone else's decision.

A custom label should be structured very small. That's one of the attractions to artists. You can better give to and serve those artists on a personal level. Many times, in a large label situation you couldn't get the personal attention you get in a custom label situation.

A lot of times the parent label handles promotion, marketing and distribution. Usually, whoever owns the custom label will be very much involved in that which will give an additional thrust to artists on that custom label.

Usually, a custom label will not put out product that is going to be in competition with each other. If you put out a self-contained up-tempo thing, usually you'll put out something soft and mellow also. Then a program director will be more apt to add both records without them being in competition with each other.

A CBS or Warner Brothers may release seven to ten albums, whereas a custom label may only release two albums a month. Thus, you can give more attention to an album.

If you are an independent label, you pay for everything and you get every dollar that is paid to you. The dollar comes to you, so you are not getting paid second hand. In lieu of that, a major label picks up all of your production costs, pressing, everything.

As a result, you get a smaller percentage of the profits made. Between 1976-78, if one had been an independent, they could have fared quite well. The record business may now be off as much as 20-30 percent.

I had a guy come by who was going to try and raise $5 million. He wanted me to be a part of his company. I declined based on the fact that I know it would be very difficult for him to recoup his $5 million at this particular time.

As an independent label, here's what you're up against: you have a pressing bill. God forbid you have a pressing bill of $50,000, and you have accounts payable to you company for $150,000. Your pressing bill is due in 30 days, and your accounts payable are due in 60 days. At the same time, there are regional and local promotion people whom you have to pay on a weekly basis.

Cash flow is one of the key things you must deal with. Sometimes, it's going to take as long as 90-120 days to collect money from your independent distributor, just based on them collecting money from their one-stops and whatever. There's a chain of command to collecting money. Whereas, in the belly of a corporation you don't get as much money back, but you don't have all those other headaches.

With majors, you're not as mobile either. They can dictate to you, "Well, *we* don't feel this particular piece of product is as strong as <u>you</u> feel it is. When you get into the record business, the game gets so big. The money can get so big that if you hypothetically owe me $2-300,000 and can keep it in a bank at 7, 8, 9, 10 or 12% for 30 or 90 days. See what you've made?

There are lots of games that are played. You can be trying to figure out how to pay your pressing bill while a guy is making 12-13 percent on your money over a 90-day period.

THE VALUE OF WHOLESALE AND RETAIL EXPERIENCE WITHIN THE MUSIC BUSINESS

Commentary by Jim Blevins

1981

Before he became an executive in promotion, Jim Blevins spent many years on the wholesale and retail side. Here, he discusses the value of those experiences.

An important aspect of working retailers is to spend time with them, discussing the merits of your products. Nine times out of ten, record companies enjoy success when they get those people behind them.

That's one of the most important things that someone who moves from the retail into a company brings as an asset, the knowledge of how that side of the business works. The retailer has to put forth the extra effort to push your product.

Retailers can exert strong influence on how a record is received. When the first ANGELA BOFILL album was released, she was a brand-new artist with a truly unique sound. People at the radio level did not exactly jump at the product. But, people in retail did, especially in Los Angeles.

We created such a storm locally from in-store play that tremendous sales were generated. It forced radio stations to take a second look, then they began to feel the full impact of it. She became a star, and it was a very nice thing to happen.

That was the first time I really felt the strong impact that retail can have on the trades and stations across the country. They forced the issue, and they played the record, and they talked about the record. It was a good piece of product, all it needed was to have somebody listen to it.

THE WARNER/ELEKTRA/ATLANTIC RECORDS DISTRIBUTION SYSTEM

Commentary by Oscar Fields

1981

Oscar Fields briefly summarizes the Warner/Elektra/Atlantic Distribution System.

The secret of the WEA distribution system is probably its decentralized branch system. You have eight shipping branches and 25 sales offices. Each branch has a manager and each functions almost like an independent distributor. That manager is responsible for his own area.

Hypothetically, a branch office in Chicago also has a sales office in Minneapolis; an office in St. Louis and an office in Kansas City. A manager's responsibility is all of those areas. He runs those areas almost independently of the other seven branches. Obviously, that branch takes on the personality of the branch manager. WEA's approach is to distribute records in each area differently, because each region is unique.

WEA's system is the most successful branch operation because the individuality of each branch manager is allowed to come into play. But, there is some flexibility that allows for the individuality of each branch to shine a little bit.

The promotion setup is unique also. The local promotion people work directly for WEA, but answer to the labels. Hypothetically, Warner Brother's local promotion people work for WEA, but take direction from Warner Brothers. Elektra promotion people work directly for WEA, but take direction from us.

It's the same with Atlantic. This allows each branch and sales office to control the day-to-day activities of each local person. That way, you have a good idea of what each guy is doing. If they were under the supervision of regional or national people, you'd never know on a day-to-day basis what they're doing.

An even greater aspect is the WEA policy of training and educating their own people. There are always educational seminars, always meetings with single specialties and product managers. In a recent three-day meeting, we wanted to educate specialists who handle Pop very well as to R&B and Country. It's that educational process that makes WEA people number one in their own market, which in turn makes the company number one overall.

THE DUTIES OF A PRODUCT MANAGER

Commentary by Mort Weiner

1981

Mort Weiner explains the duties of a product manager.

I work for a production company. I supervise marketing and merchandising for all of our products, and I handle all of the communications between 20th Century Records and RCA Records.

I supervise an advertising budget, which I have to convince RCA to spend. I initiate marketing concepts that 20th Century Records wants put forth on behalf of their products.

Then I have to formulate the marketing plans to carry back to RCA. I talk with most of the artists to relate what they can expect about what will be happening with their product as airplay picks up, what trade ads that might be running and the physical layout of what we'll be doing with their product.

In the truest sense of the word, a lot of what I do involves product management. At RCA you're the in-house manager for the record. On the international level, markets are different. What sells in that market and the methods of merchandising are quite different.

Some countries have government-controlled radio, where you can't advertise as freely. A lot of merchandising then depends on personal appearances by the artists. Videotapes are also very important.

In many instances, getting a record released internationally is a big accomplishment, because of the language barrier. Records in English are not popular in certain parts of the world. But, when the artist gets over there and works, an appeal is developed.

Edwin Starr is a big artist over in Europe, whereas Stephanie Mills, who, at one time, was big here in the United States, has not scratched the surface internationally. Once an artist creates an image, he/she hangs on much longer over there.

When you're involved in marketing and merchandising, you have to maintain an even temperament, be firm and positive all the time. An artist wants to learn merchandising and sales in one day. Whereas you can't suggest the title of a tune or what is appropriate artistically, they will freely suggest to you what should be done to market their product.

THE KEY TO DISTRIBUTION
Commentary by Stan Lathan
1981

Stan Lathan describes the key to distribution.

The key to distribution lies with knowing each individual market. We have a problem with product: there is a timing factor. We're in an industry that's almost totally dependent on another industry to expose our product—that's radio. With the tight economics of today, most (retailers) say, "If the record's not being played in my town, why do I have to have it in my store?"

With an unknown artist, we have got to go to the consumer and create a demand. Once we do that, it's up to distribution to saturate a market thoroughly. Not only having product in, but having it exposed, putting it on sale, making it the feature item of the week, putting displays up, promotions running among the local retailers themselves.

That's all a part of distribution's function. The distributing arm is the sales force. Those people dispense the product and actually write the business.

Regarding the difference between independent and in-house distribution, I can safely say that it's always nice to direct your own people. With independents, they always belong to somebody else. Having in-house distribution at Columbia, MCA or WEA means that they direct their own sales force to work their product.

Independents are in competition with other labels distributed by an independent. He might have 4*0 different companies of like product.* It's like, whoever's the hottest at the time usually gets the most attention. It's one of those things where you build a rapport with them, and they work your product and your catalog.

Unfortunately, most salesmen today don't really *work* a record. He'd rather 'work' the easy things. It's easy to go out with a Barbra Streisand, Jethro Hull or something like an Elton John.

Let him have to work a Joe Doakes, then he will really need a good sales pitch just to try and vie for that space. It's easier for them to write an order for 200 than five—they think. I try and get everything exposed.

ADVANTAGES OF INDEPENDENT DISTRIBUTION

Commentary by Miller London

1981

Motown executive Miller London discusses the advantages of independent distribution.

Independent distribution has been a strength for us, using distributors who have been in their market place for years and years. They know the consumer in the market place, his demographics, and whether a better buyer lives in the inner city or the suburbs for a particular product.

Independent distributors have the flexibility to do a lot of merchandising things that we otherwise would not normally be able to achieve through some of the branch distribution systems. They are, more or less, an interim between retail accounts and ourselves that actually sell to the consumer, and they are also something of a collection agency for us. We distribute our product directly through them.

There are a lot of rack jobbers in the business. You go into a Sears and Roebuck or a Broadway store where you see product out. It's unlike your regular retail store, unlike a warehouse or something.

With those kinds of accounts, we sell directly to make sure that we get our product in at the time that it's happening in the marketplace. They do a multitude of business since there are so many Broadway stores, chain stores, K-Marts and that kind of thing.

We go directly to those rack operations and handle those accounts in order to get our product in. On a major artist such as a Stevie Wonder, we go directly to them in the beginning. On some new artists—an artist that we're building—we tend to build that artist in a market that's more feasible.

If it's a White artist, then we'll take it through that secondary White market. If it's a Black artist, then we take it right to the Black population. We get it merchandised into those stores in the inner city.

MAKING ROUNDS WITH A WARNER/ELEKTRA/ATLANTIC RETAIL REP

Commentary by Ray Jeter

1981

Ray Jeter—making the rounds with a WEA retail rep in the Los Angeles inner-city market. Stop number one: Jefferson—Western, Mid-City Records.

My contact here is Helen Woods. She worked with Frank Jackson when he had Southwest Record Distributors. At one time, Frank ***was*** R&B product in Los Angeles—the basic barometer for sales reports on R&B product.

City One-Stop supplies the majority of these accounts with their product. Helen's my key buyer. If I want something to be broken, I'll use Helen to get a fix on the area. Mid-City is a very small store, really, but a very high volume retailer.

(Inside the store, tune changes and the song "Searching" blankets the room with its power coming out of the stereo. Coincidentally, it was one of Ray's hottest records.)

Usually, I give product to Helen. I give her the product information regarding bios of the artists, what might be current itinerary information regarding tours, who might be in town, who might be coming to town, and what some of our pushes are. Also, we have fall programs, winter programs, Christmas programs, all kinds of programs.

Visiting is a good way to give them that information because it always heads back to the streets. I just handed her the new Prince album. Prince is kind of interesting because he offers no definition. Someone described him one day as being asexual, if that means anything. He's off into his music, and I think he experiences his entire emotion through music.

(*Before leaving, Ray tests a new John Klemmer single, the magnificent ballad "Magnificent Madness." She plays it a while, brightens, then starts it over for its gorgeous intro. Ray has made a demonstrable impression with Helen—the key to his particular community-based product chain.*)

My main objection in that particular exchange was to inform her of the Monday morning release of product by Slave, Narada Michael Walden, Ray Charles, and Jean-Luc Ponty. The visit was very important because in order to make a piece of product grow, you have to begin at the roots. The roots of this industry are retail, because it is here that reveals all indications for radio and their hot items.

We reinforce weaker pieces of products—like a Bob Marley if it has some chance of making it. One of the goals of WEA is to make the weaker pieces of product as strong as the stronger items. I put up the displays myself, each display averages 45 minutes for set-up time.

Unfortunately, R&B retail is not very sophisticated in merchandising and marketing product that is brought in. They feel it is the responsibility of the record company to continue the flow of product out the door. We tend to give them support in that area.

(Stop number two, Flash Records. The longest-surviving record retailer in Los Angeles, Flash is a landmark to L.A. natives. Inside, Ray continues the pattern begun at Mid-City. He tells Mrs. Reynolds about the upcoming Monday releases.) There are some inquiries about the Doobie Brothers new album which Ray has in his possession. Once on the turntable, she critiques its merits vis-à-vis her clientele.

Other Flash employees inquire as to when he will be back and the kinds of music he'll be bringing. At his behest, they look in the back of his Datsun 280 ZX and see piled-up albums and posters. He and his counterparts with the other major labels are the closest thing to good humor men in the music world.)

Because I'm a southern boy, my conversation with Daisy (Mrs. Reynolds) allows me to get back to my roots with the South. I come by and get some collard greens and cornbread, black-eyed peas and short ribs. We talk about a lot of other things than records. We talk about the essence of life.

In our business—it's like any other—you begin first with the consumer. What makes you a consumer first is the quality of life. We talked about the short school week, and that people don't have much money between the first and the fifteenth.

It's critical in September for retailers, because the average kid's startup kit—just to get them ready to go back to school— costs between $185 and $250. When a person has three kids and a net income of $120 a week, it lets you know they can't afford to just go out and buy a Benson, a Larry Graham, or whatever.

We talk about the community, and it gives me a fix on things. Nothing really excites me, because I'm aware and attuned to this community.

The trades are supplied by retail. We could have the outcome of a piece of product on its previous piece, but that's not absolute. It we can motivate an interest in each and every piece of product, then we have a chance to really get some numbers out there. That's the name of the game in distribution.

Flash began as a family business, owned by Mr. & Mrs. Reynolds. They had two locations—one on Jefferson and one on Adams. They're still in business and tend to supply our customers with catalogs—all the old singles dating back to the Coasters and the Drifters.

(*At each stop, Ray assembles a package of current music, posters, and material for display.*)

I have a pattern about what I bring to a store. I work for three different companies—Warner Brothers, Elektra Asylum, and Atlantic. I have to make visibility very high for all three labels. In each case, I try to bring them something from each label, particularly.

Al Bergamo – President MCA Distribution Company addressing "The Anatomy of a Record Company" class at California State University, Los Angeles.

President Irwin Steinberg
Former Chairman & Chief Executive Officer
Polygram Record Operations

QUESTIONS FOR REFLECTION

Answer each numbered question with a brief essay.

1. Why is distribution so important to a record company?

2. Describe the types of distribution arrangements available today. What is your preference and why?

3. In your opinion, has the move to major label distribution been a beneficial step for smaller companies? Why or why not?

4. Why are custom labels becoming as important as they are? What are the essential differences between a custom label and a production company?

CHAPTER 11

PREPARING FOR A CAREER
The Neophyte
1981

If you've read the text as religiously as we'd have liked you to, chances are good that you know exactly what interests you in the way of a career in the business. There are many direct correlations.

From personal experience, we recommend that those of you who are college students hone up in the general area of knowledge your major field offers. Study disciplines that will give you broad training. Earn a degree in a field that could place you in many industries beyond music.

The average length of time a person is employed in the business is far shorter than elsewhere, so be prepared. You will not be young forever, and the urge to study could be a fleeting feeling.

Approach your goal correctly. If your major is engineering and that's what you want to do in the industry, balance those studies with ample measures of civil, electrical and system engineering training. Be realistic: There is no guarantee you will even get to first base in a job.

Throughout the text, references have been made about the relative ease of entry into the record business. The promotion department was mentioned early on as an access, as was the job of product manager.

Even in these tight times, that holds true. Compared to *staying in the business*, getting in is still a cakewalk. To illustrate the adaptation process, we introduce a concept called THE 3 A's "ASS, ATTITUDE, AND AVERAGE."

As with any other fraternity, sorority or benevolent brotherhood, entry into the record business takes more than a notion. It's hard enough. But, staying in is next to impossible unless one has all their survival wiles working for them. The tools we suggest are the same that got you into one or another special club. How about that old fraternity, "Felta Thigh?" the 3 A's depict the situation quite well.

Indeed, there are many challenges encountered working with a self-centered arrogant boss, and/or in a no-win situation promoting a tired-ass record. If, by some miracle, you happen to extricate yourself from underneath, or you successfully convince enough programmers of the record's merits, it was probably your ATTITUDE that got you the promotion.

ATTITUDE is an all-important issue. It is all in how you accept hardships and embark upon your successes that move you closer to your goals. The informal communication network or the 'grapevine' within the industry monitors how folks are doing head-wise. Most often, people are offered plum jobs through contacts.

A positive attitude goes far in establishing key friendships, which help an up-and-comer over the lean years. A positive mental attitude reflects an air of realism, recognizing that most people who have ever succeeded in the music industry have undergone tremendous obstacles.

For every success, there are a hundred thousand failures. Artists must not delude themselves into believing otherwise. A positive mental attitude gives impetus to continue struggling.

AVERAGE. This pertains to *skills.* Most guys in college fraternities see their grade point averages dip during the emotion-fraught time of pledging. As you enter the record business, be aware that you're green, and you may get caught up in the excitement. Once that's over, realize that your *average*—the skills you are selling—must be well honed.

If you are an accountant, be prepared. If you are a singer, take important advantage of every opportunity. If you *blow…well*, realize that there are *secretaries* at some companies who can sing as well as Diana Ross or Patti LaBelle. They may be the next people to get a shot if you mess up. Innate ability is certainly not enough. Timing, patience and interpersonal growth will likewise be seasoning.

I. The Neophyte

One fictitious day recently in the record business, a young rookie regional promotion man woke up quite excited. He was happy about his new job, with every expectation of setting the Midwest afire. His employer, the giant Megabucks Unlimited conglomerate had literally lured him off the campus of Saddleback University for a song and dance.

You need a name for this guy? Call him Fast Eddie. Fast for short, because everybody has a nickname. On this particular morning, Eddie was jazzed about his employment prospects. Since graduating, he'd learned enough to compete with the hippest guys out there. People encouraged him to stay around at least for a while. After all, the music business was booming, wasn't it?

When Eddie made it to his office, a routine memo innocently invited him to an informal coffee in the boss's office. He grinned from ear to ear after the summons. "The guy must want to reward me," he told his secretary. "Product is moving like lemonade in the desert."

Boy! Eddie was absolutely floored when he heard the real deal. "You've done an adequate job for us Eddie," the regional director intoned. "Have you been keeping up with the industry?" Eddie nodded, his mood suddenly shifted. "An adequate job," he thought. "Uh oh."

His boss continued. "Problem is…well, let me tell you in plain English, son. Megabucks sales' figures are down so low these first two quarters, they're gonna change the name to Micro-Mini. I'm gonna have to work the streets myself, and," he softened, "you're out of a job."

Fast Eddie was crushed. Within 30 seconds his whole life flashed before him. He wondered if he'd wake up from this sudden nightmare. Who'd pay his luxury notes? What about plans for promoting Megabucks product? Was he at fault? What would he do now? What kinds of games were these people trying to run him through?

Eddie thought of many unanswered questions in the space of an anxious moment. He asked his supervisor the usual postmortem questions—the *why* of the situation—then was told his termination was effective immediately.

Lop! Eddie was livid. As he gathered his belongings from his desk, he was instructed to leave his Rolodex full of contacts right where it was. That was company property.

Blown away, Eddie called his cousin who worked in Public Relations for another label. She was totally unsympathetic, having received the ax herself that day at lunch. Within a mere one-hour time difference between regions, they might have received the word at the same precise moment. Life's like that.

The illustration of Fast Eddie may seem a bit overdrawn to those of you happy and secure in your current position. In the climate of today's record industry, however, job security is a rare commodity for rank-and-file employees.

II. The Nature of Works in America

Work in America today is important for more reasons than simply deriving an income. Any professional organization has numerous roles, which are filled by an endless number of personality types, power interests and people filling out a particular structure. A wide variety of needs are available to be satisfied in a work environment directly from the job itself.

Many people are known to manifest greater emotional commitment to join than family or personal interests. Often by virtue of the way positions are acquired, they are the subject of power plays and of palace intrigues. The social networks—the 'underground grapevine'—is the predominant informal system that conveys gossip, rumors and choice information that is crucial to employee survival.

Plugging in to that hookup, or having access at least, is one way of having a peripheral view of others' mistakes before yours blows up in your face. In the square business world, education, training, and experience seem to go hand-in-hand with 'who you know' in the matter of career advancement. Planning ahead is seen as a key issue in developing a profile of longevity.

III. "In the Business"

Historically, the music business in employment practice or overall fiscal circumstances has never quite paralleled other American industries. As a leisure industry, it has always carried a glamorous overtone even when few were able to make a comfortable living.

Over the years, the industry has witnessed numerous times when sales seemed an endless cushion that provoked grand projections as in the last few years—only to fall victim to hard times as related parts of the economy slumped.

The present correlation between a soft economy and record industry trouble has numerous precedents. The grand mal catastrophe—the Great Depression of 1929—had a very heavy impact on records.

In 1930 Columbia Records did nearly $30 million in business. The next year they earned just $5 million. Needless to say, cutbacks weren't even the word for the company's response at that point. Is 'employee genocide' fierce enough? The situation had the further impact of curtailing the number of race (Black) artists signed, recorded, and promoted.

Further in time, Black music as an industry began in the late 1940s with the independent promoters, radio personalities, and liaisons. It was more of a sales and communications network than a coast-to-coast institution making up the fledgling 'industry.'

At that point, the business was a conglomeration of majors. The independents who were often organized on a shoestring were worth a fifty percent market share by the mid-50s. Employees were predominantly drawn from the streets, rather than through campus recruitment or some such. Street people were attuned with the pulse of the heartbeat, and promotion was run on a feel rather than computerized market projection basis.

The industry had little in the way of a collective corporate mentality. That began changing in the mid-60s when more dollars and public interest heightened and many corporate types were lured in.

They began applying many of the principles operational in business generally to the 'fly by the seat of your pants' mentality that had brought the business to the point it was at that time.

Some concepts were easily adaptable because the industry could stand a more organized overall structure and computerization offered potential for more accurate projection and less waste in sales and promotion.

In other areas (as some of the succeeding comments note), such as career planning and projections, and correlating training/preparation with job function, the record business still may be lagging far behind other industries. Merger conglomeration has now clouded that picture, as has the current paranoia about the future.

IV. A Must Have Survival Kit

Obviously, this entire section is intended as a coping mechanism by providing food for thought, but here are three specialized considerations one might immediately think of to maintain during these tight times. One is coping with stress.

Here's an illustration from reality. *Last Week* I hopped into a Hollywood club as the guest of a record company that had gone through a major layoff earlier that day. As is my custom, I was late and feeling pretty good. The PR person who seated me was in a particularly stressed frame of mind, worried about job security. She barked at me for being late, though it was none of her business.

I got miffed at being treated like a nobody and found out that others had been likewise accorded. Only later did I realize the degree to which she was venting her frustration and anger by indirectly projecting it onto others who were uninvolved in her plight. In her inexperience, she made us targets. Unfortunately, antagonizing people you don't know is a quick way to lose your job in spite of yourself. Be careful!

Point two is to plan ahead. The axiom in today's world is "You get a job while you got a job." Also, options are important. Planning involves skillfully assessing one's assets in the matter of what you have to sell as a commodity. Know your skills and capabilities well enough to articulate them on paper.

Remember that the record industry is tremendously overbalanced as a buyer's market because it has a much greater supply of talent than requisite demand. To make your presence felt, that résumé, demo, portfolio, graphic layout or platinum song better be jumpin'.

Adequate planning has the facility of lightening stress and giving individuals a lateral (cross-range) read on available opportunities and potential contacts.

Final point is making the break. The moment when an employee is about to take a fall can have tremendously heavy psychological impact. Preparation for leaving a job—whether done amicably, voluntarily or belly-up—carries certain ambivalent feeling of self-worth and reticence to move into the next job space and time.

ON INDIVIDUAL SUCCESS
Commentary by Bob Knight
1981

Bob Knight differs with the opinion that staying in is harder than initially getting in. He notes that cultivating a 'godfather' is absolutely essential to individual success.

I found getting in to be quite difficult, much more difficult than staying in because I've been able to survive thus far. But, it took me six years to get in. That entailed going to people like Logan's office three to four times a week, sitting down asking had he come up with any new contacts for me.

I constantly beat the sidewalks of New York, talking to radio people and people at other record companies about how to get in. There are so many people out there who would like to get in, who don't know how. They know they can go to a Capitol Records—or wherever—to try to get in, but that is just the preliminary stages. Then, you have got to start looking for someone to talk to.

You can't go through personnel. People aren't hired into record companies through personnel, so, it's tremendously difficult. The entertainment business is like a big family. It's *who you know*, totally. It is not what you have done, or what you can do. It's who you know, that's it.

Now, your accomplishments—whatever they might be—do not hurt. The things that you have done in the past do not hurt, because in order to sit down and talk with someone intelligently about your desires to get into the business, you certainly should have been involved in some aspect of the business that can relate...be it advertising or sales, something like that in another industry. But, even that doesn't mean a whole lot.

I went to CBS and everyone that looked at my résumé said, "It's tremendous, but why do you want to get into this business?" I had a feel for music, and I wanted to get in. They'd say, "I'm sorry, but we don't have anything right now." And that's how it goes forever and ever, until you find someone who's willing to sit down and listen.

Once you're in, you have to line yourself up with someone in upper management who can serve as a godfather figure for you. That person serves as a buffer in keeping all of the basically hostile and foreign forces away.

When you come in, assuming that you're a neophyte and aren't coming aboard in a middle-management position, there are a lot of meetings that are going to take place that you're not privy to—a lot of information that goes by your head.

You're not privy because you're not part of that circle. A godfather would be privy to information, to circumvent some of the negatives that are coming down about you or your area. That is essential. On the other hand, for someone to come in cold and take the perspective of, "Hey, I just want to do my work, do it well and get over."

People aren't rewarded in entertainment strictly on merit. Sure, there is some reward for merit, maybe 25 percent. Many don't want to hear this aspect of the business, but the people who are solidified politically are the ones who are able to move up. The person who comes in and just does his work, for the most part, will not go far unless he's in an unusual bargaining position.

I think in an area like accounting, it could be based on merit. But when you get down into the promotion area, into sales, A&R, into advertising/merchandising, all your line areas, you have to be politically in. In A&R, they probably look at your merits, but seldom in promotion.

This is the only industry I know of where you can be fired today as a regional promotion guy and tomorrow be hired somewhere else as a national guy, making more money. There's no penalty in that instance for the lack of excellence or achievement.

BUSINESS AND MARKETING PRINCIPLES

Commentary by Patricia Means

1981

Patricia Means successfully parlayed an MBA and a business background in other industries to her music career.

The basic business and marketing principles are the same always, regardless of what you are doing. It is a matter of falling back on basic training in addition to the marketing experience I had elsewhere and applying it to music. But it's all basically the same.

The only difference is that the marketing of music is a little bit *faster*. You have a shorter shelf life of the product. But the basic principles are the same—sound planning, knowledge of the market, what's needed, using basic marketing skills to expose your product to the market place.

(In college), There was a class called "Executive Decision Making" that has really helped. During the class, we had to come up with answers to a particular set of problems. There was no right answer and no wrong answer unlike a lot of older classes such as Quantitative Analysis Economics where there was an answer. The Management Decisions class forced you to come up with several different answers.

There was nothing that was right or wrong as long as you came up with something that was based on sound judgment. That also applies in the music world. There's no right or wrong answer. You strive to have the best solution to a particular problem, and to think through your reasons for making a particular decision. That is the class that has helped me the most.

I was interested in the music business based on my desire to get involved with something that is fast-paced and constantly changing. I get very bored doing the same thing over and over again.

It wasn't until after I got into the music business and really started to learn that, indeed, the principles of marketing (moreover of business) are applied much more than I thought. A lot of shortcuts are taken; a lot of the thinking is different. A lot of the people don't have the formal business training I had been accustomed to. The common-sense level is the same, the thinking is the same.

A PERSONAL ODYSSEY IN MUSIC
Commentary by Carol King
1981

Carol King discussed her own career odyssey. She feels that she has now "Learned all Facets of It."

I got my start into the music business from television. It was a local channel here in Los Angeles on UHF. I started at Motown, then Randy Wood came and got me for Vee Jay Records. I worked there for two years.

While at Vee Jay, I emceed shows for James Brown and Stevie Wonder. Jim Randolph got me that job when he was at KGFJ. Then he started bringing me over to the station to do commercials with Rick Holmes. We did beer commercials as well as Chinese New Year commercials. From there I became music director at KGFJ when Vee Jay folded. From KGFJ, I went over to KJLH. I got my license and went on the air awhile.

Then, I realized that I didn't know much about the marketing end of the business. I went to work at Record Merchandising, where I got experience in promotion and marketing. Warner Brothers pulled me from Record Merchandising, and I was assistant to David Banks. From Warner Brothers, Mike Thevis got me. He'd just opened up an L.A. office for GRC Records.

From GRC I developed my own business—Golden Lady Productions—on the West Coast. I was West Coast representative for all Platinum Records and a few smaller labels. I was also doing independent promotion with my company through United Artists.

They liked what I was doing, so they asked me to become full-time. The money was right and everything. I worked for United Artists, and then Bunky Sheppard brought me over to 20th Century where I've done promotion, marketing, and national Disco ever since.

I would say that I started where you're supposed to start, to learn all facets of it. It all worked out very nice because I got a little touch of everything, then I had the TV (experience) before that. One of the most important things in this business is to learn merchandising and marketing.

If you don't succeed in the music business, that knowledge will help you in any business. I think that's what's wrong with the majority of things that Blacks have started. They do not know the foundation of business.

They get in, the money is fine, they spend it, then Uncle Sam looks at them, or they fold because they don't know where it went. It's just a lack of knowledge. If we ever get to the point where we as a race know business, then I think we will never have a problem running anything on our own.

For students in school: if they want to go into this type of business, they should study business and marketing courses. A lot of times, you can work as a trainee with someone.

If you're an aggressive and outgoing person, promotion is a good place to start. If you don't get across with yourself, then the product really doesn't mean anything. I just feel that you must develop your own inner qualities as a person before you can do something else.

Dr. Van Christopher addressing "The Anatomy of a Record Company" class at California State University, Los Angeles.

"The Anatomy of a Record Company" class at
California State University, Los Angeles.

L-R Attorney David Jackson, Sidney Miller – Publisher *Black Radio Exclusive,* John Smith – Record Company Executive

L-R David Banks-Artist Mgr. & Producer, Laura Palmer-Publicist, Hillery Johnson-Artist Mgr., after a session at "The Anatomy of a Record Company" class at California State University, Los Angeles

QUESTIONS FOR REFLECTION

Answer each question with a brief essay.

1. Using your powers of imagination and reasoning, think of a few creative ways in which you can plan to then ultimately achieve a career in the record business.

2. Describe your own personal goals and objectives in detail. How does a career in the music business fit in with your overall life plan?

3. How do you personally intend to achieve the objective of your first job in the industry?

CHAPTER 12

FROM HERE TO THERE
A Layman's Guide to Success in the Music Business

Talent:
That's where it begins. Record companies have A&R (artist & repertoire) men, Arthur Godfrey had his talent scouts, and everybody in the business is constantly looking for that person—that group with 'it.'

In today's business, 'it' is often as much songwriting talent as performing talent. Since the advent of the Beatles, the music business has come to see the added plus in performing talent that can create valuable copyrights through songwriting as well as deliver performances that will sell records.

Nightclubs, dance halls, demo tapes, and rehearsal halls, all are sources for the discovery of talent—24 hours a day, 7 days a week, from any place, at any time. At some point, a professional will make a judgment that the particular talent under consideration has the potential to reach a definable and profitable market, and that leads to…

A Recording Contract:
Like so many types of written agreements, recording contracts do not have a concrete standard form. A recording artist today can expect 10 to 20 percent (of wholesale price) as a royalty with some escalation of royalty based on sales success.

Recording costs and artists cash advances are both accounted against royalties and are recouped before royalties on net sales are paid.

Often, it is the practice of a record company to hold a reasonable reserve for a specified period to protect the company when collections from distribution are not prompt.

In many instances, an artist will sign a contract with a production company who will then take on the producer's responsibility with the artist and also represent the artist to record companies.

In these cases, the artist's royalty rate is the same, and the producer's override is added as he contracts the artist's services to the record company. Music publishing is also an important aspect for artist/songwriters who could be well served to affiliate with a worldwide publisher to promote their copyrights.

A production agreement usually makes some provision for this activity. Once the terms are agreed upon, the recording contract is signed and leads to…

***The Recording Studio*:**

Under the guidance of an experienced producer, preparation for recording starts in rehearsal as the best musical material is selected and polished for the recording studio.

In the studio, the producer not only helps to direct the artist's performance, but also guides the recording engineer in using the sophisticated equipment of the modern studio to achieve the sound that best contributes to the music that the artist is creating.

Most recording is done on 24-track tape. It is not unusual for a rhythm section to record first. Then later, perhaps a horn section, lead and background vocals, synthesizers, then string and/or percussion can be added to supplement the track.

Once all of these elements are placed on the multi-track tape, they are then carefully mixed down to a 2-track stereo tape. When a final mix is completed, the resultant tape is called a stereo master. The next step is…

***Mastering*:**

The process of mastering refers to the procedures of cutting sound grooves into an acetate lacquer-coated metal disc using a heated stylus (needle) on a specially built turntable called a lathe. Not only is this a technically critical point in making a record, it is also the the last point where the sound can be substantially altered.

Sometimes, the real punching effect of the thumping beat that sells a record gains its final emphasis at the mastering stage. The lacquer disc called the acetate master is carefully packaged and sent to…

***Manufacturing*:**

Through the process of electro-plating, a 'male' plate is made of the grooves in the acetate master. This plate is also electro-plated with copper and the resultant disc impression is called a 'mother.'

This, in turn, is plated and the plate impressions of the 'mother' are used in the presses. Today compact discs are the name of the game and are digitally manufactured.

Oh yes…

***The Jacket*:**

Artwork for an *album/CD* jacket can range from simple hand lettering of type, to processed photography, to fine illustration, to oil paintings, etc. Once the art elements have been chosen, designed, and appropriate type added, the art is photo-processed, film separations are made, and from these, color printing plates are etched.

CD jackets today are made of glazed paper board, which is printed on a huge press that is capable of printing four to six colors. The printed sheets are then fed to a fabricator, which accurately cuts the album shape out, applies glue in the right places and sticks it all together.

After the jackets are printed, fabricated and packaged, they are shipped to the pressing plant where the sleeved records are inverted into the jackets. Having gone through all this, product is now ready for…

***Distribution*:**

In today's record market, CDs are distributed by both branch operations and independent distributors. CBS Records, RCA, MCA, Warner Brothers, Capitol, and Polygram each have company-owned and operated national distribution systems moving product from pressing plants to distribution depots, which is, in turn, sold by branch sales offices to retail outlets, sub-distributors (called 'one-stops') and multiple location retail operators (called 'rack jobbers' and chain stores).

There are major labels—Motown, Chrysallis, and Arista among them—who utilize independent distributors. The independent may operate from one or more major markets.

Product is shipped from the manufacturing plant to each of these independently owned and operated distributors and is then sold into the same pipeline as the branch operations use. With product headed toward retail locations, we turn to…

***MARKETING*:**

The focus of marketing is three-pronged—promotions, sales, and merchandising.

***Promotion*:**

"If the public doesn't hear the record, they won't buy it." For over 25 years, airplay has been the key to successful sales. Both independent distributors and branch operations have teams of local promotion men whose prime responsibility is to have radio stations initiate and maintain a pattern of airplay on the records that he is promoting.

Audience rating surveys and demographic studies provide information as to which radio stations can motivate sales on particular types of product. Promotion at the local level also includes contact with record and concert reviewers and feature writers for local newspapers and magazines.

This activity may have less to do with creating immediate sales, but can be important in developing and broadening a recording artist's image to the public at large.

Sales:

"Once airplay is achieved, you can't sell records if they're not in the stores." Sales executives administer, coordinate, and motivate the system of distribution. Usually, branch systems have a regional supervisory substructure in the sales management area.

With independent distributors, a label will sometimes maintain regional sales executives to closer coordinate the sales of that label's releases.

The main responsibility of the chain of sales personnel is to ensure records are available at retail to satisfy any demand that is created. Current sales practices tend to limit the number of returns that can be sent back to the manufacturer, so that the technique of placing product in such a way as it will turn over quickly without running out of stock or leaving a large overstock is more difficult than in the past.

Merchandising:

Special record racks and bins, divider cards, posters, printed T-shirts, etc., are all a part of directing the attention of the consumer to a particular album and/or a particular recording artist.

Although restricted promotion and merchandising budgets have limited the use of these items, a well-designed poster placed prominently in a retail location can be an attractive reminder that lasts many months and that constantly reminds patrons of that particular artist.

If you start with outstandingly talented performers, create distinctive and appealing recordings, effectively promote regular airplay, and get product to the consumer, you have made the journey to THE FINISH.

SECTION II

ANALYSIS
OF THE
HARVARD BUSINESS SCHOOL STUDY

CHAPTER 13

AN ANALYSIS OF THE COLUMBIA RECORDS GROUP HARVARD BUSINESS SCHOOL STUDY

While Clive Davis was president of CBS Records, the label escalated its visibility as a dominant leader in the market. Columbia was the biggest revenue producer in all areas except R&B. CBS acts topped the Country charts, Pop, Classical, the whole spectrum—except Black-oriented product.

Commentary by the Author
Logan H. Westbrooks
1981

I was hired by CBS Records the latter part of 1971 to coordinate a new R&B thrust. Clive Davis and his VP of Marketing, Bruce Lundvall, jointly made the decision to establish a Black Marketing Division, and make it work. Prior to that time, it was titled National R&B Promotion. Later, it was 'CBS-ified' to 'Special Markets.' My mission was clearly stated: Create a Black Marketing Staff to penetrate the Black Market.

(Below is an excerpt from the announcement of my appointment to the Columbia Records Organization, from Bruce Lundvall.)

It is with great pleasure that I announce the appointment of Logan H. Westbrooks to the newly-created position of Director, Special Markets. Mr. Westbrooks will be responsible for directing the overall marketing efforts of Columbia, Epic, and custom label R&B singles and album products.

To help achieve this new concept in Black product marketing, he will directly supervise the field activities of our R&B Promotion Managers and will also provide special marketing direction in all aspects of R&B product, including advertising, cover art and design, sales and merchandising. I know that you join me in welcoming Logan to CRG and wish him success in this new endeavor.

In putting together a strategy to exploit the strong selling potential of Black product, CBS executives reached into a multiplicity of directions. One place consulted was the Business School ("B" School) of Harvard University, where a research team of instructors and students was organized to study the Black music market from a quantified standpoint.

They also assembled a narrative, and it has a starkly historical ring to it, both in language and provisions set forth by which the Columbia Records Group (CRG) might make its presence felt.

Davis didn't follow the blueprint. In his comments, later in this section, he indicates that he had no knowledge of the document. He began the move into Black music marketing based on pure intuition. It was the executive Larry Isaacson, a 'B' school alumnus, who is credited with commissioning the study.

Regardless of whether Davis referred to the document in the early 1970s, its words ring prophetic. In less than a decade, CRG increased its impact on Black music a thousand fold. In 1971, there were two progressive Black-oriented acts recording steadily for the label—Sly and Santana. By 1980 the total numbered over 125, one-third of the largest artist roster under contract.

In this section, we intend to establish the significance of CRG's move into Black music, analyzed in context of the study. Pages and paragraphs (noted in parentheses) refer to source document.

The study first came to the general public's awareness during the Stax Records' controversy. CBS and Stax got into a hell of a dogfight—$60 million worth—and the document was presented as evidence of the conglomerate's alleged intentions to constrict the smaller label.

THE CBS/HARVARD 'B' SCHOOL STUDY

The significance of CBS's moves should be well framed in light of subsequent events. The action of the largest record company in the world to establish a forceful presence in progressive Black music began a chain of events among all the majors. The reaction became a greater focus and better-structured handling of Black music as commercial product.

The initial actions of CBS were copied throughout the industry. Suddenly, every company doing even *traces* of R&B business had a Black Music Marketing Division with a token executive force. Whites still maintained the lion's share of control and power. The motives? Clearly financial as the 'B' school study notes.

Sixty million pretty little green bucks were going untapped as a market base, because Columbia and most of the other majors were ignorantly under-exploiting Black sounds at the time. Other benefits the 'B' school study outlined were ancillary to the market potential.

These involved the power to institutionalize Black commercial music as a legitimate Pop art form, more jobs for Blacks, other fringe benefits. Shall we name one direct result? CBS now has a consistent power base with acts like Earth, Wind & Fire and numerous Philly International acts.

As a sidebar, the move signaled the value of conducting such formal research. The projections were based upon the battery of analytical mechanisms brought to bear.

The team's multi-variant approach to record industry business established a standard, and CBS was quickly able to adapt the information into its game plan. With such massive sums of money at stake every day, why weren't more companies using such an approach?

ELEMENTS

The research of the 'B' school was referred to as "A Study of the Soul Music Environment Prepared for Columbia Records Group." The Harvard team was officially named the "Columbia Records Project Group."

The narrative was comprised of 24 pages with an 18-page section of market projections, revenue graphs, market size estimates and buying analyses of potential consumers. The final agreement is an addendum of specific action recommendations aimed at pushing CBS/CRG over the top. The findings were indeed overwhelming.

The *introduction* outlines the problem in a straightforward discussion. The *objective* of the research was to examine the feasibility of expansion into R&B in light of the organization's then current structure and the strategic and financial implications of the move. The *scope* of the study analyzed historical developments of Soul music, and its internal development and relationship to the music world at large.

The innate conclusion is as follows: the recognition that a large under-exploited Soul market existed, which CRG had not tapped into significantly. In order to do so, they would have to modify and broaden current efforts in that market.

The institutionalization of Soul music, created by the establishment of an autonomous entity within a label such as CBS, then, had a solid foundation. The resulting industry wide game plan for Black music marketing has always emphasized the reflexive relationship of *increased visibility* to *increased viability*.

Therefore, the CRG study not only established a blueprint structure but also detailed on a yearly basis the mechanisms for filling in the content. The study predicts such realities as pervasive development of custom labels and the dwindling of the all-Black segments of the vendor side of business effecting R&B promotions and retail wings of small but experienced independent labels.

One obvious side effect of commercializing music industry wide was the de-emphasis of traditional Folk music, Blues, and other low-selling genres. As a direct result of the changed climate in the 70s, such artists were virtually eliminated from major concert bills, and big city radio playlists.

Additionally, every possible outlet has become a selling space for product. The dichotomy between music as 'art,' and music as 'product' was misconstrued during this time. Standards of greatness, and the lion's share of accolades are pretty much saved for the superstar sellers.

The other realities of great relevance were as follows: at the time of the study, local Jazz clubs were dying. Acoustic artists went lower and lower on the priority list, judged non-commercial. Suddenly, 'accessible,' as in *pop, poop*, and *pap* became an important word in radio jargon.

With more money at stake and according to the axiom, "It takes money to make money," the break-even point for success escalated. Production budgets doubled, trebled, quintupled, depending on which side's cost analysis one subscribes to.

Bigger business begat bigger demands. Poor Herbie Hancock. He's seemingly caught in a vice. *Headhunters* went double Platinum once upon a time, and now everything he records must reek of such potential.

The analytical process began when Clive Davis recognized that formalizing the structure of Black music would provide a direct result of multiplying sales and power. The concomitant image development afforded CBS the opportunity to trumpet each move of positioning visibility as a breakthrough.

A more subtle variable was the action of time and space. The early 1970s were alive with the remnants of the Black consciousness movement, now filtered into the public and private sector. Every university in the land had at least a token manifestation of Black visibility.

Shrewd businessman that he is, Davis simply did what was appropriate business-wise in his own bailiwick. Black visibility in CBS's promotion machine equalized major scale success.

The ANALYSIS in part of the 'B' school research was very well drawn. Implication derived from stated facts are clearly constructed, allowing opportunity to assess the study from a variety of perspectives. For purposes of illustration, here is a sports parallel: The study called for expansion in similar ways that ball clubs and ball players interact in this era of *free agency*. The below study recommendations follow the roman numerals, CBS acquisitions follow in parenthesis:

I. CBS was urged to purchase an already-developed talent roster (PIR, STAX)

II. Revive and re-establish proven talents (O'Jays, Lou Rawls)

III. Take breaking groups and break them bigger (Earth, Wind & Fire, Harold Melvin & the Blue Notes)

IV. In-house development (Teddy Pendergrass, Sly, Santana, Heatwave, Webster Lewis)

V. Buying into breaking trends (Fusion through Miles Davis and all his major 'alumni.' Weather Report, Mahavishnu Orchestra and Headhunters, and PIR's characteristic sophisticated smoothness).

VI. Allowing success to begat success (ARC and other custom labels, Michael Jackson's "Off the Wall" album, artist generated)

The time frame for implementation offered a correlation between these moves, some of which called for outright acquisitions; while others utilized the label's vast pre-established image-building and act-development capabilities. Literally considered, the study offered an ongoing working plan which remains viable today as an overview.

The INTERNAL DYNAMICS section offers a range of information on the structure of record promotion, dimensions of the hit-making process, even a section on payola. The summary finding noted the importance of Black radio as providing access to a large, ever-growing consumer pool; and offering the most effective way of getting a record onto a Top 40 playlist in these days of 'crossover.' A central point of discussion regarding the industry's internal dynamics also emphasized the value of strong product to overcome payola potential.

A key section identified and highlighted CBS's varied competitors for Black consumer dollars. Specialized national companies were noted as the most formidable opposition, with Motown, Atlantic, and Stax specifically tagged as Soul market leaders.

"They are entrenched," the student noted, "and control half the total market. They have the most established Soul artists, with management and professional staffs with the most experience and understanding of subtleties."

Thus was established the *nature* of the competition—strong independents relying heavily on the strength of personal networks, well established to promote and to market the records, with an intense profoundly-drawn awareness of the music itself.

The study *unequivocally* highlighted the nexus of power of the major independents: by the early 70s, they were in a crucial gate-keeping function to regulate traffic within Black music, while the lesser players could only react to shifts in trends. CBS's entrée signaled attention shifts and the re-prioritization of those relationships. Ultimately, major labels acquired a majority of the talent rosters from *Indie* labels.

The study stressed that in the short run, CRG would be in direct competition with the well-established independents, who were planning to increasingly diversify into Pop and MOR from the strong R&B power bases.

Another key area noted was the suddenly keen competition for the limited, though heavily experienced, Black employee talent pool in promotion, management, as well as artists. CRG was, therefore, urged to put together a long-term benefits package because other competitors were less likely to do so.

On the basis of organizing a well thought out, well planned, and well financed initiative aimed at long-term market penetration (rather than short-term profits from an opportunistic 'creaming' program) the *impetus* for developing a successful Black Music Marketing Division was laid out in black and white. Using success aids the success axiom, the 'domino theory' took its natural course and lesser labels quickly followed the lead of the industry flagship.

The study was no less explicit in detailing the means for exploiting resources currently in the marketplace. Accordingly, the presence of smaller independents represented an 'opportunity' rather than a threat. Indies offered a source of ready resources that money could buy, quickly shoring up CRG's short-run lacks in the Soul music field.

A sampling of surveyed resources graphically illustrates the means by which CRG and the other majors tentacled into the echelons of the Black music industry. Indies were judged ready sources of (1) 'hot masters'; (2) talent with national hit and image potential; (3) experienced personnel and staff, especially in promotion and production; (4) a source of captive independent producers; and (5) proprietary product which CRG would serve as the distribution arm.

Therefore, a blueprint for establishing linkages to achieve the ultimate, major objective: ***market dominance***. CBS had to put forth capital as an initial step to buy its way into Black music on the short end. On the long end, the artistic dimension would be added to establish appropriate creative trappings.

The *ANALYSIS OF COLUMBIA RECORDS* assessed CRG's then-present capabilities. The study observed the label had never been a market force in Soul, despite earlier short-lived and sporadic forays with Okeh and Date. It was, therefore, judged that CRG knew little or nothing about the projected market, Black artists and related professionals in radio.

The study also described 'a historic neglect' of the Soul market. In all fairness to Columbia, that statement is hardly accurate. Bessie Smith was a Columbia artist as early as 1923 and her recordings of "St. Louis Blues," "Downhearted Blues" and others sold seven million 78s between 1923-28.

Here's what the study suggested as remedy, which the company subsequently followed closely: A 'significant' financial and organizational commitment, hiring 'experienced Soul personnel' in the areas of A&R, production and promotion. *Significantly, these were the only areas specifically targeted for input.*

Enrichment and promotion of the present talent roster, while increasing the ante for talent and development was something that arose as an issue. As a parallel action, CRG was urged to "build productive relationships with the trades and with Soul radio personnel," and screen independent producers to establish "an authentic, commercially viable, reproducible and distinct Columbia Records sound."

The final statement notes that the process had heavy potential to incur financial loss in the first few years of development. The study stopped short of advocating a proportional amount of new hiring in support positions. Emphasis was placed on deriving maximum goods and services by amalgamating the best talent tributaries into the parent system.

The RATIONALE justified the move on several counts:
1. Significant profit potential and appropriateness of timing at that point in the early 70s. Columbia shouldn't forfeit any market share to its competitors. Soul music was then credited with a seven percent market share and CRG's only consistent chart makers in that area were Santana and Sly.

2. The 'crossover' potential of Soul was also cited. At the time of the study, the Billboard Hot 100 consisted of 20 to 35 percent Soul performers and has remained steady in that regard since.

Therefore, a protracted campaign with Soul music as the backbone would greatly expand CRG's already dominant power and influence. Soul stations offered a more than ample amount of music for ultimate access to Top 40, especially in these times of tighter formats.

Lastly, the study noted Soul music's role as an indigenous American art form rooted in Africa. From that base, a plan of action with recommended strategies was put forth.

Three broad approaches were advanced. The expansion of external resources by adding to the then ever-present roster with more custom labels and outside product resources were one of the broad approaches.

3. Creation of an in-house Soul music production matrix, and the establishment of a semi-autonomous group to handle Black product.

The aims of this strategy were to immediately penetrate the market while developing a broad base for future action. The group considered two alternative sets of recommendations that, in historical retrospect, are great food for hindsight judgments. The team rejected the idea "of acquiring a presently strong company based on the anti-trust threat," with speculation being that the three leading companies were unavailable at the time.

CRG went against the advice, entering into a distribution deal with Stax that ultimately led to the legendary Memphis-based Indie's demise. Alternative two, also discounted by the study group, called for acquiring already established talent.

This approach was frowned upon because of the high costs of contracts, the risk of diminishment, and the in-house base structure not yet developed in A&R, promotion and artist relations, possible competitors' reactions, and the cynical reality that payment of large dollars to new talent might stimulate jealousy among current acts.

Such *ad hoc* judgments and negative projections were ultimately alleviated. Wilson Picket, one act noted, was never signed by CRG, but lesser-priced talents with innovative potential were 'discovered' and promoted proportionally to their commercial worth.

In that way, CRG was able to benchmark the Jazz Fusion movement, re-break LaBelle as the vocal trio of the 70s, and showcase Michael Jackson, a growing innovator as the decade closed. The Harvard Study—and resulting Black Music Marketing—outlined a structural underpinning.

The team recommended an organizational structure, based on specific guidelines. These were the necessary functions seen as appropriate.

1. Decision making in signing and talent acquisition, with adequate budget an obvious corollary

2. Independent talent and product evaluation powers

3. Responsibility for artist coordination and product management

4. Maintenance of beneficial rapport with radio

5. Integration of the Soul music sales force within the existing structure

6. Integration of the Soul music group with other functional arms of legal advertising, physical production, graphics, the *rest*. The formal organization, consisted of the Director of the Soul music group, responsible for overall management, an administrative coordinator acting as an 'integrative liaison,' between the Soul music group and the rest of CRG and requisite functionaries in promotion, A&R, sales, and product management.

The narrative following the skeletal detailing is likewise revealing. The Soul group was not intended as a separate entity, but rather as BMM's role became, in actual reality, a coordinative function.

Under the arrangement, Soul artists could utilize the new umbrella regardless of which Columbia label they recorded for, however, the *intent* for the mechanism was clear. Simply stated: to create an atmosphere conducive to Soul music flourishing, rather than lay out extensively rigid guidelines.

It was also judged conceivable that an artist might have an album worked through the Soul music group, then have the next effort promoted through the existing structure depending on the nature of the sound. *That* provision, interestingly enough, was precisely the means by which Soul artists quickly became visible on Top 40 AM.

THE PIR GROUP STUDY

Artists promoted under the Soul music banner were assigned to a definite label, with a group's style being a particular consideration in choosing an outlet. The Soul group's autonomy was underscored by its stated chain of command: its director reported to the CRG president, which allowed for flexibility and a tangible manifestation of a top-level serious commitment to marketing and promoting Black music.

The independent nature of the group was offered as an opportunity to eliminate potential conflicts from working in an environment unable to appreciate or understand Black music, or requirements for success in that sector of the business.

Once again, note the subtle parallel between projected actions for CRG to take and the influence of the Black consciousness movement at the time. Such key words as *autonomy*, and actions like *reporting directly to the president* had similar overtones as the action in Black studies departments, Black employee associations, and the rest.

'Autonomy' had another less-recognized element, however, the longer an entity stayed 'autonomous' in corporate situations, the longer they stayed out of the power networks and access to normal means for surviving.

As a corporate entity then, Black music marketing was intended as a tactical means to an end rather than a viable power base in and of itself. Control remained vested within the top echelon. The Black music marketing effort that resulted afforded tremendous new opportunities.

The 3-phase overlapping strategy for ***implementation*** entailed establishing a marketing position through existing custom label operations, including Epic and the associated labels, expansion through internally generated product, and the ultimate creative development of a distinctive 'Columbia Soul Sound.'

When queried, Clive Davis noted that his interest in Black music was an 'intuitive' thing. He says that he never consulted the 'B' school study.

It was purely intuitive judgment reasoning on my part. At the time of the early Motown hits, they weren't major sellers of albums. I noticed the Black motion pictures were coming out such as "Shaft" and one or two others that were getting a large audience. It appeared to me that the time was ripe to sign artists with potential who could develop into album sellers, as well as singles sellers.

You don't make much money in the record business off singles, you do if off albums. I had been waiting a very long time for Columbia's A&R staff to develop a Black sensibility, listening to the promotions and marketing people say that they could do it with a White staff.

In listening to the various arguments of our Black A&R staff we had there saying that they were coming up with hits, but the White staff could not break them—and the White staff saying they could break the hits, but they weren't being given the hits by the A&R staff, I decided that I would be able to come up with a hit, and yet who had not been able to develop major artists' names—who had hit singles but never developed a career, long-term artist image, namely Gamble & Huff.

I sought out Kenny Gamble and Leon Huff, and decided to make a commitment to a Black promotion and marketing staff. In the space of a year and half I made the deal to sign Kenny and Leon for Philadelphia International Records. Of course, that led to the O'Jays' record and the Billy Paul contract from Warner Brothers for $75,000.

I attracted the Isley Brothers, who were unhappy on their current label. I brought in Herbie Hancock and the Manhattans. Putting all those names together, that constituted the nucleus.

The success was so strong. I remember flying Earth, Wind & Fire to London to our world-wide convention. We flew them over to perform, to show (people) what the potential combination of strong R&B fused with Jazz influences could be. I had worked with Miles Davis during the *Bitches Brew* concept, I had worked with Billy Cobham to fuse with John McClaughlin in the Mahavishnu Orchestra, and then I signed these other artists.

Everything exploded all over this place with Gamble & Huff, and with Earth, Wind & Fire's first and second albums. Obviously, the Isley Brothers did well from the beginning since they had established a name for themselves previously.

It was not based on any *blueprint*. It was based on awareness that there was no obstacle in looking where CBS could grow. But in looking at my herculean task to see how the growth could keep on going, it was clear that it was very hard to get a larger share of the middle-of-the-road or the Rock markets at that point. And the market that they had *no* share of was the Black market.

With the awareness that there had been an increase in the disposable income of Black people in general and the fact that there was an increase in Black films and Black stars developing, I saw no reason why there could not be a Black album market as well.

I went straight ahead on creative feel, intuitive reasoning and common sense, *not* because I had any study or blueprint. I've never read that study, I've never seen it, and I've certainly never used it as a blueprint. (The study) did not form the basis for any move that I made. Regarding Stax, I just happened to have gotten a call from Al Bell. He asked if I was interested. That's all that happened.

People have said that I pioneered and (influenced) the established company, that's when I got the NATRA award (then NARAS) …it's the same thing, really, as what happened after Monterey with Joplin, Blood, Sweat & Tears, and Santana.

Obviously, after we did that, every record company established Rock departments or contemporary Rock departments. They made a turnaround in what their previous sensibility had been in the Rock world after what we had done, and they made it similarly after we broke through and pioneered in making large companies' presence felt in Black music.

JOHN SMITH
1981

Veteran executive John Smith was a key aide to Al Bell during Stax Record's heyday. Here, he discusses Stax's relationship with CBS during the early BMM days.

Regarding Stax's relationship with CBS, as with any deal, there are certain lines or certain languages expressed as to how the deal is to work. I guess that is the letter of the contract, but the spirit of the contract was totally differently.

When two individuals such as Al Bell and Clive Davis sat down and worked out how they were going to work together, all the mechanics were not put into the contract, for whatever reasons. I don't know if you can put certain things in the *spirit* of a contract.

When Clive Davis left CBS, the relationship changed instantly, *that day*. We found out that Clive had been locked out of his office. And when he got off the elevator, there were guards there to escort him out of the building.

We knew about it within a half hour after it happened. So then, we, at Stax, developed certain fears about what was going on because the deal really had been made with the man, based on the integrity of the man, and all of that.

So, some of the first things we found, in addition to the chaos surrounding the company when the president was let go, was that *there was* a period of reorganization and adjustment, insecurity. There's a new guy coming in to bring his entire regime. Information was scant and second-level management was attempting to cover their asses.

A lot of the CBS executives were attempting to ingratiate us with strokes, and what have you, because of what we represented dollar wise to CBS. At that time, Stax was actually CBS's biggest Independent custom label entity. Philly International was in the process of trying to get their land legs. They were still a little wobbly at that time.

We were *there*, off the tremendous success of Isaac Hayes with *Shaft*. It was just an out-and-out smash record. The spirit of the deal, and the initial working relationship came as a blessing from the top. If Clive Davis says, "We're going to get behind the deal and support it," it's going to filter down to his subordinates.

When Clive Davis left, Goddard Lieberson took over. He was less into the music, I think, than Clive Davis. He was more corporate oriented, so the relationship changed. With that, you're dealing with a Black entity in Memphis, Tennessee, that was everything but corporate. Stax was very personalized, a family kind of operation. Any relationships that were entered into were based on more than a person's talent or ability. It was 60-70 percent ability and 30-40 percent vibes.

When the deal was made, there was a tremendous amount of interfacing, a lot of meetings between CBS and Stax in Memphis. We felt that it was *super* important to have the meetings in Memphis, where they'd have the opportunity to see our offices.

Part of our strategy was to drive home the one key point that we were not a production company; we were a full-service record company with an advertising department, a publicity department, and so forth. We were highly departmentalized.

We didn't just have an A&R department and a promotion department. We did other things. We had enjoyed a lot of success, and we weren't about to have a company like CBS come down to Memphis and tell us they were the experts in Black music. By our past successes, we felt that we had demonstrated that we were the experts. CBS was trying to get into it, but we were already there.

It was vitally essential that CBS respected that we were a full-service record company, and they were to deal with us accordingly. They had to respect us, if this deal was going to work.

You can't base it on the prospect that you're giving out another "Nigger" deal. You know how those kind of deals go inherently. They're either designed to fail, or are under-capitalized.

That's a key, central difference between record companies making a serious investment in Black marketing departments, and the social programs of the 60s and 70s that ultimately failed. The social programs failed because participants didn't have enough training, whereas, the business world is more training and opportunity-oriented.

In the example of a record company, the relatively few people that were allowed into the larger corporate structure could develop the expertise and filter into population and help generate tremendous revenue for the company, if given the opportunity.

The prospect of an incredible return argued well for giving opportunities to the Vernon Slaughters, Paris Eleys, Win Winfords, and the various other people who have actively made CBS such an impressive Black music market force.

In the case of social action programs, gains were made grudgingly. It was a student-developed idea to have a Black studies program, whereas the idea for a fiscally successful Black music marketing setup came right from the top—from Clive Davis himself. That speaks *tremendously* for the relative reception each idea received.

As soon as many of the people who had objections could see their own destinies were directly tied to the success of Black music, because the Pop albums they were giving promotional priority to became loss leaders and Black music divisions are not able to tolerate losses from a political standpoint.

These people supported Black music promotion. Once things settled down, Jim Tyrrell and Ron Alexenburg were charged with the day-to-day responsibility for making Stax/CBS work. We were assigned to Epic.

The daily contact with them was unreal. We spoke to them six to seven times a day, constantly on top of what was going on in the marketplace—anticipating problems and working them out. We saw an attitude of really trying to make it work.

Those who were there working with it, saw their futures with the company tied to the relationship. Some were looking into the future, some were looking at the presidency, and the president was looking at being Chairman of the Board. It was a chain reaction, and we were courted because we were the big cats on the block.

CBS was also concerned with its image at the time. They flatly refused a Richard Pryor project because they didn't understand the dollar impact, the dollars that could be generated for them on this comedy was always kept underneath the counter.

They were afraid of it, and once they listened to it, they were absolutely certain that they didn't want to be a part of it. So, they missed an album that was super, super big in the interests of image.

We went through independent distributors with it. Stax Records had six labels, CBS only took three of them—Stax, Volt, and Enterprise. Three labels that Stax retained and distributed independently were Truth, Respect, and Partee.

Truth was a Gospel label and CBS didn't want anything to do with that. Respect featured the Rev. Jesse Jackson, and Partee had Moms Mabley and Richard Pryor. These were distributed through independents.

Excerpted from a Columbia Sales Meeting in San Francisco in 1974, the following is a Special Markets Presentation. Note the sophisticated tone blending 'sociology' with sales demographics.

Black music began in fields and small clubs, and when it came time to record it, John Hammond and others brought it into the studio, but when it came time to merchandise it, it turned into something called 'Race' Records.

A sample of the sophistication of CBS's move into Black music marketing

In 1920 Columbia Records made 'Race' Records. The Okeh label produced music especially for Black audiences, and only released it in outlets in Black communities. In 1973 that same music has become classics for the entire industry. In fact, the concept of Black music has exploded beyond the boundaries of color. As late as the 1950s, Black records were covered by White artists and turned them into Pop hits.

In 1973, Black music is only defined by the artist who makes it, because everyone loves and listens to it—and most of all buys it. Billy Paul, Harold Melvin & the Blue Notes were also Pop hits. Since las year's convention, we have earned over $50 million on Black albums and singles. Billy Paul's "Me & Mrs. Jones" sold 2,000,095 singles. The O'Jays' "Love Train" hit 1,407,000 singles. And Harold Melvin & the Blue Notes, "If You Don't Know Me By Now," was at 1,506,000. Billy Paul, the O'Jays, and Harold Melvin & the Blue Notes won six Gold records for albums and singles.

And within the last year, the relationship between Columbia Records and Leon Huff and Kenny Gamble and their family of labels, has been one of the most spectacular success stories of the entire music business. Gamble and Huff have turned out an unprecedented string of hits.

And with artists like Isaac Hayes, the Staple Singers, Johnny Taylor, the Manhattans, and Sly, Columbia, Epic, and the Columbia custom label family have had a spectacular year of hits. In fact, the Black singles market has become one of the strongest foundations of the entire music industry.

R&B singles have sold up to one million units in the Black market alone. "I Miss You" by Harold Melvin & the Blue Notes did 600,000 singles with very little Top 40 airplay. The Manhattans had sold over 200,000 records before "There's No Me Without You" even reached the Pop charts. The Manhattans had sold over 100,000 records in one market—New York City—and that was on R&B airplay alone.

Ten years ago, there were 30 R&B stations. Today there are over 250. And as Harold Melvin & the Blue Notes proved, their ability to sell records is undisputed.

They have also become the most important staging ground for #1 Pop hits. "Crying in the Chapel"—the Orioles 1953 hit—was probably the first song to break from the top of the R&B charts into the Top 20 of the national charts. Still, that was at the time when Elvis Presley was covering R&B hits.

The White audience was given Black music with White singers. Slowly, that changed. From the 60s, more and more Black singles and albums crossed over. Black artists like the Supremes began to enlarge their White audiences. Today, Al Green plays Philharmonic Hall. Stevie Wonder does the Rolling Stones tour. Black artists like Aretha Franklin, Isaac Hayes, Sly Stones and the O'Jays have consciously broken down all the barriers.

Today, singles and albums constantly jump from the R&B charts onto the Hot Pop charts. Black crossover records have become one of the most invigorating ingredients in our Hot music. And there is a new force that has speeded the growth of crossover records: 'Black Underground Radio' like WBLS FM in New York, WHUR FM in Washington, and WDAS FM in Philadelphia.

Five years ago, this concept in FM radio programming barely existed. Today it is one of the most important places for Black music to meet with both a Black and White audience.

The Black Program Director is where Earth, Wind & Fire have found a potent new home. In New York, Philadelphia, and Washington where Earth, Wind & Fire have had concentrated Black FM airplay, they have also had their most enormous sales.

Black FM stations have become a vital new force in selling Black records, especially Black albums and crossing them over. Actually, in major metropolitan areas, where there is a tremendously high percentage of Black population, crossover R&B hits should not be that difficult to obtain.

But, of course, there are still the inevitable problems of moving a record from R&B to Top 40. The response from White programmers is sometimes a song is 'too Black,' whatever that means. They may pass a record for fear that their playlist is beginning to sound like the local R&B station. Or they may just want to hold off, waiting for a response in other key White markets.

Today, Detroit and Cleveland are probably the most responsive markets to R&B airplay. CKLW is always influenced by the record sales off Detroit's two Black stations. And the point is that every White programmer should be made as responsive as possible to the enormous sales generated by R&B airplay.

Actually, if the truth was told, every programmer should be sensitive to Black records immediately upon their release. There is no reason to wait for Black re-orders and bullets on the R&B charts.

Black songs should be considered like any other songs. But largely, that is not the case. So, we point with pride to our successful ability to cross over records. It has been nothing short of phenomenal.

In addition to our tremendous success with Columbia acts, Earth, Wind & Fire, and, of course, the Gamble and Huff acts, we've made four new distribution deals. Tommy Records with Tom Bell; T-Neck Records; the Holland Dozier Holland label; and the monster, Stax, with their family of custom labels.

Reviewing; we've got some of the most talented producers and leaders in Black music. Men like Al Bell, Jim Stewart, Tom Bell, and Holland Dozier Holland. And we've got the most amazing line up of Black artists ever assembled. Freda Payne, General Johnson, Chairman of the Board, the Isley Brothers, Albert King, Eddie Floyd, Rufus Thomas, Carla Thomas, the Barkays, Luther Ingram, the Staple Singers, and the giant Isaac Hayes.

We can expect enormous sales from these artists, possibly greater sales than ever before, because these artists enjoy the benefit of a new and important Black media. Today, we have music publications like *Soul* and *Soul Sounds*. There is also *Essence* and *Encore*, and teeny bopper magazines like *Black Stars* and *Right On*. National publications like *Ebony* and *Jet* have begun to carry music features.

And Don Cornelius' *Soul Train* is the only TV show in the country that breaks records. Magazines, newspapers, radio, and TV have become instrumental in the growth of Black stars and Black sales. Two years ago, Columbia Records was doing a minor business with Black one stops. Today, Black one stops have become some of our biggest accounts.

But now, Columbia Records must face some very new and different merchandising problems. The small Black merchant is like no other in the record business. Records are sold in every kind of conceivable outlet—in furniture stores, barbershops, candy stores. Racks are set up wherever they can fit. And each of these stores cater to small insulated neighborhoods, sometimes as small as one block.

Obviously, the record industry does not have the man power to service each of these stores individually. But, that's just a cop out. There is still a lot that can be done. We have an obligation to ourselves, to our artists, and to the Black community.

It's now clear that records are not reaching the small merchant fast enough. He has no personal relationship to this company. In the past, he has gotten no help in merchandising, he gets no help with advertising, he does not know how to expand his record business. He doesn't sell catalog, and he doesn't know what catalog will sell.

They must be full line with both White and Black catalog. They must be in the neighborhoods. They must: service the neighborhood stores with new speed and increased selectivity. Black merchants want to buy from Blacks.

They are often intimidated by the huge White Columbia Records image. Studies have shown that 70 percent of Black singles are sold out of small Black merchants' stores.

These are valuable retail outlets. Important retail outlets that still feel disconnected from the major record companies. In New York, Chicago, and Los Angeles, we have created a program of local detail men to make a connection between the local merchant and the record company.

The detail man will help merchandise. He will provide point of sale material and samples. Along with the Black one stop and Black promotion merchandise, he can help the merchant to sell catalog.

A personal human connection has to be created between Columbia distribution and the people who retail our product. It's also up to each Columbia branch to enlarge its involvement in the Black community. We have to encourage Black retailers to come in. We have to help them expand their business, and find out the best way to finance expansion.

We also must know the best advertising media for the Black community. What radio, what print will be the most effective and how the Black retailer can use it. With that in mind, Columbia has launched a huge Soul promotion.

We have created a newspaper supplement that can be tied into every account, even the smallest Black stores that have never gotten sales material before can use it.

The promotion will feature Isaac Hayes, Johnny Taylor, Sly, Earth, Wind & Fire, and the Intruders. It will include hits and catalog. Here, we are creating a direct connection with dealers. We are creating sales, and we are showing the small retailer that catalog is a viable product.

There was a time when Black music was ascending to ultimate heights, it was it. Changes in taste throughout the English Rock invasion diverted attention away from it, but Black sales remained at consistent high rates. Now Black music has grown even further.

The Black record market is capable of enormous new sales, and Black music has found tremendous new acceptance in White markets. A little over two years ago, Columbia, Epic, and the Columbia Family of Custom Labels made an enormous commitment to Black music. And today, thanks to our enormous growth and success in Black music, we can honestly call ourselves the Family of Music.

MARNIE TATTERSALL
1981

Marnie Tattersall was a graduate student at the 'B' school during the period of the study. She was one of the first students hired into the BMM team.

I got involved in the study because I was at the business school and had to do a research report. It's a half year requirement. There wasn't a whole lot unusual about the request for the study. Many companies are able to develop fresh, bright ideas through student research at a very low expense. I think it cost less than $5,000 for the whole thing, including personal expenses, airfare, meals, hotels, and taxis. I did most of the interviews and footwork.

I think CBS came to us because Clive Davis was Harvard Law and Larry Isaacson had graduated from the Business School. Clive's interest (in Black music) was already headed that way, but the study validated the direction. There was, however, strong divergence on CBS's part from our recommendations regarding budget. I see that as a factor of corporate racial life in this country.

Six of us were involved in the study for six months. Most of the data was derived through personal interviews, with the math part coming from a small sample in the Boston area. Priorities were established by our professor as an academic exercise. All of us during the time envisioned ourselves as already in the corporate world in our training.

I agree that Clive Davis was a key component in the *Establishment* delving into Black music. Having talents like Kenny Gamble and Leon Huff available made it even easier. Unfortunately, most Blacks who were hired in haven't integrated into areas outside of their home discipline (sales, promotion, etc.). It's sad, and not generally true among Whites.

MARNIE TATTERSALL
Thoughts on the Harvard Report 45 Years Later
2017

When I participated in the Harvard Report for Columbia Records Group over four decades ago, I took the project seriously even though I didn't fully realize the role it would play in my life.

MY BACKGROUND

I was born in Sri Lanka, and I'm a preacher's kid. My father was a Methodist missionary in Sri Lanka and my mother was a native of Sri Lanka. My background and viewpoint is different, having lived in other countries (Sri Lanka, England, U.S.A) and being exposed to other cultures and religions since birth.

We immigrated to the United States when I was 11 years old. We lived right outside Portland, Oregon, and I considered myself a country bumpkin. I didn't get into Black music until I went to college where I was introduced to Wes Montgomery and other Jazz artists. Then came Rock & Roll like Chicago. I loved it all.

After I graduated from college in 1970, (with a Bachelors in Business Administration), I applied at the brokerage firm of Merrill Lynch, Pierce, Fenner & Smith. The man who interviewed me told me quite frankly, "There aren't any farmers in Oregon who would trust their money to a woman, can you type?"

Well, I couldn't type, so I applied for and was accepted into the Harvard Business School MBA program. In a roundabout way, I can attribute my dream career in the music industry—that I love—to the 70's sexism of Wall Street.

I was one of about 30 women in a class of 700, and Harvard Business school had only been admitting women for about 45 years at that time! I found myself in class with Efrem Zimbalist III, Teddy Roosevelt IV and Joseph Perella, who became extremely successful in mergers and acquisitions.

I wasn't used to being around those types of men, and I was very intimidated. That intimidation, however, forced me to come out of my shell, speak up, and contribute my perspective, opinion, and analysis to situations that I was a part of or involved in. I didn't have a scholarship, I didn't get a free ride. I had to pay for it myself by taking out student loans. That gave me the determination to work hard and make the most of my education.

THE STUDY

"A Study of the Soul Music Environment Prepared for Columbia Records Group"—The Harvard Report, as it is called—was to research and analyze the prospect of Columbia Records Group (CBS Records) penetrating the Black music market. The study was initially the brainchild of CBS record executive Larry Isaacson.

Larry Isaacson

Larry Isaacson was a Harvard MBA who was working at CBS Records. He was the liaison between CBS Records and Harvard. I think he's the one who came up with the idea to do the study and pitched the idea to Clive Davis, (then President of Columbia Records/CBS records, and a Harvard Law graduate).

He suggested to Davis that he could get the study done by letting a group of bright young Harvard students do it, rather than hiring an expensive consulting firm. Because we were students, the study was practically free to CBS except for travel expenses, which were minimal.

Davis gave the greenlight for the study. Once the pitch was made to Harvard by Isaacson, it was then offered to interested students. Isaacson, Logan Westbrooks, and Bruce the professor met with the students at Harvard. Westbrooks became the contact person and the liaison between CBS and the Harvard students. He provided the lead questions and directed us as to what type of information to look for. He then selected the cities, radio stations, and retail outlets for us to contact.

We were to diagnose, evaluate, determine the feasibility of, and recommend a strategy to accomplish CBS Records' goal of penetrating the Black music market. The basic intent for the study was to validate what Davis was already doing, and that was to bring in more Black artists to CBS Records. He had already signed a distribution deal with Gamble and Huff and their company Philadelphia International Records (PIR).

Isaacson felt the study would be good as validation for the effort. Westbrooks noted that Isaacson believed getting this report started, finished, and validated would help him (Isaacson) get recognition and lead to his upward mobility within the company.

Under the Columbia Records banner head, there was Columbia Records, there was Epic Records, and there were others. Columbia Records itself, Clive Davis was the head honcho of all of it, including Epic and everything else.

There was an open president position at Columbia Records, and, per Westbrooks, Isaacson had apparently thought that bringing in the Harvard Report would maybe help him become the president of Columbia Records. Well, it didn't happen. He did not become the president of Columbia Records.

HARVARD STUDENTS INVOLVEMENT

Companies would come knocking on the door of Harvard Business School and ask for students to work on projects for them. CBS was not the only one. I, along with five other MBA students volunteered for this particular project.

As graduate students, we had to fulfill our thesis requirements. We could either come up with our own or work on a project for a company. So, that's how we got into it—to fulfill a requirement to become Harvard MBAs.

Now, that said, certainly I had a love of all kinds of music, including Black music. The other people I was working on this project with also loved music, but they were basically not interested in going into the music business. I was thrilled at the opportunity to get into the music business after I had toyed with the idea of going to work on Wall Street. Many people who graduate from Harvard Business School start their own companies or end up on Wall Street.

Love of music, however, was not a prerequisite to be a part of the project. In fact, the study was specifically about the business aspect of music and not necessarily music, in and of itself.

CONCERNS OF CBS

One of their concerns about delving into the Black music market was the image. For example, in Rock & Roll it was called it sex, drugs, and Rock & Roll (and Payola). In R&B it was also called sex, drugs (and Payola). It had been easier for Columbia Records—other than when it went into Race, Jazz, and Gospel music—to stay away from Black music and Black promotion.

From what I saw and learned, Black promotion and what was done to promote things within Black music was really no different from what they did to promote White music. There was sex, drugs and Payola in White music and in Black music.

THE GOAL

The project took six months to complete. Based on our research, we estimated that it would take three years for CBS Records to overcome Atlantic and Motown. It actually happened within six months. But again, that's because Gamble and Huff was such a power house. And right off the bat, there was the O'Jays with "Backstabbers." There was Harold Melvin & the Blue Notes, there was Billy Paul. It was that whole genre of music right off the bat. And I was honored to receive Gold records since I was involved in the marketing of that music.

Those songs just came out of the box and they were hits. And they were hits because of one of the important things we learned in our study—that CBS Records was such a distribution power house. With them being able to distribute Black music, they would start to have hits because they were a distribution arm par excellence bar none.

ARTISTS FLOCKED TO CBS

After the success of Gamble and Huff and PIR, people were coming out of the woodwork trying to get deals with Columbia. Columbia was also very active in its own Artists & Repertoire and pulling people in. When I joined the label, they didn't have a lot of Soul music, but they had a large group of Jazz artists.

John Hammond was a legendary A&R person at CBS at that time and had been there for years. He not only brought in Bob Dylan, he brought in the Jazz trumpeter Miles Davis, Count Basie, and many others. The Jazz depth within CBS was huge, and it was basically because of John Hammond, as I recall and in my opinion.

One of the groups that signed with CBS Records was Earth, Wind & Fire. How they actually got to CBS, I don't recall. People in the business at that time—which was about some 40 odd years ago—knew that CBS was THE distributor. So, if you could be connected to CBS, more power to you. There were many artists and people with record labels that were looking for distribution deals with CBS.

DISTRIBUTION

Distribution was crucial for success—responsible for getting the music to consumers. The bigger the distribution channel, the more music lovers could be reached. CBS's distribution channels were international.

CBS already had the distribution deal with Gamble and Huff. A few years later, they made a distribution deal to market Stax Records.

Stax, of course, was much more established. It was a full-fledged record label, whereas Gamble and Huff was a production company. They produced hot music that went to the top of the charts.

I think it's safe to say that most people—artists and labels—in the business saw it as an opportunity. They wanted to get on top of the charts, make money and become famous. Major distribution was necessary for that to happen. That's the main component CBS could provide to them.

Now, in terms of others like Motown, were they liking this concept? I don't think so. Was Atlantic liking this concept? I don't think so. They knew that they would now have serious distribution challenges vis-à-vis CBS being the number one record distribution company at that time.

RECOMMENDATIONS

CBS did not accept all our recommendations. One, in particular, was my suggestion that CBS Television should broadcast Don Cornelius's show *Soul Train*. I felt so strongly about it that I wrote a separate Addendum to the report. There were six of us, and I was the only one pushing for it. That's why I wrote it separately.

They passed on *Soul Train* because this report was being done for CBS Records, not CBS Television, which is a whole different entity. They could do, and did do, and knew they could successfully get into the Black music business without taking on Don Cornelius. Not that there-was anything wrong with Don Cornelius, but they had never even done Dick Clark's "American Bandstand." So, it was no big deal to them or their success.

It was only me that made that recommendation, it wasn't the team. And that's why, interestingly, in that report the only name mentioned of somebody who worked on it was me because I did that Addendum. I describe myself as a progressive activist, and I campaign for something I feel strongly about.

That doesn't always mean I'm right. For instance, this is not a part of the Harvard Report, but it's an example of my advocacy. After I was hired by Westbrooks to work at CBS, I campaigned for something that, in retrospect, was a dumb thing.

Billy Paul had "Me and Mrs. Jones," which was a huge Pop hit. On that album (*360 Degrees of Billy Paul*) there were other potential Pop hits. We could help choose what the next single should be. And many of us—particularly me—thought that "Am I Black Enough for You" was the next best song. We thought it was the most sensible song, so we advocated that it should be the next single from that album.

It turned out to be a big mistake because that decision took a man who had just crossed over into Pop and pulled him way into 'blackness.' It was very difficult to cross over into Pop, and we should have kept him in Pop. The song didn't even do that well. There were people who liked it, but it didn't do well on the charts. "Me and Mrs. Jones" was #1 on the Billboard Top 100 chart. "Am I Black Enough for You" was #79 on the same chart. If success is based on numbers, you can see the stark contrast.

CONTROVERSY

I wasn't aware of any controversy about the Harvard Report, but I've read where we were criticized years later for 'helping' a huge White company jump into a place where only Black labels like Motown and Atlantic had been. But then again, Motown was Black, Atlantic was not. Atlantic was Ahmet Ertegun, Herb Abramson, and Jerry Wexler. They had Aretha Franklin, Archie Bell & the Drells, and others.

I don't know, but most people who had the benefit of being involved with that ride would probably feel that it was a good thing. I'm not sure. Do I feel that CBS had anything to do with Motown's eventual changing, I don't think so. I think Motown was going to change anyway because one brilliant impresario—Berry Gordy—could not hold on to it forever and ever in a vacuum.

IN CONCLUSION

Bottom line is that our thesis project "A Study of the Soul Music Environment Prepared for Columbia Records Group" was simply a feasibility study and suggested marketing strategy for success. There has been a lot of confusion surrounding the Harvard Report, some even insinuating a nefarious intent.

Our project did not discuss or have anything to do with Black music aesthetics—we were not trying to pilfer or plunder a culture. But, we did all believe that Black/Soul music should have more exposure and "cross-over." We were graduate students who approached our stated project with clarity of purpose primarily focused on obtaining our MBAs. I don't think anything more than that should be read into it.

All in all, I'm pleased with the path I took. I didn't feel like I wanted to end up on Wall Street making rich people richer. I'm not driven to make money. I'm driven to do things I love and to have a good time. And I certainly did all that in the record business. I had a blast. And the same thing when I went into the film business, I enjoyed it.

One thing I've always been thankful for is that I loved all my professional jobs, which is not the case for so many people. Around the time I got the gig working for Westbrooks—and I was the only person from the team interested in going to work for CBS.

I once saw a poster with a Walt Whitman quote: *"Most people lead lives of quiet desperation."* I bought that poster and kept it on the wall in my office at CBS Records because every day that I went to work, I did not lead a life of quiet desperation. Quite the opposite.

VERNON SLAUGHTER
1981

Marketing executive Vernon Slaughter rounds out the discussion with this optimistic assessment of the Black music industry.

The concept of Black music marketing was developed by CBS to enable it to effectively market records by Black artists, and to reflect the Black consumer's point of view in terms of marketing. Underneath that structure, since marketing is generally an umbrella term that encompasses several areas, promotion is the most important and there is also merchandising and artist development.

Bringing together a group of experts, and working within a team concept, enables CBS to develop penetration within the Black music market place, and to set up the foundation for crossover success. Black music marketing could not exist within a vacuum. It was not created as such and could not exist if it was in a vacuum. The purpose was to provide the foundation for initial market penetration.

Another important aspect was to develop a sense of commitment to the Black community, putting something back in rather than just taking it out. The Black music department served all those different functions quite well.

At every other major record company, with the obvious exception of Motown, the Black music marketing or special marketing departments were formed as a direct result of CBS's success in this area.

There will continue to be a nucleus, a core of individuals who are specialists, who understand the idiosyncrasies and ever-changing nature of the market place, and who have the expertise to act in order to achieve the same objectives (as before). Not, as I've said earlier, in a vacuum, but in tandem with the other elements of the record company.

It is true that the concept of special markets was borrowed from other industries like General Motors and other companies. Obviously, it was the result of two things: First, the recognition by CBS of the amount of money available in the Black market place. Secondly, there was the social pressure manifested during the 60s and culminated in the early 70s. I agree that there is an obvious parallel with other social institutions.

The changes that Black music marketing have gone through recently also reflects the parallel of *retrenchment*. In situations like this, the question always pops up: Does big business influence society, or is it a reflection of society? It's almost a question of what comes first, the chicken or the egg.

I think they're both tied in sociologically. You can't talk business without talking sociology. I think there will always be a need and a desire for Black individuals to stay within this framework of marketing to the Black consumer.

I also think there are certain points that have to be stressed. One, a majority of the same techniques apply to marketing to anybody—White, Black, purple, green whoever.

Therefore, the positive aspects of creating these departments was to give individuals like myself a real start to opportunities which I probably would not have had otherwise. The point is, I feel that I am qualified to market any other forms of music.

There are individuals at many other companies who have come through these departments and are just as qualified. Black music departments provided a necessary training ground for Blacks getting into the business, and there will be a continuing need to do that.

At the same time, and I realize I keep saying the same thing, but nothing can work—nothing lives in a vacuum. Only in tandem with the other elements of a record can Black artists achieve the level of success that they deserve. As specialists, our job is to set up the conditions and set up the foundation.

Ultimately, the success of the record company dealing with Black artists is based on their ability to enhance upon the foundation that is laid down by the Black music marketing experience.

L-R Ron Alexenberg, Leon Huff, Clive Davis, Kenny Gamble signing of the CBS/Philadelphia International Label deal.

QUESTIONS FOR REFLECTION

Answer each question with a brief essay.

1. What lessons do the CBS-Harvard Study point out, regarding the potential relationship between academic research and music industry needs?

2. Why was CBS so influential with its move into the Black music area?

3. In an evolutionary sense, what stage does the marketing of Black music seem to be in? Fully integrated with the system? On the periphery? How important has Black music become as a market force?

CHAPTER 14

THE HARVARD REPORT

HARVARD UNIVERSITY

GRADUATE SCHOOL OF BUSINESS ADMINISTRATION

GEORGE F. BAKER FOUNDATION

Soldiers Field
Boston, Massachusetts 02163
May 11, 1972

Logan H. Westbrooks

The findings contained in this report are the result of an investigation of the Soul music environment and analyses of relevant data conducted by the Columbia Records Project Group. The analyses led to three major conclusions pertaining to Columbia's present and desired postures in the Soul music industry:

(1) A market opportunity for CRG exists in this area.

(2) CRG's previous efforts in Soul music have not been adequate.

(3) Several changes in CRG's organization and orientation will be required for success in the Soul music market.

To expand on the above conclusions, it was estimated that a market of approximately $60 million at manufacturers' prices exists for Soul music recordings. CRG's previous efforts have been hampered by an organization staffed by personnel oriented to the popular music field which differs fundamentally from Soul music in the critical factors required for success. In order to become a significant factor in the Soul music industry, CRG must establish an internal Soul music group and improve the quality of Soul music product released on recordings.

Respectfully submitted,

Creative Marketing Strategy
Columbia Records Project Group

THE HARVARD REPORT

A STUDY OF THE SOUL MUSIC ENVIRONMENT PREPARED FOR COLUMBIA RECORDS GROUP

I. INTRODUCTION
  Purpose
  Scope
  Major Conclusions

II. ANALYSIS
  Definition of the Market
  Size
  Historical Development
  Evolution of Soul
  Impact on Other Sectors of Popular Music Culture
  Role of Specialized National Companies in
    Broadening this Market
  Internal Dynamics
  Airplay/Playlists/Crossover
  Payola
  Competition
  Analysis of Columbia Records Group

III. RECOMMENDATION AND RATIONALE

IV. PLAN OF ACTION

I. INTRODUCTION

Purpose

The objectives of this study were:

1. To examine the feasibility of an expanded Columbia Record Group (CRG) Soul program.
2. To evaluate CRG's present organization in the context of the requirements for that expansion.
3. To examine the implications of such an explanation for CRG from strategic as well as financial perspectives.

Scope

The Soul segment of the music market has been analyzed from the standpoint of its historical development, its internal dynamics, and its relationship to the broader world of contemporary music. CRG's general approach to the music industry has been reviewed, with particular reference to its efforts to date in the Soul market.

This study has confronted limitations inherent to any quantitatively-oriented analysis of the record industry: the sources of information are limited and widely dispersed. Despite these limitations, the degree of uncertainty associated with the resultant conclusions is not inordinately high.

Major Conclusion

The primary conclusions resulting from the study are:

1. A market opportunity exists in the Soul segment of the music market.

2. CRG's past efforts to cultivate this market have lacked virtually all of the elements critical for success.

3. To capitalize on that market opportunity, CRG must significantly modify and substantially broaden its current efforts to cultivate that market.

II. ANALYSIS

Definition of the Soul Market

A definition of the Soul market is critical both to the determination of its size and composition. The issue is very complex, and there is no generally accepted definition. Efforts to define it in terms of a 'certain sound' lack precision. Defining it in terms of specific artists can be problematic because a given artist may produce a Soul record one day, and a Rock record the next. At the same time, artists do manifest tendencies in one or another direction. A rough typology based upon three broad tendencies is one way to suggest the Soul market's boundaries:

SOUL CONTENT OF ARTIST'S REPERTOIRE

Almost All	Mixed	Almost None
James Brown	Isaac Hayes	Miles Davis
Wilson Picket	Joe Williams	Johnny Mathis
Aretha Franklin	Roberta Flack	Gloria Lynn
The Chi-Lites	Fifth Dimension	Mills Brothers
Clara Ward Singers	Sly & the Family Stone	Thelonious Monk
Joe Tex	Lou Rawls	Dionne Warwick

Another way of getting at the definition of Soul is by enumerating some of its features:

- It is characterized in many instances by a raw, driving beat that is as much viscerally as aurally experienced.
- It enjoys great popularity among Black people.
- It is generally though not exclusively produced by Black artists

Finally, from the standpoint of convenience, it can be defined as the kind of music which is likely to appear on Billboard's "Soul" Chart, and the kind of music likely to be programmed on Black listener-oriented radio stations such as WILD Boston, WWRL New York, WJMO Cleveland, WVON Chicago and KGFJ Los Angeles.

Size

Beyond the problem of market definition lie difficulties in quantifying the market because of the virtual absence of relevant published data. None of the companies in the Soul market, nor in the entire record industry, for that matter, are free-standing, publicly-owned. They are either subsidiaries or divisions of conglomerates, or privately held. As a consequence, published information is scarce. The sources analyzed (Appendix A) suggest a market on the order of $60 million at manufacturers' prices, broken down as follows:

Albums	$30 million
Singles	$30 million

Factory prices of $2.50 and $0.50 for albums and singles respectively yield this unit size for the market:

Albums	12 million
Singles	60 million

The size of the total recorded music market has been estimated at $1,660 million for 1970. Since that figure is based upon average 'suggested retail price,' it is necessary to convert Soul albums and singles into equivalent figures, $5.50 and $0.90 respectively, to determine Soul's share of the total recorded music market:

Albums	$66 million
Singles	$54 million
TOTAL	$120 million

$120 million / $1,660 million = 7.23%

This estimate is considered to be on the conservative side, since it excludes those sales of artists in the 'Mixed' category, which are considered more in the Rock than Soul area. A less restrictive approach would probably assign a total market share on the order of 10% to Soul music.

Historical Development of Soul Music Market

For the purposes of this analysis, there are three broad trends in the historical development of Soul music which are especially relevant:

1. There has been an evolution of Soul from a series of isolated, local-regional styles, sounds, and artists towards a more homogeneous and stylized sound almost national in the scope of its popularity among Blacks. And with this has come the emergence of Black artists with a national following within the Black community.

2. Soul music has had a significant and continuing influence on other sectors of the popular music culture in the United States and Great Britain, initially through the medium of White artists who first covered, then later interpreted Soul music for White audiences. Ultimately this influence broadened through the medium of Black Soul artists themselves as they belatedly received exposure and access to White audiences.
3. Aggressive, innovative, specialized national companies highly focused on Soul, have played a key role in broadening the market for Soul music both inside and outside the Black community.

The historic disinterest in the Black record buying market by the major record companies gave rise to a tier of small independent record companies which catered to it. At that time, the Black market consisted of local/regional audiences with particular tastes.

The companies which emerged in a given region tended to concentrate particularly on styles with local associations. These independents were small and almost seriously under-capitalized. They relied almost entirely on the ingenuity of their owners, who functioned as their own talent scouts, producers, promoters and distributors.

They were essentially running their record companies out of the back trunks of their cars. Operating from a small and uncertain base, they had few resources with which to expand their operations. Almost all of the important ones attempted to break into the national market.

Not until 1953 did one of these succeed in reaching the White market with a Black vocal group. 'Jubilee' made this breakthrough with its 'Crying in the Chapel,' by the Orioles, which made the Pop music Top Twenty. By and large, however, these independents had short life cycles. Even the ones who were able to survive, such as Atlantic, suffered because they did not have the resources with which to expand their promotional and distribution networks. Thus, local hits remained that: local hits, because of the difficulties in achieving more exposure.

The treatment of Black artists and writers by the major record companies during this period can be described as racist. Cover versions of R&B hits by White artists were common practice in the 1940s and 1950s. As an example, many of Elvis Presley's hits in the 1950s, when he was a dominant force on the music scene, were nothing but cover versions of hits in the then fairly small Black market.

The lack of interest in the Black market exhibited by the major record companies also had implications for Black artists. It meant that unless a Black artist was willing to sever his ties with Black music, and instead work in the field of popular music, he would be unable to gain wide exposure.

The disinterest in Black music was not, however, universal. In the 1950s Decca had an interest in Black music. It was in fairly close touch with tastes and styles in the market and evidently appreciated the potential of the music. Mercury, too, participated in this market. But in contrast to the activity of these two companies, the reaction of RCA, Columbia, Capital and MGM to Black music was almost total indifference.

Internal Dynamics

An examination of how the record music market works, from the point at which a record is released by a record company, to the point at which the consumer makes his purchase reveals that radio is the critical link. For the record to sell, it must receive exposure; practically speaking, that means that the record be played on the radio. To do that, the record must get on a playlist.

What looks like an unbreakable circle is involved here, since one of the principal ways a record can get on a playlist is by generating sales. What provides the break in the circle is that part of the playlist which is set aside for new releases which the program director considers to have "hit potential." And it is this part of the playlist which becomes the target for all of the record promoters.

There is a very important difference between Top 40 and other types of stations, such as Soul and Easy Listening, with respect to this discretionary part of the playlist. The difference is that it is much easier to promote a new release on to a Soul and Easy Listening playlist on the strength of the product, the artist or the promoter, before that record has received any airplay.

The discretionary part of Top 40 playlists, on the other hand, is more often selected from among those new releases which have gotten on and stayed on other playlists, such as Soul. A recent study of the record industry underscores that point: "Approximately 30 percent of the records heard over Top 40 stations are selected from "down home" Blues programming of the Negro oriented stations found in most major cities, which program strictly "Rhythm and Blues" stations, it is likely to be co-opted by the Top 40 programmers and exposed to their wider audience.

The Negro audience thus serves as a test market for many of the selections that reach the Top 40 stations. Records having strong sales in the ghetto record stores as a result of airplay over R&B stations will soon be heard by Top 40 listeners."[1]

This is not to suggest that new releases are impossible to promote onto a Top 40 playlist before they have made other playlists since new releases of established artists, especially when they are following up on a recent hit, are almost certain to get some, and perhaps considerable, airplay unless the record is poor. The record company can create interest in a new record and anticipation for it by heavily promoting and advertising it before it is released.

The fact that 30 percent of the Top 40 is composed of records which have "crossed-over" from Soul stations underscores the strategic importance of Soul stations as one of the most effective vehicles for getting onto the Top 40. What this means is that the competition among promoters for Soul airplay involves far more than simply the prospect of record sales to Black consumers.

In sum, Soul radio is of strategic importance to the record companies for two principal reasons: first, it provides access to a large and growing record buying public, namely, the Black consumer. Second, and for some of the record companies more important, it is perhaps the most effective way of getting a record to a Top 40 playlist.

The critical importance of Black radio for the reasons just mentioned, coupled with the fact that Black DJs still have some, though diminishing discretion in the selection of records to be played, and the widely shared belief that Black DJs are seriously underpaid has led to widely held beliefs within the industry that payola is pervasive in Black radio.

Until recently, Black radio was considered to be the last remaining pocket of payola. A recent Jack Anderson article, however, suggests that if anything, payola is pervasive throughout the entire record industry. Anderson's article has generated considerable discussion from the industry and the government, and the issue is likely to remain alive for at least several months.

With respect to payola in Black radio, this study has identified considerable suspicion, but no evidence. Payola, of course, is difficult to document. This study cannot conclude that there is no payola in Black radio. It can be concluded, however, that some of the assumptions concerning payola might usefully be examined:

1. There have been important changes in Black radio in that there is a growing trend toward professionalization.

2. There is not as much of a discrepancy between the salaries that White and Black DJs receive, as was formerly the case.

3. The playlists of Black radio stations are getting tighter, and DJs have diminishing discretion over what is played.

4. More careful distinctions must be made between those expenses which can be considered legitimate business related expenses, and those which are nothing more than subtle forms of payola.

5. Though payola may now and in the foreseeable future continue to be a significant problem for those companies interested in cultivating this market, but unwilling to violate Federal Anti-Bribery Act to do so, it is not a decisive one.

The recent Anderson article, coupled with the immediate industry reaction, underscored the industry's reluctance to call attention to itself and to face another government investigation. This situation is likely to provoke caution and to put radio on its best behavior over the short run, at least, as a way of warding off new government investigation and legislation.

For companies interested in cultivating the Soul market, but unwilling to participate in the more obvious forms of payola, the time would appear to be opportune to move into this market. Whatever payola problems there are likely to be less salient until this current payola discussion declines.

The major internal dynamics of the industry may be summarized as follows:

1. The importance of Black radio as an avenue of access into the Black consumer market, and as a springboard into the Top 40 Charts through the phenomenon of crossover, is likely to continue. In the case of the latter, it is likely to increase to the extent that Top 40 playlists become even tighter and shorter.

2. In the short run, industry and government scrutiny of payola in the record business is likely to drive what payola there is deeper underground and reduce its immediate importance as a key obstacle in Black radio. In the long run, the growing professionalization of Black radio, and the increasing specialization between the DJ and Program Director functions is likely at least to change the locus of payola, and ultimately to reduce its overall importance.

3. While this study is inconclusive regarding the form and volume of payola in Black radio, it does conclude that, while undoubtedly a formidable obstacle, payola is not an

insurmountable one, and that a persistent and politic promotional force, using good public relations and consistently high quality product can probably go a long way toward overcoming the obstacles posed by payola for companies who are not willing to engage in that practice.

<u>Competition</u>

An expanded CRG Soul program will have to compete for the limited available airplay with three types of firms:

1. Specialized national companies, principally Motown, Stax, and Atlantic

2. Major national record companies, such as RCA, Capitol, MCA

3. Smaller independents

The specialized national companies will provide the most formidable competition. They have an entrenched position and control half of the total market. They have most of the established Soul artists. Their management and professional staffs have extensive experience in this market, and a deep understanding of its subtleties. They operate through a highly sophisticated personal and informational network which they have built up over a period of many years.

Finally, they have a profound understanding of the art form with which they work, and of its commercial possibilities. In fact, they have helped to shape it, thus are in a position to change and manipulate it while the rest of the competitors can only react to its seemingly unpredictable evolution.

CRG can expect to find itself in competition with these firms in markets which CRG presently dominates as these firms, their base in Soul well established, graduate their artists into other markets, such as the Middle of the Road and Pop.

A dominant position in Soul has provided these companies with the financial and management resources, and the consumer visibility to broaden their product lines and move into other, related markets. This underlines another element of the Soul market's importance. In a sense, it has provided these firms with the base from which to challenge the majors in other segments of the popular music market.

Second in importance will be the other major national firms which, like CRG, can be considered late-comers into this market. In the short run, should CRG decide to expand, it will find itself in competition with these firms for the limited available Black professional and management personnel who are experienced in this area. It will also find itself in competition for available Black artists, especially from those companies which may be out to "cream this market" rather than build for the future.

CRG should not find itself at any particular disadvantage with respect to these firms. It will find that they are as uninitiated and uninformed about this market as it is. Thus, an expanded CRG Soul program could quickly achieve a decided advantage over other major record companies entering this market if it did something they are not likely to do: to put together a well thought out, well planned and well financed initiative aimed at long term market penetration, rather than short term profits from an opportunistic "creaming" program.

It could also achieve an edge by providing its Soul initiative with the flexible decision making capability which its major record company competitors are not likely to have.

The small independents will represent more of an opportunity for CRG than a competitive threat. An expanded CRG program might well look to these small independents for a number of things which could strengthen its overall position.

These small independents could provide a source of product, in the form of "hot masters;" talent which could have national potential; experienced personnel for CRG's staff, in the areas of promotion and production; and serve as a source of captive independent producers.

Finally, CRG, with broadened distribution in the Black community, which an expanded Soul program would bring, could serve as a distribution arm for their proprietary product under a custom label program.

Analysis of Columbia

There are two facts which must be taken into account in examining CRG's present capabilities for broadening its Soul efforts:

1. This market has never been important to CRG. It has never systematically cultivated it.
2. Its incursions into this market, as with the Okeh and Date labels, have been sporadic, half-hearted and short-lived.

As a consequence, CRG knows little about Black consumers, Soul artists, and Black professionals in the music and related businesses, such as radio. Aside from isolated White professionals in its organization, it has little knowledge about how this market works.

It is not tied into the strategic sources of information about what is happening inside that market. And the almost total absence of Blacks at the professional and managerial levels in its organization until recently has denied it of what could have been a valuable resource for relating to that market.

CRG's historic neglect of the Soul market has brought upon it some problems in respect to its image in this market. Interviews with people in the Soul music business indicate that CRG is perceived as an ultra-rich, ultra-white giant which has for the most part chosen to snub Blacks in the business. Blacks in the trade feel that CRG has heaped upon them the ultimate insult; that of ignoring their existence.

Even when the slight involved seemingly superficial things (CRG fails to invite them to functions; DJs say they do not get free tickets to shows from CRG as do White DJs) these are seen as manifestations of a broader pattern. Further, they perceive a degree of arrogance in CRG promotion personnel who try to get airplay for a Soul product viewed by Black radio personnel as sub-standard. That these promotion personnel until recently were almost always White did not help matters.

Given CRG's present situation, an expansion in its Soul program aimed at establishing a dominant position for it in the Soul market would require a significant financial investment and organizational commitment. Time would be needed to build a base organization and to get it functioning as a cohesive unit. Experienced Soul personnel would have to be hired in the areas of A&R, production and promotion.

The present Soul roster would have to be enriched and promoted more heavily. This program could involve significant talent recruitment and development costs. Time would be needed to build productive working relationships with the trades, and with Soul radio personnel to open up the channels for the promotion and distribution of Columbia's Soul product.

Time and money would be required to sift through a variety of independent producers in order to single out those with whom a long-term relationship might be compatible. Considerable experimentation might be required to sort out an authentic, commercially viable, reproducible, and distinct Columbia sound. Such a venture aimed at long-term market penetration would probably incur losses for several years before achieving profitability.

III. RATIONALE

This raises the question of whether CRG should undertake such an expansion. The major conclusion of this study is that it should do so for several reasons:

1. The potential for profitability could be significant. Exhibit 1, based upon a level of activity provided for in Exhibit 2, estimates that the Soul program should achieve Break-Even within three years, and an Operating Profit of $1,401K by the fifth year.

2. The time is opportune. Whatever pressures there are for payola in Black radio will probably subside in the short-run, perhaps long enough to allow CRG to broaden its participation in Soul.

3. As the dominant firm in the recording industry, there is no reason why Columbia should forfeit any segment of the total market to its competitors. The Soul music market is not inconsequential. As noted above, it represents roughly seven percent of the total recorded music sales at the retail level. At the present time, CRG has but two artists, Sly and Santana, who get on Soul Charts with any consistency. And it is important to realize that they get on Soul Charts more as Rock acts crossing over into Soul, rather than as Soul entries. These two acts aside, CRG has but two or three artists with significant Soul potential.

4. Soul music has broad national appeal which extends far beyond Black consumers. Billboard's "Hot 100" which is based predominantly upon a sample of White-consumer-oriented retail outlets, will rarely have as few as 20, and can have as many as 35 records on any given week which also appear on Billboard's "Soul" Chart consisting of the Top 50 Soul hits. In short, CRG's miniscule program not only deprives it of product for Black consumers, but also limits its ability to compete within the full range of the "Hot 100." It is a commentary on Columbia's strength that it is able to

maintain its dominant position on the "Hot 100" even though it has virtually no entries for a music segment which constitutes roughly one third of that chart. A successfully expanded Soul program would strengthen CRG's already dominant position on the "Hot 100" to the point of making it practically invincible.

5. Soul radio stations offer the most effective and most direct way of getting on Top 40. This will become even more true as Top 40 playlists become tighter. By remaining marginal to this market, CRG is denying itself of one of the most direct routes for getting certain kinds of records onto Top 40.

6. Soul music is one of the very few basic art forms which is indigenous to America, although its own roots may be traced to Africa. It has been, and probably will continue to be, a vital and influential force on contemporary popular music. And Soul is by no means a static music form.

   It too will continue to change. Companies able to work successfully in this art form will be in a position to relate more dynamically to its impact on other forms of popular music, such as Pop and Rock. This will be especially important as these three music styles converge upon one another.

IV. PLAN OF ACTION

Recommended Strategy

The recommended strategy encompasses three broad areas:

1. Expand external sources of product by augmenting present custom label activity and increasing outside product resources.

2. Develop an internal means of Soul music product generation.

3. Establish a semi-autonomous Soul music product group.

The recommendations provide a means for immediate expansion of CRG's activities in the Soul music market, and a basis for coordinated, broader scale future action. The suggested actions will enable CRG to become exposed to more product offerings from varied sources while developing the internal capability to evaluate, cultivate, and promote Soul music talent.

This expansion of quality product offerings and intensified efforts in the solicitation of product will establish CRG's interest in Soul music to industry members, and contribute to the creation of a more desirable image within the industry. Consequently, increased lines of communication will be opened with industry product sources.

Two alternative sets of recommendations were considered. The first was the acquisition of a company presently strong in the Soul music business. This strategy is not a feasible one for Columbia for the following reasons:

1. The dominance of the CBS organization in the communications and entertainment industry could possibly precipitate anti-trust action if it were to attempt the acquisition of a major company in the music industry.

2. Of the three companies strong enough to offer Columbia a base from which to operate, Atlantic has been bought out by

the Kinney group, Stax was acquired by Gulf and Western, and it is rumored that Motown is not in a position to contemplate an acquisition at this time.

The second alternative, which was the acquiring of presently established talent was similarly discounted because of the following:

1. The costs of acquiring such talent would be high (it is rumored that Wilson Pickett had announced his availability for $500,000).

2. There is a risk that the performer may not produce for Columbia at expected levels of quality.

3. The base structure required to support top talent does not exist within CRG at this time. This approach would, therefore, necessitate a delay until the proper internal support has been established at CRG.

4. An approach such as this might precipitate competitive reaction if pursued vigorously.

5. The payment of significant dollar amounts to newly signed talent might lead to jealousies among artists presently under contract and escalation of their money demands.

Recommended Organization

The analysis of the Soul music industry indicates that the following functions will be critical to the success of CRG's Soul Music Group:

1. Decision making responsibility and authority for talent signings and product acquisition. Implicit in this is the assumption that the group will have an adequate budget.

2. Independent evaluation of Soul music talent and product.

3. Capability for arranging product and coordinating artist's activities within the specialized context of the Soul music form.

4. Establishment and maintenance of beneficial relationships with Soul music radio stations and dealers.

5. Coordination of Soul music sales activities with the existing sales force.

6. Integration of the Soul music group with other functional activities within Columbia, which will be necessary for support (e.g. legal, advertising, physical production, sales).

The formal organization as shown in Exhibit 4 would consist of a Director of the Soul music group, an Administrative Coordinator, Manager of National Promotion, Manager of A&R, National Sales Coordinator, two product managers, three secretaries, and twelve field promotional men.

Responsibilities

DIRECTOR OF SOUL MUSIC GROUP – would be responsible for overall coordination and management of group activities and for decisions involving talent signings and product acquisition. In addition, budget responsibility for the group would be held in this position.

ADMINISTRATIVE COORDINATOR – would act as integrative liaison between the group, and other companies within Columbia Records Group. Also, would control administrative arrangements internal to the group.

MANAGER OF NATIONAL PROMOTION – would be responsible for directing the efforts of the twelve field promotional men toward the establishment of relationships with Soul music radio stations, and dealers, and the coordination of national promotional campaigns.

MANAGER OF A&R – would perform the functions of seeking out, evaluating and developing Soul music talent. In addition, this person would handle artist relationships.

NATIONAL SALES COODINATOR – would coordinate the sales effort for Soul product with the present sales force which would be used to distribute Soul music product.

PRODUCT MANAGER – the two product managers would arrange for the packaging and merchandising of Soul product, plan national promotional campaigns for the Soul artist, and work closely with the promotional staff in their implementation.

FIELD PROMOTIONAL FORCE – would consist of four regional and eight local promotion men, and would be responsible for maintenance of relationships with Soul music radio stations, distributors, and retailers.

The proposed organization is not intended to be an additional internal label, but rather a coordinating activity for Soul product which will be able to release artists on any of the Columbia labels. The intention is not to establish rigid guidelines for the handling of Soul music artists, but rather to create the proper atmosphere for the kind of music being produced by the artist.

For example, it is conceivable that a given artist might have one record arranged, produced, and promoted through the Soul music group, and the next through the existing organization, depending on the nature of the sound.

However, overall responsibility for an artist should be specifically assigned to one of the Columbia Records Group organizations at all times, to minimize lapses in the artist's development. In the case of talent presently under contract, the desires of the artist in addition to the sound should be considered before the decision is made on which group handles the product.

The Soul music group should be semi-autonomous with the Director reporting to the President of CRG. This arrangement will provide the flexibility determined to be so important in earlier sections of this report, while manifesting top management commitment to the Soul music business. In addition, the independent nature of the group will eliminate potential conflicts resulting from having to work within an environment which does not include an understanding of either the Soul music art form or the requirements for success in this business.

Implementation

The adoption of the recommended strategy is intended to be accomplished in three phases:

1. During phase one, emphasis should be placed on establishment of market position by expanding the existing custom label operation.

2. In phase two, market position should be further established, and industry reputation developed by utilizing more externally generated product.

3. When the third phase is reached, emphasis should be placed on internal product, and the development of a distinctive Soul music sound for Columbia.

The three phases are not intended to be mutually exclusive, but rather interactive and continuous as shown by Exhibit 5. The purpose of this sequential arrangement is to indicate to the industry Columbia's interest in Soul music, and thereby attract more talent and product while providing some initial operating results.

The three-phase approach is in effect a tactic of BUYING TIME WHILE THE REQUIRED INTERNAL SUPPORT ORGANIZATION IS STAFFED AND DEVELOPED.

An added benefit will be the opportunity for acclimatization of the present CRG organization while the Soul music group is being gradually developed. During this period, an educational process can be started which will be directed toward the minimization of organizational problems.

EXHIBIT 1

YEAR	1	2	3	4	5
MARKET SIZE	$60MM	64MM	69MM	74MM	79MM
ESTIMATED LEVEL OF MARKET PENETRATION	2%	4%	5%	7%	10%
CONTRIBUTION AVAILABLE	$559K	1,193K	1,608K	2,433K	3,711K
LESS:					
FIXED COSTS	$830K	870K	915K	960K	1,010K
DIRECT COSTS	300K	500K	650K	900K	1,300K
	1,130K	1,370K	1,565K	1,860K	2,310K
OPERATING PROFIT (LOSS)	(571K)	(177K)	43K	573K	1,401K
CUMULATIVE PROFIT (LOSS)	(571K)	(748)	(705K)	(132K)	1,269K

Assumptions:

1. Market will grow at a compounded annual rate of 7%.
2. CRG will achieve a 5–1 singles-albums ratio for the first three years, and a 4–1 ratio for years 4 and 5.
3. Fixed costs will increase at the rate of 5% per year.

EXHIBIT 2

PROPOSED ANNUAL OPERATING BUDGET

1. FIELD PERSONNEL:

Regional Directors (4) @ $60K	$240K
Promotion/Sales Personnel (8) @ $25K	200K

(These figures include salary, fringe benefits, travel, entertainment, and all other expenses required to support a professional staff man in the field. CRG sources indicate travel and entertainment expenses amount to roughly three times salary for Regional Directors, and roughly one and one-half times salary for other professional staff.)

2. HEADQUARTERS PERSONNEL:

7 Professional Staff, including Director of Special Markets, National Promotion Director, Manager of A&R, National Sales Coordinator, 2 Product Managers and Administrative Coordinator	210K

(These figures include salary, fringe benefits, travel, entertainment and other related expenses.)

3 Clerical/Secretarial @ $10K	30K
3. OTHER HEADQUARTERS EXPENSES	50K
4. DISCRETIONARY BUDGET FOR TALENT DEVELOPMENT	<u>100K</u>
Total	$830K

5. RECORDING, PRODUCT PREPARATION AND PROMOTION COSTS:

Year	1	2	3	4	5
	$300K	500K	650K	900K	1,300K

NOTES TO EXHIBITS I AND II

1. Unit contributions are assumed to be as follows:

	Singles	Albums
Factory Price	.53	2.50
Less: Variable Costs	.30	1.25
Contribution	.23	1.25

Variable costs are of two types: 1) those variable to manufacturing, which includes manufacturing, warehousing, plant returns, transportation and obsolescence, 2) and those variable to selling, which includes artist and copyright royalties, union fees, sales commission and cooperative advertising.

Contribution is defined as sales revenue less variable costs.

2. Contributions for the several singles-album ratio at the different levels of market penetration is computed by dividing sales revenues by the appropriate weighted sales figure, and then multiplying the resultant figure by the weighted contribution. Weighted sales and contribution figures are derived as follows:

Singles/Albums Ratio	1-1	3-1	5-1	7-1
Singles sales	.53	1.59	2.65	3.71
Album sales	2.50	2.50	2.50	2.50
Weighted sales	3.03	4.09	5.15	6.21
Singles contribution	.23	.69	1.15	1.61
Album contribution	1.25	1.25	1.25	1.25
Weighted contribution	1.48	1.94	2.40	2.86

Thus, if market penetration = 5%, and singles-albums ration = 3-1

$60MM x 5% = $3MM
$3MM / 4.09 = 733.5K Aggregate units
733.5K x 1.94 = 1.423MM
Total Contribution = 1.423MM

3. The proposed Operating Budget includes two categories of costs: First, those Fixed costs which are incremental to CRG as a result of the expanded Soul program. Thus, it does not include an allocation to general corporate overhead. Second, Direct costs, which include recording costs, such as studio time and talent costs; album preparation; and advertising and promotion expenses such as trade and radio promotion peculiar to a specific product. CRG's estimates, based upon historical experiences, is that they average roughly half of variable costs. In light of the start-up character of the proposed Soul programs, and the likelihood that these Direct costs, in relation to Variable costs, will exceed CRG's historical average, at least initially, an alternate method for dealing with these costs has been used. Funds have been budgeted based upon probable level of recording and promotional activity.

4. Operating profit is profit before interest, taxes and allocations to general corporate overhead.

Exhibit 3a
PROBABLE REVENUE

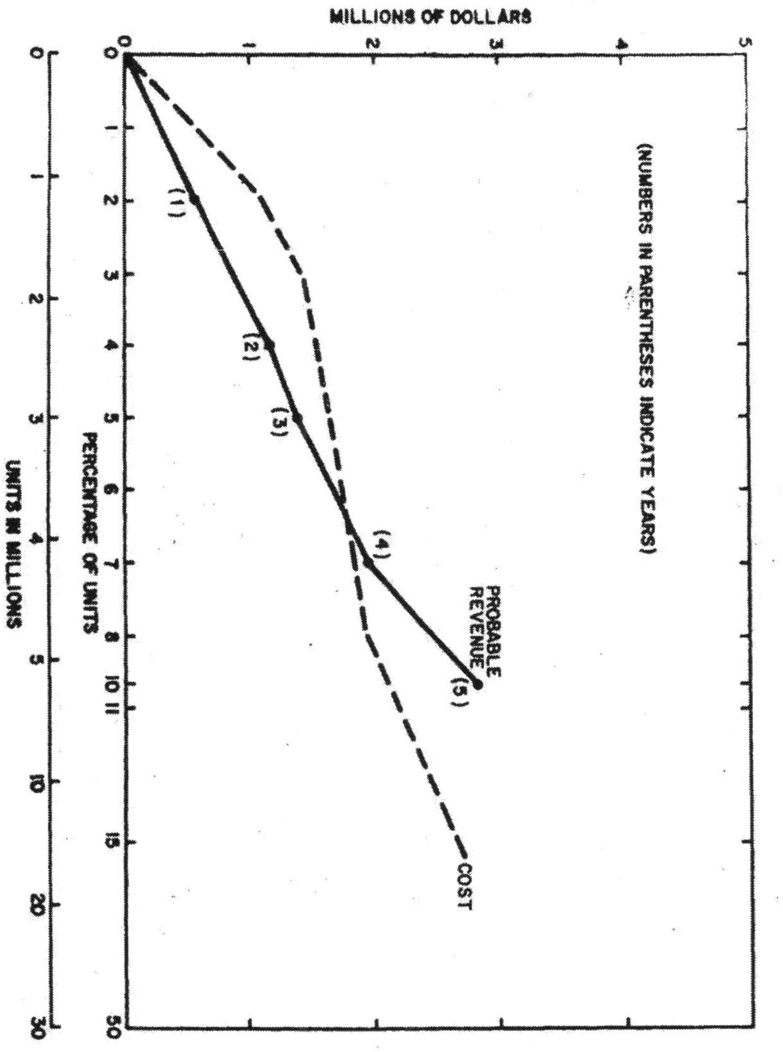

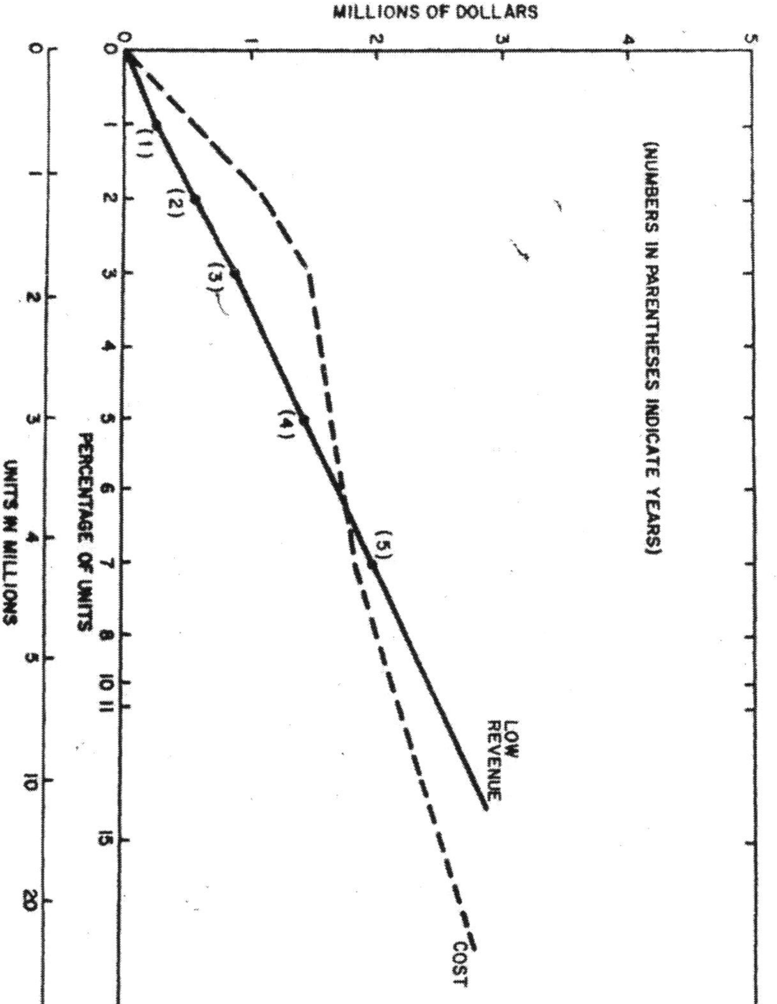

Exhibit 3b
LOW REVENUE

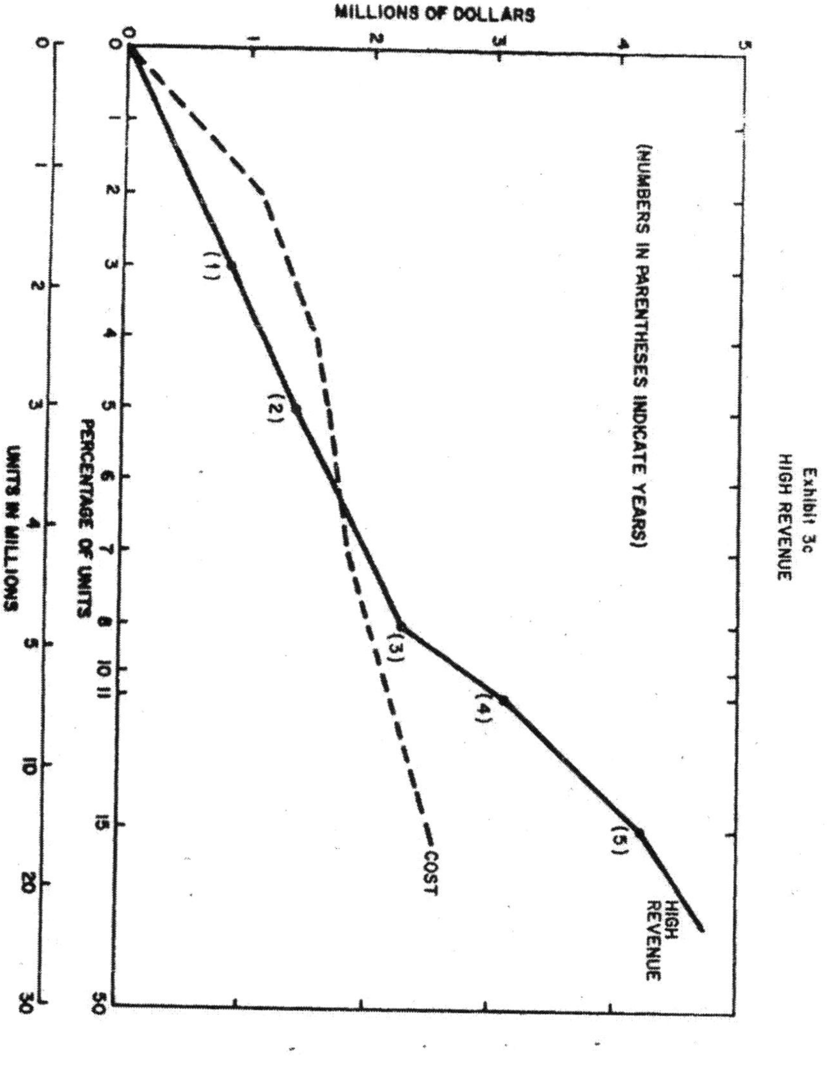
Exhibit 3c
HIGH REVENUE
(NUMBERS IN PARENTHESES INDICATE YEARS)
MILLIONS OF DOLLARS
0
1
2
3
4
5
PERCENTAGE OF UNITS
0
1
2
3
4
5
6
7
8
10 11
15
50
UNITS IN MILLIONS
0
1
2
3
4
5
10
20
30
(1)
(2)
(3)
(4)
(5)
COST
HIGH REVENUE

Exhibit 4
ORGANIZATION CHART FOR NEW SOUL DIVISION

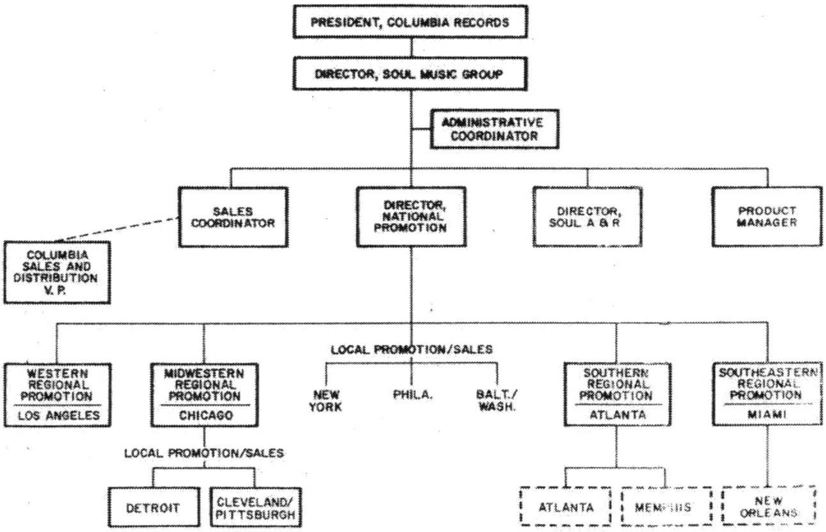

Exhibit 5
ENTRY PHASE OVERLAP

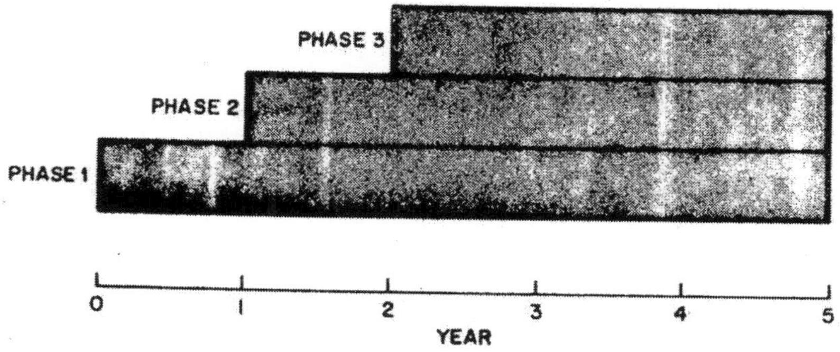

APPENDIX A

ESTIMATE OF SOUL MUSIC MARKET SIZE

The base from which the Soul market size estimate is determined is the total market estimate of approximately 175 million units each in singles and albums. For the years 1967-70 Soul music artists captured 22% of the RIAA audited Gold singles awards. Non-audited firms are assumed to add another 60% to sales giving Soul singles 35% of the total singles market. This percentage on extension gives:

.35 x 175 = 61MM Units

Market research data from CRG indicates that over the period 1967-71 Soul albums averaged 3% of total album sales. An examination of RIAA data for specific artists (i.e. those having Gold album awards) over this period suggests the CRG indications are too low by between 30 and 40 percent. (The error results from the composition of the panel used in developing CRG's data.) For the estimate, it is assumed that Soul albums constitute about 7% of the total album market which is upon extension:

.07 x 175 = 12.2MM Units

To mitigate spurious accuracy, the above unit estimates are rounded to the figures presented in the text of:

Singles	60MM Units
Albums	12MM Units

The prices used in arriving at dollar volumes are given during the text discussion of market size.

A check was made using Billboard data on market share along with a confidential disclosure of one competitor's volume.

APPENDIX B

A broad based representative consumer survey was beyond the scope of the project. However, a telephone survey was undertaken in which 750 Black college students in the Boston area were contacted.

Black college students cannot be construed as being representative of the population of Soul record consumers. They are, however, a very important sub-segment of that group because:

a. They do make a significant number of purchases.

b. They have a great influence on tastes and trends within the Black community.

This survey was conducted by four college educated women from the Harvard Business School community. Analysis was performed through the use of the AQD (Analysis of Quantitative Data) package, which is a new program authored by Professor Robert O. Schlaiffer of the Harvard Business School.

The objectives of this survey were information oriented rather than action oriented. We have not reached any conclusions or made any recommendations based solely on this survey. For this reason, analysis was performed on only 278 of 750 responses. A disk file containing all 750 responses has been made available to you. Graphs and charts displaying information obtained are attached.

APPENDIX B (cont'd)

Age vs Factors Which Attract Consumer To Rhythm & Blues

AGE	SOUND	ARTIST	LABEL	OTHER	TOTAL
16-18	96%	4%	*Results indicate label is unimportant in selection process	---	100%
18-20	89%	11%		---	100%
20-25	88%	9%		3%	100%
26-30	81%	19%		---	100%
31+	50%	38%		12%	100%

*Number of Respondents to Survey by Age Group

Under 16 years of age		3
16-18	"	29
18-20	"	114
20-25	"	75
26-30	"	45
31+	"	12
	TOTAL	278

APPENDIX B (cont'd)

Age vs How Person First Gained Knowledge of a Record

AGE	RADIO	FRIEND	STORE	OTHER	TOTAL
16-18	86%	14%	---	---	100%
18-20	84%	14%	---	2%	100%
20-25	64%	23%	11%	2%	100%
26-30	61%	33%	3%	3%	100%
31+	63%	13%	12%	12%	100%

Age vs Outlet Where Records Purchased

AGE	SMALL LOCAL RECORD STORE	DEPT. STORE	BOOK STORE	DISCOUNT STORE	OTHER	TOTAL
16-18	55%	14%	17%	14%	--	100%
18-20	47%	17%	11%	25%	--	100%
20-25	35%	15%	24%	26%	--	100%
26-30	31%	19%	20%	30%	--	100%
31+	41%	0%	41%	18%	--	100%

APPENDIX B (cont'd)

Age vs Purchasing Outlet While in High School

AGE	SMALL STORE	DEPT. STORE	BOOK STORE	DISCOUNT STORE	OTHER	TOTAL
16-18	79%	11%	10%	--	--	100%
18-20	72%	15%	8%	1%	--	100%
20-25	61%	15%	14%	--	--	100%
26-30	68%	11%	7%	--	--	100%
31+	75%	--	--	--	25%	100%

* Some totals do not add up to 100% due to rounding.

Age vs Frequency of Purchase

AGE	WEEKLY	BI-WEEKLY	MONTHLY	EVERY FEW MONTHS	TOTAL
16-18	25%	14%	21%	32%	92%
18-20	18%	28%	27%	28%	101%
20-25	9%	27%	27%	38%	101%
26-30	13%	9%	28%	50%	100%
31+	13%	---	38%	50%	101%

* % do not equal 100% due to rounding.

APPENDIX B (cont'd)

Frequency of Purchase vs Amount Bought in a Month

TIME	2 RECORDS OR LESS	5 RECORDS OR LESS	10 RECORDS OR LESS	TOTAL
WEEKLY	16%	37%	47%	100%
BI-WEEKLY	22%	51%	27%	100%
MONTHLY	35%	41%	24%	100%
EVERY FEW MONTHS	55%	33%	10%	100%

ADDENDUM

Submitted by:
Marnie Tattersall

At this research group's first meeting with CRG personnel, it was stated that CRG wants to be "Number One" in Soul music sales, profits, and number of artists on contract. This addendum is offered with some specific action recommendations which could be helpful, in conjunction with the recommendations in the body of this report in getting CRG to this goal.

A best estimate of current market position In this segment looks like this:

Market Positions

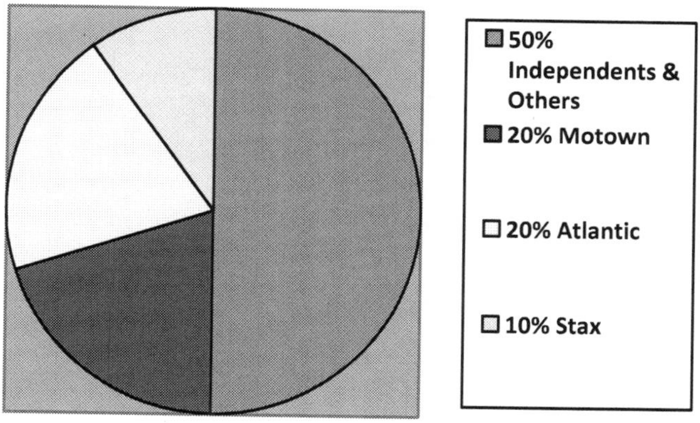

If CRG reaches its goal, the market will probably look like this:

Market Positions

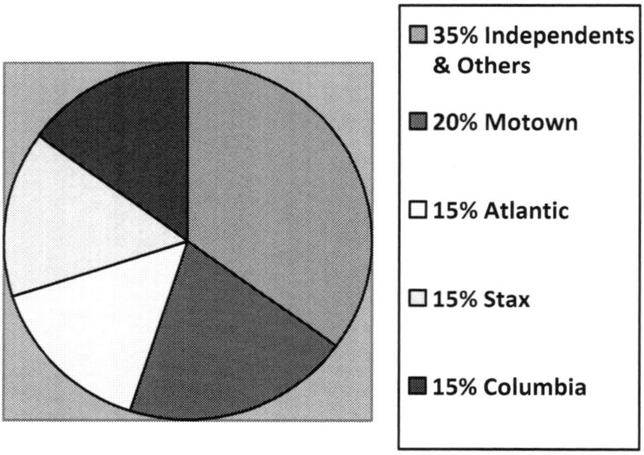

In essence, it is not unlikely that in order to be "Number One" in this segment, CGR will have to capture about 15 percent of it. This will not be easy, but it is not an impossible goal. If all CRG's resources are brought to bear in a concentrated effort, it is my feeling that CRG can reach this 15 percent in five years. In other words, CRG could be as large and dominant as Atlantic is in this segment by 1978.

To do this, however, will require higher market share goals and concurrent direct cost budgets than are presented in the body of this report. The following is what I see CRG being willing to spend and set as its yearly sales goals in order to produce and market the quality product which could make it "Number One" in five years.

Year	1	2	3	4	5
Market Size	$60MM	$64MM	$69MM	$74MM	$79MM
Estimated Level of Market Penetration	3%	5%	8%	11%	15%
Sales Volume	1.8MM	3.2MM	5.5MM	8.2MM	11.7MM
Contribution Available	840K	1,490K	2,570K	3,840K	5,600K
Less: Fixed Costs	830K	870K	915K	960K	1,010K
Historical Direct Costs	368K	658K	1,120K	1,590K	2,310K
Start-up Costs	200K	150K	--	--	--
	1,398K	1,670K	2,035K	2,550K	3,320K
Operating Profit (Loss)	(558K)	(180K)	535K	1,290K	*2,280K
Cumulative Profit (Loss)	(558K)	(738K)	(203K)	1,087K	3,367K
Unit Sales:					
Albums	350K	620K	1,070K	1,770K	2,570K
Single	1,750K	3,100K	5,350K	7,100K	10,300K

* Represents 19.5% operating profit on sales.

Assumptions: Same as in Exhibit 1.

With this goal in mind, the following are some of the kinds of actions which could be beneficial in terms of creating a more desirable image for CRG and in stimulating sales.

Program Director Convention

It was suggested by one of the program directors interviewed for this report, that if CRG is really serious about getting into the Soul market, it will have to start showing it. He suggested that a good way of establishing rapport between CRG and Black P.D.s and D.J.s would be to sponsor a conference for the ten or fifteen key Black P.D.s in the country. The purpose of the conference would be to announce CRG's desire to enter the market, to ask their advice, and in general to have a "rap session." The people he recommends inviting include Curt Shaw, WABQ Cleveland, the current president of NATRA; Bob Jones, KDIA San Francisco; and LeBaron Taylor, WDAS Philadelphia.

Radio Station Relations

Some of the things being done to gain favorable rapport by other companies in this market—in lieu of illegal inducements—which were cited by station personnel as being desirable include:

- Occasional visits by artists and record company executives
- Purchase of air time to advertise current product or concerts
- Purchase of advertising space on the station's complimentary "Hit List"
- Use of stations D.J.s as M.C.s for concerts
- Invitations to local press parties

Concerts

As mentioned in the report, exposure has been and continues to remain a real problem for Black artists. While expenses for a touring Black act do not differ significantly from a White act, there is still usually a sizable difference in audience. This makes promoting Black concerts a usually much less profitable proposal, which has led to a dearth of popularly priced live Black performances across the country. There are several things that CRG can do to help its Black artists in this area.

- Help out with concert tour expenses
- Recommend top flight booking and management agencies
- Work with and encourage Black concert promoters
- Sponsor or co-sponsor free or token-charge concerts
    1. other record companies, i.e. ABC are already doing this
    2. it is rumored that companies such as Coca-Cola and 7-Up are interested in this area
- Encourage the billing of Soul acts with Pop acts
    1. i.e. Van Morrison with the Dramatics
    2. very little of this is being done to date—with the result that White audiences are seldom exposed to live Soul performances

Soul Train

Television is considered a White medium. There is increasing pressure for minority programming from Nicolas Johnson, FCC Commissioner to the recent Black caucus on media. The result of this White orientation is that few Black artists get national television exposure; yet television is such a powerful medium for exposure that a recent BILLBOARD article suggests that television spots may become tomorrow's medium for advertising new musical acts and albums.

It is my feeling that the young White audience of today is not half as hung-up on seeing and "digging" Black artists as are the older White generation who control television programing. Thus, if more Black-oriented programs and Black artists were given national exposure, the effect on ratings may not be as detrimental as feared.

With CRG entering the Black market, it would be in its, and, therefore, CBS Incorporated's best interest to do what it can to influence and encourage more Black exposure on CBS television in particular, and on other television networks and stations in general. (It is interesting to note that NBC and RCA worked together to bring out color television.)

A case in point is *Soul Train*—an independently produced Black "Dick Clark" type show out of Los Angeles. Because it has been refused by the national networks, it is showing on a haphazard basis in whatever cities it can find a marginal station willing to program it. In Boston, for example, it is programmed on Channel 56—where it is gathering a significant audience—despite the fact that many potential viewers do not have televisions which receive more than twelve channels.

Were CBS television to syndicate this show, with only minor alterations—such as using several different cities for location, and including occasional White 'Soul' acts—it could pick up a substantial young Black, and White, national audience. It is only a matter of time before some network picks it up.

There is also ample demand for a television concert series; the poor sound quality argument not withstanding—it is no worse than most radios. One evidence of this is the positive sales that CRG experienced when it programmed parts of its annual promotion movie on Seattle, Washington, television. It is rumored that a sizable department store chain in New England would like to sponsor a similar show but has not been able to find the material.

Thus, it is essential that CRG realize the potential power of television to cultivate the audience for Soul music, and to positively influence Soul record sales.

Radio

Again, in reference to the exposure problem as well as the payola scare, it should be realized that CBS Radio owns seven AM and seven FM stations, as well as providing programming for some 246 radio stations across the country. None of this is Black programming

—even though a considerable opportunity exists for more Black-oriented radio programming. (A separate report is available on this subject.)

Were CBS Radio to offer Black programming of the kind desired—which would include more album exposure—the programming would be profitable. CRG could benefit by having a radio outlet which—while not doing it any favors—at least could not refuse to play 'Columbia' records; and album airplay will generate significant album sales over singles airplay which is the vogue on most current Black radio.

<u>"Discount Record Stores"</u>
Mom and Pop record stores are particularly important to the Soul music market because a much higher percent of Soul product is purchased through them than is the case with White or Pop music.

One of the basic reasons for this is that the geographic dispersion and travel patterns for Blacks are different from those of Whites. Thus, a large portion of the Black record-buying public does not have the same access to rack outlets as do Whites.

Currently CRG owns record retail outlets in various cities, but none in the ghetto areas of these cities. At first glance it would seem that establishing these stores in ghetto areas would only succeed in putting the Mom and Pops out of business, while creating unneeded ill-will and trouble.

Nevertheless, it would be very desirable for CRG to have such outlets, because it could have a direct pulse on what is happening at the Black retail level—a pulse so important that Atlantic and Motown are in daily contact with their key inner-city retailers.

A way of getting around the ill-will that could be generated by CRG ownership of ghetto record stores would be to establish stores on a franchise basis. An arrangement could be worked out whereby young Blacks who are looking for opportunities to own their own businesses, but do not have the capital, could manage the stores and pay for them out of earnings.

If the owner/managers belonged to the community in which they set up shop, they would have the advantage of knowing the community, little opposition could be voiced because these young people are as entitled as the Mom and Pops to start their own business, the venture would help build Black capital, the community would benefit from lower prices and wider variety, and CRG would not only get the information it needed, but its image as a leader in minority business development would be enhanced.

Public and Industry Image

As mentioned in the report, CRG does have a real image problem with regard to entering the Black market. This image can and should be changed, but it will take some doing.

Following is an example of what one other company in the business is doing. The company is Atlantic Records—part of the Kinney group that is now considered such a powerful threat to CRG's total market dominance.

- Atlantic invariably buys a table for the company when a Black station recommends a local Black charity event.
- Last Christmas, Atlantic gave away three thousand dollars worth of turkeys to the poor in Philadelphia through WDAS radio. The turkeys were purchased from a local Black turkey grower and said simply, "Season's Best Wishes from WDAS and Atlantic Records."

The positive feedback that is generated at the station level and from the recipients for these types of action is phenomenal. CRG will have to start thinking about engaging in similar "public spirited" endeavors. If not for the simple reason that these actions should be taken, then they should be done for defensive strategic reasons—besides, they are tax deductible. The concern that record companies should start putting back some of the money they have been taking out of the community for so long is getting strong enough that it is rumored a coalition in Harlem is being organized to boycott record companies that do not engage in this.

These are some of the things CRG should consider doing. One word of caution though—they must be done tastefully.

- Support Black charity functions
- Contribute food to the poor through radio stations and perhaps the Panthers.
- Establish minority music scholarships as grants.
    1. These could be set up at schools such as New England Conservatory or Julliard.
    2. They could be administered by CRG to promising individuals, i.e. winners from the Apollo amateur contests, so that they could spend a year or two taking lessons from masters or traveling to countries such as in Africa to be exposed to native African music. The musicians chosen, and the world of music could only benefit from this type of opportunity; not to mention the rich potential for future CRG artists that this could offer.

In closing, I would like to add, Black music stands to gain as much as CRG from a whole-hearted CRG attempt to participate in the market. It would be a shame for CRG not to live up to its potential.

The Black Music Marketing staff assembled to implement The Harvard Study

Seated L-R - George Chavou, Fred Ware, Bill Craig, Vernon Slaughter, Granville White, Logan H. Westbrooks, Richard Mack, Ralph Bates, Speedy Brown, Richard Outler, Chuck Offuitt, Jerry Griffith Standing L-R – Armond McKissick, Leroy Smith, Marnie Tattersall, and Glen Wright

The Results

Harold Melvin & the Blue Notes with Clive Davis and Kenny Gamble & Leon Huff receiving their first Gold Single on Philadelphia International Record Co.

BIBLIOGRAPHY

A Study of the Soul Music Environment Prepared for Columbia Records Group, 1972

Collins, Lisa. *Gospel Music Round-up: The Bible of the Gospel Music Industry*. Eye on Gospel Publications, Los Angeles, CA, 2002

Cook, Davey D. *Rap History*.
http://www.daveyd.comraphist10.html, 1985

Guralnick, Peter. *Feel Like Goin' Home*. Canongate Books. December 2003

Hurst, Walter E. and Hale, William Storm. *Your Introduction to Music/Record Copyrights, Contracts, and Other Business Law*. Borden Publishing Company. Los Angeles, CA, June 1974

Korda, Michael. *Power: How to Get it, How to Use It*. Random House Books. New York, NY, 1975

Oliver, Paul. *Conversation with the Blues*. Horizon Press, London, 1965

Terkel, Studs. *Working: People Talk About What They Do All Day and How They Feel About What They Do*. Pantheon Books, New York, 1974

Walker, Andrea K. "Hip Hop's Appeal Benefits Radio One" in the Baltimore Sun. Baltimore, MD, August 5, 2003

MAGAZINES / TIPSHEETS
(Main Offices Listed)

Airwaves, New York City
Advertising Age, Chicago
Billboard, Los Angeles/New York City
Black Radio Exclusive, Sherman Oaks, CA
Blues and Soul, London, UK
Broadcasting, Washington, DC
Broadcast Communications, Prairie Village, KS
Cashbox, New York/Los Angeles, CA
The Gavin Report, San Francisco, CA
Goodphone, Sherman Oaks, CA
Impact, Philadelphia, PA
Jack the Rapper, Orlando, FL
Jet, Chicago, IL
Mickey Turntable, Boston, MA
The Mix, New York/California
Music Connection, Los Angeles, CA
Neworld, Los Angeles, CA
Performance, Los Angeles, CA
Radio and Record, Los Angeles, CA
Record World, New York/Los Angeles

INDEX

F

G

H

T

U

W

ABOUT THE AUTHORS

DR. LOGAN H. WESTBROOKS is one of the first African Americans to work as a major label Music Executive. His impact in the music industry is undeniable. Dr. Westbrooks is recognized as a pioneer who paved the way for African America Music Executives of today. Dr. Westbrooks is also a businessman, real estate investor, and a producer of three short films.

Other books by Dr. Logan H. Westbrooks:
The Harvard Report

The Anatomy of the Music Industry:
How the Game Was & How the Game Has Changed

The Anatomy of a Record Company:
How to Survive the Record Business, 1st Edition

Available on AMAZON.COM and LOGANWESTBROOKS.COM

Westbrooks Curated Exhibits

Original photographs, personal papers, awards, and memorabilia from Source Records and his career in the music industry are archived at Indiana University in Archives of African American Music & Culture (AAAMC) in Bloomington, Indiana.

Other original items will be on display in the exhibit for African American Music Executives at the National Museum of African American Music (NMAAM) in Nashville, Tennessee.

***

DR. LANCE A. WILLIAMS is an anthropologist and Jazz critic. He has written over 300 articles on American culture and published in the prestigious Latin American Journal, Folklore Americano. He has over 35 years of experience as a Department Vice-Chair, Assistant Professor, and Instructor at several colleges and universities in southern California.

46881569R00203

Made in the USA
Middletown, DE
11 August 2017